The Psychology and Education of the Young

of the Young

A GUIDE TO THE PRINCIPLES OF DEVELOPMENT,
LEARNING AND ASSESSMENT

by

Margaret Munro, M.A., M.Ed.

*Lecturer in Psychology,
Jordanhill College of Education, Glasgow*

HEINEMANN

LONDON

Heinemann Educational Books Ltd

LONDON EDINBURGH MELBOURNE TORONTO
AUCKLAND SINGAPORE JOHANNESBURG
HONG KONG NAIROBI IBADAN

SBN 435 80620 3

Published by Heinemann Educational Books Ltd
48 Charles Street, London W1X 8AH
Printed in Great Britain by Morrison and Gibb, London and Edinburgh

Contents

v

To the only true begetters of the following
pages, the students of Jordanhill

Preface

Applying psychological knowledge to teaching is an individual skill and therefore deciding what is significant enough to go into a general survey of educational psychology is an individual matter too. Teachers and intending teachers may find particular topics they want to be informed about given little space. I should like to believe however, that my choice of content does not distort too seriously, for any reader, the general design, which is to interpret, as far as possible in non-technical language, the various psychological viewpoints of the present day and show how they relate to classroom activity and to the wider changes in educational policy and administration which are taking place.

May I suggest to students (with all due allowance to individual study habits) that they will probably get the best out of the book by reading it through as a connected whole and not by separate topics. A difficult patch might profitably be skimmed over on a first reading and returned to in the context of the subject matter as a whole. Allowance has been made for this treatment in particular by the end summaries to the various topics, but also in a general policy of 'cross-reference'. Awkward points are sure to recur in later contexts and different wording, with a reminder of their first appearance. The following topics, for example, in the first half of the book are likely to need several re-readings. In Part 2: Chapter 1 (4), the explanation of the standard deviation (pages 34 ff); Chapter 2 (3), on how correlations are calculated (pages 51 ff) and Chapter 6 (3), on Piaget's use of the symbols of abstract logic to express his ideas (pages 162 ff).

The student will not find anything more difficult than these anywhere in the later part of the book, although a higher degree of understanding and sophistication is expected in himself by the time he is ready to attack it.

———

In writing this book I have benefited greatly from the help and interest of my friends on the College staff. I am indebted in particular, to certain members of the English and Mathematics departments for information on matter and method in their subjects, and to my immediate colleagues in the Psychology department for the liveliness of the 'shop-talk' which has put me in the way of many a useful new idea. The College Librarian and his staff have received, with unfailing courtesy, my unpredictable demands upon the contents of their shelves and upon their professional help in tracking down essential references. One last important acknowledgment is to my husband, an admirable listener and encouraging critic.

M. M.

PART ONE

Introductory

I

How the Science of Behaviour can be of Service to the Teacher

Psychology is the science which has human behaviour for its subject matter, a definition unlikely to surprise students opening a book, or settling down to listen to a lecture. Like most people nowadays they will have their ideas about psychology, so much of its vocabulary has worked its way out of the textbooks and into ordinary conversation. Behaviour is an acceptable name for human activities in general, which is what they expect the subject-matter of psychology to be. They also expect the kind of orderly treatment which justifies calling it a science. The information will be the result of careful observations and some-times of experiments, so that general statements can be made about behaviour, describing the forms it takes and explaining what causes them. In this way it will be possible to predict the outcome of certain conditions, what sort of behaviour will result from them. It may even be possible, with psychological insight, to shape the behaviour a little by providing the right conditions, which is what teachers are trying to do all the time.

How far does the subject-matter of psychology allow of scientific treatment? Can enough information be collected about some aspect of behaviour, and arranged in a systematic way that justifies making generalizations? A psychologist would give a cautious yes to this sort of question, and probably quite a confident one if he was being asked, for example, about scores on an intelligence test! Supposing the cir-cumstances are known, can psychology make any really useful pre-dictions about what a living individual will do? Or can it explain an action any better than the common-sense way? No psychologist, of course, would answer this kind of question with a downright yes. But a downright no would be wrong too. Explanations can be useful even when they are not complete explanations and actions can turn out very much as expected, though not exactly so. A teacher may teach something well enough in the end, and the pupil may learn it without benefit of psychology, but he may learn it better and quicker (and

3

perhaps without tears) if his teacher remembers some psychological principle, and gives it a trial.

Psychology is not an exact science, but we may describe it as a science of probabilities, though this sounds rather alarming and will be the better for some non-technical explanations. Psychological information, as in any other science, is collected by observing an adequate number of examples of the thing one is interested in. It might be the use of speech by three-year-old children playing together, or how someone's learning speed is affected by tiredness or stress. The observer then moves on to the next stage, of tidying up his observations, listing and sorting them, drawing up tables and graphs. Reliable statements of a general kind can then be made. He can say that the social talk of other three-year-olds is *likely* to follow the same patterns but he cannot say that they will all certainly talk to each other this way. He will probably not be surprised by anything he hears, but he would be very surprised indeed if he had happened to guess their very words beforehand. And as for our tired, worried student, while one can tell that his performance is likely to be affected, *how much* will not be certain. It will depend on other considerations which had to be left out when we were observing simply the effects of tiredness or stress on speed of learning. How near is the examination, for example? Does he like the subject? Has he formed the habit of shutting out distractions?

Everyone will see that these other considerations are important and cannot be ignored for long. Human actions are not simple, and this is something that will have to be discussed presently. Meantime we need only say that we cannot allow for all the things that affect what someone does at any one time, so we can never give a perfect explanation, or foretell it exactly, as a physicist can foretell the behaviour of a certain weight dropped from a certain height on a windless day. But when a certain kind of human action has been seen to happen often enough in certain conditions, we are justified in calling it a normal one and one very likely to happen again whenever the conditions are the same. Knowledge like this would come in handy if the behaviour were something we should like to see repeated (or avoided!) in the future. And just about the most comforting thing one can say to the mother of a four-year-old is that tiresomeness at this age is common enough to be very nearly normal; she is not bringing up a juvenile delinquent nor does she have to start reckoning her own mistakes. Of course, no age phase is guaranteed to end punctually on the next birthday, but end it will, though every child takes his own time about it. Family life would be easier to organize if he did not, but it would be a good deal duller.

Indeed, in at least two of the fields in which psychology has been useful, namely medicine and education, the lack of exactness is no real disadvantage. Neither doctors nor teachers can reckon cause and effect in a cut-and-dried way. Every doctor knows that the same cure works differently, and sometimes surprisingly, with different patients. The co-operation he gets from them will be different too. It is a whole person who is ill, not just a bit of his body or mind; it is a whole person who diagnoses and prescribes, not some single cell of the doctor's intelligence where the facts from a medical textbook are stored. And as long as this is so, the doctor must work through a series of judgements and understandings very far removed from mechanical rules. His experience will help him; it will never tell him precisely what to do. The only part of his behaviour which can be precise in this way will be the skills which his fingers have learned, but where to apply these skills will be a matter for judgement as well. It is like manipulating the gears of a car, which is one thing, and guessing the state of the traffic when the lights have changed—which is quite another.

Of course, neither doctor nor teacher is working blind. Every case history is unique, every teaching situation is unique, but the skill of the doctor and the teacher is in comparing it with others which have been like it. This is the process which psychologists have called insight, and means that someone is working partly by rule and partly by departing from the rule to suit the present differences. It is hardly ever just one or the other alone. Occasionally, if it is a small item of behaviour that is being taught, a teacher may make use of a simple educational method that she has learned from someone else. It has always worked when she used it before and it does not fail this time. And occasionally too, the conditions are so peculiar, as when her governess first met Helen Keller, or Gladys Aylward found herself in the middle of the prison riot, that the teacher has nothing but the resources of her own personality to help her. But these are the two extremes.

For almost everyone work is most satisfying when it is somewhere between. Familiar routine can be a pleasant relaxation for teacher and class, but only for a while, and doing something new and difficult may be lively but may produce too high a failure ratio. A teacher, like other professional workers, feels happiest when he has knowledge to give him confidence but uses it as he himself thinks fit. This is his privilege, and he would not welcome a set of rules which took it away from him. But more knowledge will not do that. On the contrary, the more he has, the richer will be his choice of what to do next. His psychological insight he can put to work for him, as a real part of himself and his own individual teaching knack.

Between psychology and teaching there is a natural bond. The aim of one is to explain human behaviour and remove harmful misconceptions about it which would hamper the teacher, whose aim is to alter her pupil's behaviour in a way which she believes to be for the better. Of course there is a lot of psychological knowledge which is not directly put into practice by a teacher, although it may be interesting and of value to himself as a person. And of course teaching is not only applied psychology. Though it will help the pupils' arithmetic if the teacher has read some of Piaget's work and knows how their number concepts are likely to be formed, he also needs to know more arithmetic than they do! But the overlap between the two is so great that education and psychology have been called two sides of the same thing. Behaviour changing, becoming more complex, or clearer and simpler, taking on new shapes and forms, losing others; this is what psychology describes, while the teacher's very job is to steer these changes.

Think, for example, how the infant teacher induces the five-year-old to adapt his conversational repertoire to the new situation of school, framing her own talk so that the answers and comments she gets from him gradually take the shape she wants. Think how cunningly she helps him to collect many simpler performances into one complex behaviour pattern. The hand movements which draw the letter shapes are joined into continuous writing and the writing flow is metered out by spacing and punctuation. Meantime another ascending series joins speech sounds to ideas, and spoken ideas to the rules of simple syntax, so that he can now achieve a sentence—an astonishing feat, when you come to consider it, for a human being who has been only five years alive and communicative for little over three of them. It makes the final level seem well within reach, when handwriting, language, and inventive thinking are all combined in written composition, and yet it will take almost the whole of his primary-school career to build this last complicated behaviour out of all those earlier ones.

In this sort of learning (which is sometimes called a learning hierarchy because it goes on from a lower grade of organized behaviour to a higher one) our pupil retains all his gains and keeps on using them. But sometimes, as has been mentioned, the teacher wants his new behaviour to oust the old one, preferably for ever. For instance, supposing an increased alphabet was used to shape early reading responses there will be a right moment for dispensing with it. In the same way she might persuade a cross child to exchange his screaming fits for a better way of dealing with his frustrations, which will need a different kind of psychological insight and classroom craft.

These are all examples of deliberately engineered changes in a child's behaviour. Any ordinary school day would produce a dozen more, especially of the kind we normally call learning, since coping with a temper tantrum is luckily more unusual. They are all alike in this way, that they depend for their success on the teacher's supply of knowledge and experience and his good judgement in using them. Sometimes the knowledge is more exact with some well-tried rules to proceed on; other episodes—and I suppose the tantrum would be one—require more individual techniques. Teaching is a matter largely of human relationships and is full of situations for which exact instructions cannot be given beforehand, by a psychologist or anybody else. Reading the directions is a good start to mending a fuse or building a boat or even teaching a beginner how to skate. There are no directions one can look up for comforting a child heartbroken because a pet has died. Nor are there any on how to win an argument, make an audience laugh, or quell a riot in a class of thirteen-year-olds. If someone tried to do any of these things by the book he would be behaving out of his own character and this is a sure way of failing. Losing one's temper might be effective for some situations, but a naturally gentle young woman cannot lose hers to order, and if she tried the pupils would probably laugh at her. A reserved girl lamely trying to imitate a talkative, high-spirited one would embarrass herself and everybody else. Some teachers like quiet and orderliness and in this atmosphere they and their pupils do their best work. Others like more vigour and stimulation in the classroom. Both preferences are perfectly justified.

This is probably the right place to recognize an important part of a good teacher's equipment. Over the years teachers gradually become entitled to have their own standards about the behaviour and abilities of children. Their expectations of what a boy aged nine can do will become more valid and a better guide to planning next week's lessons. This is very like a psychological survey. It is a process of recording many observations, the only real difference being that it is done in an informal way instead of by tests and measurements, and the records are inside the teachers' heads and seldom written down. Now, no one in his senses would deny that teaching experience is necessary, or that the pronouncements of experienced teachers are often dependable.

But it would be unwise of teachers to rely altogether on this. Their views will be bounded by their own interests, even if these are wide, and by the kind of pupils they have happened to come across, and while there may be no harm in this as long as their teaching lives remain much the same, education is a rapidly changing world and teachers need help in keeping up with it.

The reply of one exasperated mother is now an educational classic. Interrupted in a thorough job of spanking by some bystander's smug enquiry: 'Have you never heard of psychology?' she contents herself with: 'Yes, but this is quicker.' For all we can tell she may have been perfectly right and the well-read bystander perfectly wrong, at least for her own immediate purposes. But there are educational purposes for which we are right to turn the tables and say that psychology is quicker. Certainly a full-scale, carefully conducted educational survey takes time and effort. But it will scoop up a wealth of relevant information which no individual could possibly collect in a lifetime of ordinary human contacts. Whatever the questions being investigated, the answers found will be explicit and scientifically reliable, and they can be made available to any teacher in the time it takes to read them.

What has been said so far about the usefulness of psychological knowledge to a teacher can now be summed up. Some of it is indispensable. Without it professional equipment would nowadays simply be incomplete. Sometimes it can be applied direct to a straightforward teaching routine, so saving unnecessary drudgery and making success nearly certain. Oftenest it will have to be fitted in with the teacher's own personality and experience. In every case it makes for an increase in professional confidence.

2

The Subject-matter and Methods
of Psychology

1 Human behaviour

The first chapter made several references to the meaning of the word science as it can be used about psychology. We have found that it means observing human behaviour, its subject-matter, so as to increase the stock of reliable information about it, and that the aim of the observation may be to describe some piece of behaviour accurately or to explain what causes it to occur. No psychological statement can be properly made unless it is justified as far as possible by the observations. It must be made clear, too, whether it is an exact statement or a statement about likelihoods if it is going to be of any use, for instance to a teacher in the classroom. These are general principles of psychology and therefore of educational psychology as a particular branch of it.

You, the reader, may or may not have a natural liking for the understanding of scientific method, but there is no doubt about the interest of psychology's subject-matter. Human behaviour is probably the most interesting material ever presented in scientific form and most students approach the subject favourably. The student's job is to work at this interest when the subject becomes thornier and thinking about it does not come so naturally as expected. The job of the textbook is to indicate how this should be done, although it is the very thing which gives psychological matter its special liveliness that sometimes has to be ignored for psychological purposes. I mean, of course, the endless and often baffling variety of human actions.

Many psychologists take it for granted that behaviour as defined by psychology means animal behaviour as well as human. Some, especially those interested in a certain kind of learning, have made it their special study. Because an animal's behaviour is less varied it is easier to observe the same things over and over again and much information has been classified since the days of Pavlov and Thorndike. Some of it is clear and definite and helps us to trace the outline of corresponding human actions. There remain, of course, very large areas of human activity

9

for which there is no really helpful correspondence to be found, one
of the most obvious being the human power of operating with *symbols*
of concrete things and events as substitutes for the things themselves.
One would probably think first of language and numbers in this connection, but human beings have also been known to laugh at witty
music like Walton's 'Façade' or stand silent and moved before Dali's
'Crucifixion', though one is just noises of assorted pitch and the other
daubs of pigment upon canvas.

Now, anyone asked to pinpoint the *difference* between animal and
human behaviour would probably mumble something about intelligence, which indeed human beings have been priding themselves upon
from about the time they were forced to accept proof of their animal
connections. Fortunately, there is a comfortable gap between, for
example, the responses of an adult chimpanzee to speech sounds and
those of a two-year-old child with quite ordinary mental powers,
and if intelligence means successful adaptation of action to situation
and a making-over of the environment to suit oneself, then human
beings have been remarkably intelligent.

On the other hand, cats show a timely capacity for appreciating
danger and streaking out of its way. Cuckoos neatly shelve their
parental responsibilities and beavers make excellent arrangements for
living afloat, as they prefer to do. Animal ways have a compactness
which is pleasant to watch. Within the limits of their needs they are
successful. But these needs are fixed and simple and one animal has no
occasion to vary its methods very much from those of another of the
same species, so that we have a very good idea of how it is going to
progress through life. Furthermore, there are times when the life
needs of animals are temporarily satisfied and these tend, upon the
whole, to be intervals of inactivity. Animals do not set up for themselves
a great many unnecessary goals to keep them busy when free from the
urgencies of food-seeking, caring for young, or bolting into safety.
Of course some animals are more restless than others; experimenters
have noted that they occasionally seek stimulation for its own sake.
Some even play a little (and it is worth noting that man finds these
species the most endearing) and our nearest connections, the primates,
are shrewdly inquisitive. But self-imposed activity like play is only a
tiny part of the lives of most animals; and this must be remembered
when we apply patterns derived from animal study to human behaviour. It makes a difference even when a human being is limited (in a
learning experiment for example) to making one simple response
which an animal might manage quite well. It matters far more when

there are no artificial conditions and he is behaving in an ordinary human way with dozens of options to choose from in his environment.

A favourite of many novelists is the quick, panoramic view of how two or three of the characters in the story are employed at the same moment of time. As the town clock strikes three, a young man is installing the aerial for someone's new television set, two miles away his wife is humming a tune as she wheels the baby out on its afternoon airing, and somewhere else his eight-year-old son is shouting encouragement to his side in a game organized by the class teacher. It would not be at all difficult to collect a handful of more spectacular employments. While the life of a British provincial town is ticking comfortably along, somebody in Japan is skin-diving for pearl oysters, somebody is being projected into orbit in a one-man satellite, and nearer home a brain surgeon is completing the last delicate manoeuvre in a four-hour operation.

The human scene is the delight of novelists, newspaper columnists, historians, television scriptwriters, and all their devoted audiences. It might be called at times the psychologist's despair. Yet its variety is exactly his business, too. He has to come to terms with it, as indeed all the practitioners who use psychological ideas also have to do, the teachers, the doctors, the personnel workers in factories, the advertisement copywriters, the social workers in child-guidance clinics. He is in one way more closely concerned with human variety than any of them. His ultimate job is to find some explanation of it.

You may have looked at one of Brueghel's 'landscapes with figures' and felt almost appalled at the amount of detail. Yet all you have to do is take it in. You do not also have to describe each item according to a plan and attempt to connect it to a complex of other features. And the human scene goes one better than the Brueghel one by not even standing still to be looked at! It is not surprising that psychologists would be delighted to find the key to even one corner of it and be able to pass on confidently to the next—to be able to say: 'All children will acquire this mathematical concept by manipulating this designed material' or 'The causes of juvenile anti-social attitudes can be regularly assigned to the following six categories . . .' But in fact hardly any corners have been definitively tidied up and we are very far indeed from a systematic plan for classifying and understanding all the forms of human behaviour.

2 *Some psychological aims and methods*

Psychology has been in existence just long enough for present-day psychologists to realize fully the size of the task that is shared out among all the well-known subdivisions like psychiatry and educational psychology; and to take it for granted that in psychology, as in any other science, some investigator will carefully confirm the results of his observations and experiments only to have to modify them or even to see them overturned by new discoveries. Like checking and confirming, modification is normal scientific procedure, but it gets more prominence in psychology than in most sciences, partly because it is so often just when psychological findings are put to practical use that the new discoveries are made. Thus with the new psychological insight there has to be a revision of policy as well. Readers will find some examples of this in relation to the changing psychological concepts about the nature of intelligence and its development, with corresponding changes in methods of transfer from primary to secondary education.

Psychology cannot help being a practical science. Even if psychologists were not anxious to improve their own conclusions by trying them out, other people would do it for them. The relationship between psychological investigation and practice has nearly always been a reciprocal one. For example, a teacher nowadays can hardly avoid being aware of the immense programme of educational research that is going on to implement, confirm, modify, and even at times to refute by practical examples Piaget's huge schematic account of the growth of scientific and logical thinking in children. Piaget's own experiments are not designed, except incidentally, to teach, but to check how the progress of children's mental development accords with his own system of explanation; but that system is all the time being modified and expanded so that it can contain other educational findings than his own.

The work of Freud is another famous example, perhaps the most famous of all, of how psychological insight gradually becomes more comprehensive while at the same time accommodating itself to the results of practical application. Freud began his medical career as a neurologist and when his interest shifted to psychological medicine he brought to bear his scientific methods of observing, recording, confirming, and classifying upon the individual behaviour of patients. This particular psychological method is called the clinical method; firstly, because its aim is the practical one of providing effective treatment (which can, of course, be educational or psychological as well as medical in context) and, secondly, because it is the whole behaviour of one unique individual that is the subject of study. It is very different from the techniques of survey and measurement which tend to be concerned, as we shall see in a moment, with a very large number of individuals who are not differentiated from each other except by the one performance that is being surveyed.

But although it is observation of individual behaviour and of behaviour in the round, it is not haphazard. The clinical psychologist, like the psychiatrist, checks each observation according to a plan for confirming or modifying his conclusions. The interview may be quite informal in appearance (though very methodical in purpose) or it may be formally structured in a manner resembling Binet's individual testing techniques where the dialogue is prescribed beforehand. The examiner must speak his lines like a well-rehearsed actor, and although the child is often allowed to respond spontaneously, his responses are rated against reliable established standards. Similarly, in the extension of these observation techniques from individual to inter-personal or group behaviour, the speech and actions may be recorded as they spontaneously arise (in writing by the observer, or perhaps with the help of tapes, cameras, and closed-circuit television, or one-way screens) or alternatively certain types of action may be entered on a chart as they occur over a specified interval. But in the first case the record is subjected to careful analysis and evaluation. A very famous record of this kind was the one made by Susan Isaacs of the conversation of children during the activities in her school.

Clinical and group observation techniques are one solution to the problem of studying individual behaviour and inter-personal behaviour in a systematic psychological manner. The great problem of individual behaviour for psychology as a science is its unpredictability. There are too many factors involved for an individual's actions to be forecast accurately from *general* behavioural laws. The observational methods, therefore, tend to fulfil the psychological function of describing behaviour systematically, and of providing general guides only as to the kind of actions you may expect of human beings in certain conditions; for example, from an adolescent who had no 'authority figure' in the early years of life, with whose restraints he would gradually identify and so become socially responsible; or from children in a certain age-group during free play or when subjected to rigid, though benevolent, patterns of adult dictatorship; and so on. Readers will have conjectured that the psychology of development, and particularly of social development, must often rely upon information collected from observing the *whole* behaviour (or *global* behaviour as it is sometimes called) of an individual human being in relation to a situation as he perceives it, or in relation to other individuals.

In this difficult study, neighbouring human sciences like anthropology can often provide useful hints to psychologists. Cultural anthropology considers different tribal customs such as the status of adolescents in a certain primitive society, or community attitudes to competitiveness or aggression. If there are wide cultural differences in these respects with correspondingly wide personality differences in the members of two respective cultures, a measure is offered of the social as opposed to the innate factors in behavioural development. Conversely when a human practice is found many times over in different social and geographical contexts, it points to the existence of a general human trait, or a general human need for which some provision is necessary. For example, all human communities do in some fashion prepare their children for adult competence, whether this implies a few simple, traditional skills or an advanced sophisticated technology like our own which requires highly specialized and differentiated kinds of training. Think of a young aborigine learning his cunning at the heels of an experienced hunter, and then think in how many thousands of guises this typical human pair, the teacher and the pupil, must have made their appearance since the start of history.

Now, individual action is unique because it is a unique *blend* of many separate variables. Thus, to put it very simply, one person's action can be generous, brave, and enlightened; another's kind and courageous but misguided; and another's none of those things. And these variables in one person's behaviour will happen at certain times and in certain strengths because of certain conditions and events—things like his age, his bodily capacity, his intelligence on the one hand; on the other such things as opportunity to learn the behaviour and the occurrence of the right stimulus to trigger it off. Like other sciences, psychology makes use of certain techniques for isolating a 'bit' of behaviour, such as a single performance, and by controlled experiment endeavouring to establish what conditions are likely to make it happen or to make it take a particular form.

One well-known technique which we shall come across more than once later in the book, is 'matched groups' by which, for example, we compare the performance on a common test of a trained and an untrained group. Experimental studies of this and other kinds have been particularly useful in the psychology of learning and the psychology of development, although findings must be cautiously applied. In almost any human performance, the factors excluded from the experiment for the sake of scientific accuracy have a way of breaking in and modifying the expected result, particularly if it is a complex performance. The most reliable and consistent results are usually to be found in relation to fairly simple and uniform kinds of behaviour that can vary only in a limited number of ways between individual and individual. Memorizing and manipulatory skills, for example, are easier to study experimentally than the conditions that bring about problem-solving and social responsiveness, although both of these have been the subject of learning experiments.

By far the largest body of experimental work has been done upon the simplest forms of living behaviour. These are either single random responses which become gradually adopted as habits through being consistently reinforced (for instance a pigeon can be induced to peck repeatedly at a selected key-spot which happens to release a food-pellet, and a rat to turn regularly to the right at a Y-shaped junction) or else the involuntary responses that are sometimes called reflexes. A reflex action can be made to occur over and over again in the same way as often as the appropriate stimulus is applied; for example food inserted in the mouth makes it water; a sharp tap below the knee-cap makes the lower leg jerk forward. Since there is a fixed connection between stimulus and response it is easy to control experimentally; and if the response is shown to be made to something *other* than the natural stimulus, as for instance we may find our mouths watering at the sound of preparations for a meal, then some form of learning may be presumed to have occurred.

These learning, or conditioning experiments (as they are often called) are most often carried out on animals, as we have seen, and the manipulated responses are of those kinds which are the most rigid in the human behavioural repertoire, and the least readily combined into an *intelligent* plan of action. While their relationship with behaviour is important, it is by no means straightforward—that is, with behaviour which is goal-directed, interested, and discriminatory, all the qualities which give behaviour in general its individual stamp.

The techniques so far mentioned include systematic observation of behaviour under clinical conditions, sometimes with formal tests and records, sometimes with plans for categorizing and evaluating the behaviour; experimental investigations to establish a connection between foregoing conditions and certain actions or performances; and formal scientific experiments with single responses that can be easily manipulated. These last have, as we shall see in a later chapter, an important bearing on more complex kinds of learning and adjustment.

All these psychological methods are of course in use in educational psychology, along with many others which will be mentioned later, since they are best understood in the context of their special uses and the educational discoveries they have made possible. But one other method ought to be mentioned here, since it has provided by far the greatest amount of the information customarily associated with the subject. This is what may be described as survey and measurement. Details of this will be considered in the next chapter but in brief it may be said that the behaviour under study must be a clear-cut simple trait, ability, or performance, and individuals are graded on a fixed numerical scale for this one item. We call it a *variable* because it varies in quantity over a great range of cases, some showing higher, some lower ratings.

Needless to say, it is not the whole person who is being rated, only this one performance, the rest of his individuality being temporarily ignored. You can however collect a constellation of scores and measures which add up, not to the whole person, to be sure, but to something usefully informative. The limitations of the methods of survey and measurement will be considered, along with their advantages, in the next group of chapters; and it is just when these limitations are understood that the findings can be put to their best use. It is the optimistic outsider and not the informed educationalist who reads more than was ever intended into the meaning of an intelligence quotient, and its function.

Although the prime subject of psychology is human behaviour, we cannot exclude from it the study of other kinds. Useful insights into corresponding human activities can be got from observing animals and by comparison with their limited patterns the characteristic feature of human behaviour is also emphasized. This is the endless variety of objectives and the means of attaining them. It presents a peculiar problem to the science of behaviour, which aims at a systematic description and classification of all these behavioural forms and an explanation of the conditions of their occurrence. Some of the principles of psychological method have been indicated, particularly as applied to the investigations in educational psychology.

The variety of the human scene is the combined effect of the behaviour of individuals. By definition, therefore, educational psychology is fundamentally concerned with describing and explaining the development of individuality. We are going to trace the origins of it in the innate and maturational differences between individual children as part of the general theme of the next six chapters. In the second half of the book we shall be dealing with the individualizing effect of different kinds of interaction between a living person and his environment.

Under the general heading of the psychology of survey and measurement there is first to be considered the enormous range of individual differences in measured abilities and educational per-formances, with a preliminary chapter on the measurement and sampling techniques by which it has been discovered. Survey methods, also, have laid down the lines of normal maturation and also of the modifying trends brought about through environmental and social pressures. Therefore the chapters on the psychology of growth, on cognitive development, and on the socialization of behaviour can also be included under this heading. The environmental and social variables, however, are so numerous that many other methods of investigation will be mentioned as well. Case-histories, for instance in Bowlby's and Goldfarb's work (which see), group experiments and clinical observations of individual performance (which were essential to Piaget's findings)—all provide information reliable enough to be generally applied to large numbers of children.

The first topic to be considered in the next part of the book is the equipment which every living human being has for apprehending his environment and making effective responses. Making use of this equipment is part of the great process of adapting to the environment which we call learning. Firstly, there is the learning of the general forms of competence, learning to recognize and understand the environment, learning when to respond and how to plan responses. Readers will find this divided among such topics as perceiving and attending, perceptual conditioning and thinking. This will be followed by two chapters on the more specific kinds of learning such as acquiring habits and memorizing, with a note on recent educational techniques and their psychological basis. Certain school subjects will be referred to along with the relevant forms of learning. The important subjet of language learning has been given the last chapter in this group to itself, since there is hardly any learning pattern which is not illus-trated by this particular human competence. By the same token, frequent references to language will have to be made throughout the book in the context of other learning, and of individual social and cognitive development.

PART TWO

The Psychology of Survey and Measurement

I

The Methods of Psychological Measurement

1 What is measured

Psychological measurement has the same subject-matter as any other branch of psychology, but because of its special purpose has to make a good deal of use of mathematical ideas and calculations, which seem at times to take it very far away from human behaviour. Nevertheless, its purpose is to explain behaviour better by setting down information in an orderly manner, and this is the best way to understand its methods, complicated as they may seem at times. This kind of psychology is sometimes called *psychometrics* and it includes many things which will have a familiar sound, like intelligence testing, and others, like correlation ratios and the graph of normal probability, whose right to be in a psychological textbook will certainly need some justification. Psychology in general is justified by its usefulness and there is probably no psychology more useful than the psychology of measurement has been. It has developed in the service of state education, and has had to keep pace with its very rapid expansion over the last hundred years, and in particular the last fifty. During this period educators have been ransacking all the facts and figures that psychologists have been able to provide, and have been waiting to put into practice every scrap of knowledge about children and their development almost as soon as it came to light.

When should a pupil be promoted to secondary school? How should spelling be memorized? Can we afford to postpone reading lessons to the age of six and a half? To questions like this, vague generalizations are no sort of answer. When a county is planning the size of its schools, or the kind of instruction that will be wanted, the percentage of children in a given intelligence range must be pretty exactly known, and this is only one of many policies which need dependable psychological information based on research.

To fulfil these exact expectations a psychologist must severely limit himself. Behaviour must be studied in a way which students at times may find difficult and abstract, denying them all the imaginative insights and inspired guesses which make psychology naturally attractive. But only for a time. The quantitative approach can bring some interesting things to light, and for this reason, as well as for its usefulness, its methods deserve to be understood.

Some of these methods can best be explained through their actual uses, and will therefore be dealt with in the chapters on educational assessment and intelligence testing. But there are some general principles of measurement which educational psychologists take for granted and it will be as well to get them out of the way as early as possible so that the student can do the same.

In any psychological survey there are three things to be decided. Firstly, what is to be measured and how the measuring is to be done; secondly, how big the survey must be in order to give adequate information; thirdly, how the results are to be summarized. These are not independent problems, of course, but luckily we can consider them separately.

The first step in measuring something is to isolate the one feature about it which is to be measured, and this, of course, means ignoring all its other properties. When cardboard boxes are being sorted for size their colours do not matter, whether they are of sludge-grey uniformity or as varied as the stained-glass windows in Chartres Cathedral. Exactly the same thing applies when we come to the measurement of human beings and their behaviour. We do not 'measure' a whole person, or behaviour in the round. We pick out and measure the separate items of which personality and behaviour are presumed to be constructed, such as physical features, traits and characteristics, skills and performances. And of course such a measure, in itself, tells us nothing about the excluded features.

This may seem obvious, especially when some human characteristic can be directly measured. But there are not very many of these. Apart from the bodily measurements like height and weight, only a few very simple skills can be directly observed. Most psychological measurement is indirect. There is no known way of measuring a personality trait like introversion or a mental property like reasoning power. We can only set tasks and ask questions in the expectation that someone's *performance* in them will reflect his tendency to be introverted or his ability to think out a problem. We are measuring the *effects* of the characteristic, not the characteristic itself, and this, of course, is quite normal scientific procedure. We do not count up the temperature of a room. We count up the slight alterations in the length of a column of mercury in a thermometer, although we do not call them units of length but degrees.

Now the expansion and contraction of mercury is a very faithful index of temperature changes. But when we decide to measure ability to do arithmetic we have no guarantee that the performances we choose to measure—such as adding up columns of figures correctly, thinking out space relationships, and turning verbal problems into figures— do in fact represent arithmetic ability or can be taken as a true index of the way that ability varies from person to person. That is why in psychological measurement it is often necessary to remind ourselves that what we have measured is a carefully singled-out performance which must not be taken as implying more than it does, because almost certainly it does not represent the individual's whole range in even one ability, let alone tell us anything else about him.[1]

Still, it is only through sample performances that psychological measurement can be done at all, and these performances tend to be selected in the light of ordinary common sense and common observation.

If we analyse arithmetic ability into a large number of single skills, as indicated, it is likely that we shall come back in the end to a composite score which represents the individual's ability fairly adequately, and this analytic method, whereby the complex activity is unravelled into separate strands, makes the actual measurement much easier. We can take each performance as a single *variable* which differs in amount between one person and another, and these amounts can be measured, if we wish, in quite small units.

It is a different matter, however, if the performance is a complex one which cannot be broken down in this way, but must be evaluated as a whole. Many psychologists doubt whether *measurement* can be done at all in these circumstances. A sweet-tooth has no trouble in choosing between a bag with six peppermint humbugs in it and one with only four. The first is demonstrably better to the precise extent of two humbugs. But how does anyone enumerate a preference? By how many units does an artist prefer Rembrandt to Josef Albers, or does a little girl like a golden-haired doll that talks better than a dark-haired

---

[1] We must always remember that the measure of a characteristic or ability we arrive at in this way is no more than the total of the separate measurements. It will be a valid estimate only if the choice of variables was representative—a point on which disagreement can arise! The difficult question of validity is mentioned again on page 44 and page 50.

doll with a wardrobe of pretty clothes; or a teacher rank one child's pretty fairy story higher than another's well-thought-out explanation of how a steam engine works?

The usual technique for these *qualitative* judgements is to arrange the performers in rank order, or order of merit, making no attempt to quantify the exact degrees of difference between them. An individual's score is then awarded simply in accordance with his position in the group. Suppose, for the sake of example, it was somehow or other impossible to measure heights in units of length, it would still be possible—on the evidence of the eyes—to arrange twenty children in a row with the tallest at one end and the shortest at the other. We could then 'award' a height-score of 20 to the tallest child and of 17 to the fourth tallest and so on. We do not, of course, know by such means how much taller one child is than another. We only know that there are three points of difference in their comparative scores, which is not the same thing at all.

This is a serious shortcoming of the technique, but the comparative method is the usual, and often the only way of quantifying those differences between individuals which cannot be directly measured and cannot be broken down into single performances. A score, or rating, of this kind gets its value from its position in a descending series. It may have only a restricted, local value like the 'best' performance in a classroom; but such a score may have a value in respect of the whole population. An intelligence quotient, for example, really states someone's ability level in the whole population to which he belongs, which brings us now to the consideration of how widely psychological measurement must be done to achieve representative results.

2 Surveys and samples

Most psychological measurement is carried out in order to establish the true facts about a whole population. By a *population* is meant all the members of a certain very extensive human group; for instance, all the children under the administration of a local education authority who have their eighth birthday in the first half of the current year, or all the employees of a large industrial concern with branches in the north and in the home counties, or all the married couples in Wimbledon who have three or more children of school age. Sometimes such a population may be surveyed entire down to its uttermost member, if it is strictly defined like an age group in school, or localized like the third example. But populations do not stay fixed for very long; they shift about all over the place and shed and acquire members so rapidly that their limits can never be defined. You might, for example, want to establish the general musical views of the audiences who stream to the Royal Albert Hall in London on summer evenings. You may even want to legislate for a population which is not even in existence yet, like the population of British universities in 1980. In such cases you can only take a sample. Even when the actual numbers and location are known, a sample is often preferred, if only to avoid the labour of measuring and sorting out the facts about the whole enormous category. In any case, as statisticians have been patiently telling us for years, there is usually nothing to be gained by so doing.

The function of a *sample* is to provide information which can be taken as true of the whole population, because the sample represents it so well. The best sample in the world cannot give us exact information down to the last individual, but it will give us a very close approximation, and a close approximation would be the best you could do even if you did measure the entire population. This is because the 'true' facts will have changed in the interval between the measuring and the recording. Everyone knows that the national census becomes, strictly speaking, out of date overnight. None of the groups contain exactly the same number of members or all of the same individuals as when the returns were made, simply on account of the ordinary human events of birth and death. In the same way you cannot hope to establish the 'true' average height of all the fourteen-year-old boys in a large community, because every day of the week a number of them will cease to be fourteen and another number will qualify for inclusion by ceasing to be thirteen. Of course your information will remain approximately correct, because changes cancel out and the general pattern does not alter. To establish such a pattern a good sample does equally well.

Now what is a reliable sample? In the first place, readers will expect that it ought to be an unbiassed one. This means that the examples must be picked out from the whole population by some system which has nothing to do with the thing that is to be measured. If you tried to find the average male height from the members of the police force you would be far out, because your sample would be a group already selected in part on a criterion of height. Similarly you would not try to establish the language norms of an adolescent age group by taking all your cases from the third year of a grammar school in a middle-class residential suburb.

On the other hand, picking out cases quite at random on a hit-or-miss basis does not necessarily tell us anything significant. There is nothing magical about the fact that one or two cases have been picked out by sheer chance, although advertizers often speak as if there were. If you asked an unknown school class a question, chose one child at random to answer it, and got a brilliant answer, you would have no right to assume that the whole class was brilliant on the strength of this one remarkable result. All you would know is that there was at least one bright child in the group. You would not know how many more.

The same thing holds as long as your sample is too small. It is easy to see the absurdity of a 'sample' of one; but it is just as absurd to argue anything from a small sample just because you have made it up at random. Random choice begins to matter only when the sample is big enough, which brings us to the second property of a reliable sample, its size.

Now 'big enough' will not always be the same thing. The size of a sample depends, of course, on the size of the background population and the number of cases we can get at of the thing we are investigating. One of the difficulties in medical research is that not enough cases can be got at to establish the general nature of some disease, or its cure, and in this respect at least, educational surveys have a great advantage. Their 'populations' are often easily located and the sample from them can be made up with a fair certainty of adequate numbers. For instance, it would be a gargantuan task to give an individual intelligence test to every last eleven-year-old in the country, but if you decided to test all the children born on certain days in the appropriate year you could calculate beforehand how many children you would be likely to include, and such a system of choice would of course be unbiassed for the object of the survey, since as far as we know there is no relationship at all between a baby's intelligence and the date of his birthday.

You may also wish to *stratify* your sample, that is, to include in it representatives of the different groups in your population on the basis of ordinary observation, and as far as possible in the right proportions, which will also affect its size. Having made up your 'random' sample in this far from random manner, how do you know when you have been successful?

Roughly speaking, a sample is big enough and representative enough when the results of the measurement fall into a definite pattern, and this pattern does not change when we examine more cases, or even when we do the survey over again with a fresh sample. Now, some times a pattern turns out surprising, but, generally speaking, in psychological measurement this does not happen. The pattern of the results does not usually contradict ordinary common-sense observation of the characteristic we are measuring, but simply confirms scientifically what has been expected already in a vague, general sort of way. Long before Binet, teachers must have taken rueful note of the difference between thick-headedness and quickness in the uptake, and been thankful, on the whole, that most of their scholars were run-of-the-mill. Binet's findings about the wide spread of intelligence were impressive, but they were not revolutionary. There was nothing in them that flatly contradicted common sense.

The reader will see, then, that common likelihood or probability is one way of deciding whether a sample has been well selected. We must spend a little time now on considering this useful auxiliary to psychological measurement.

3 The patterns of probability

When something in the past has happened often it is likely to happen again. On the strength of this probability, you would be wise to take your umbrella with you on an October morning, even if it is not positively raining, and you might risk leaving it at home on a June day that begins cloudy. Of course, you can quite easily be caught in a sudden shower on Midsummer Day, because *probability* means that there are other possibilities. Certainty means that you must include in your prediction all the possibilities there are. Sometimes there is only one. It is, for instance, certain that everybody now alive will one day be dead. Sometimes there are two, so that if you predict that a penny which falls flat will come down *either* heads *or* tails, you are certain to be right, having named both possibilities. Sometimes there are many possibilities, and to be perfectly right about what is going to happen we must mention *all* these possible alternatives. This adds up to total certainty, or unity, and each of the separate possibilities makes up a fraction of this.

They are not equal fractions. Some of the possibilities have a bigger share of the total certainty and are therefore more likely to happen than others. For instance, if we throw two coins, 'both heads' can only happen in one way, 'both tails' can only happen one way, but 'one head, one tail' can happen by two possible arrangements, left hand coin a tail, right hand a head, or else vice versa. So 'one head, one tail' has half of the four possible arrangements and is therefore more likely to happen.

Similarly with *ten* coins. There are actually 1,024 possible arrangements in which ten coins can fall, but there is only one possible way in which they can *all* be heads, and one possible way in which they can *all* be tails, whereas there are *ten* possible arrangements of 'one head, nine tails' since that one head can be in any one of the ten positions. So the probability of 'all heads' is $\frac{1}{1024}$ which is a minute share of the total certainty, whereas the arrangement 'five heads, five tails' can happen by any one of 252 possible arrangements, and its share of the total certainty is the fraction $\frac{252}{1024}$.

Total certainty of prediction in this case means saying that if you throw ten coins they will fall in *some* ratio of heads to tails varying from nothing to ten, and if you put some money on every one of them you would certainly get a fraction of it back. But betting even on the midmost term (the five to five ratio) which has the biggest fraction of the whole possibility, is still pretty wild speculation, since it leaves 722 chances out of 1,024 that it will not happen.[1]

Nevertheless, if we give all the possibilities a chance they will eventually turn up, and in the right proportions. This simply means, for the present example, throwing the ten coins often enough, which would have to be several thousand times, although a thousand throws would give *approximately* the same pattern of results. The largest number of throws would show a five to five ratio of heads to tails, the two next largest six to four and four to six, and the pure or extreme cases would occur most seldom and probably only once. We would say that just over a thousand throws would be a representative *sample* of all the throws of ten coins that are ever likely to happen in the world, and that the results of it could be taken as typical.

This pattern of results, with the majority of the cases falling at the average, and the actual numbers tapering off to the two extremes, is called *normal distribution* since the results are distributed, or spread out, according to normal likelihood or probability. It is, as most readers will know, the most familiar pattern in human measurements. Whatever the variable may be, whether it is size of head, speed of reaction, or age in months for the first spoken word, there are far more occurrences of the middle values than of any other, and extreme cases have the smallest share of all the occurrences—exactly in accordance with the mathematics of probability. It is not difficult to

[1] Many readers will have long since recognized in all this the expansion of the binomial $(a+b)^n$. The present informal explanation is felt to be necessary for bringing out the significance of *probability* in the results of psychological measurement.

reason out why this should be so. Suppose, for the sake of argument, a man to have equal numbers of tall and short ancestors, then he has about twice as many chances of inheriting average height (one 'tall' gene with one 'short' gene) as of extreme tallness (two 'tall' genes) or extreme shortness (two 'short' genes). Of course the biological laws of inheritance are nothing like so simple; there are very seldom only two alternative ways that a human characteristic can turn out; and there are other factors besides inheritance at work on individual differences. Nevertheless, wherever there are a large number of possibilities and a great variety of factors which bring these about, the pattern remains the same. There is a strong tendency for 'compromise' cases to be favoured and for extremes to be left with a minute share of the pattern of results.

Human traits which can be directly measured fall into the pattern of normal distribution. It is reasonable to assume that non-tangible characteristics, such as mental abilities, are distributed throughout the population in the self-same way, although it cannot actually be demonstrated by direct measurement. But when the results of a psychological survey take this approximate form, then two things are supposed to be confirmed. First, the measuring devices have been sound; the tests and performances selected have done their job. Secondly, the sample chosen from the population has been large enough and representative enough; the results are approximately the same as though the whole population had been tested. They can be taken as giving the 'true' facts about the whole population in respect of the characteristic that has been measured in the survey.

Of course, patterns in results do not appear of their own accord. As we work our way through the sample the cases pile up haphazard and in no sort of order. The results must be arranged and summarized so that the pattern gets a chance to emerge. This is exactly what statistics do for psychological measurement, so to complete the chapter we must consider some of these useful devices.

4 Summarizing the results

Educational statistics can be useful at several levels—that is to say, they can be more or less precise according to what is going to be done with them. An informal summing-up like 'Oh, about one in four, I should say' may be helpful if you want to provide for the pupils who will drink ginger-beer instead of orangeade at the Christmas party. A teacher's statistical needs in the classroom lie somewhere between this sort of invaluable working guide and advanced psychometrics. Some of the devices mentioned in this and later chapters can be used quite properly by a class teacher who wants to get the maximum of useful information out of his own tests and assessments; others involve elaborate computations which can only be done on large-scale surveys where precise and scientifically organized results are wanted; but their purposes and the way these are achieved can be readily enough appreciated by anyone interested in modern education and prepared to give a little thought to them. The actual terms used, and their meanings, should be familiar to teachers as a matter of course, and luckily, although the formulas are usually a neater way of expressing them, there are few ideas in educational statistics which cannot be put into quite ordinary words.

A teacher who has just read through a batch of essays is interested in getting them into some order of merit to see the general trend of the performance. This is a statistical procedure. But a teacher will also be very interested to see whose name appears on this week's best effort and how the quiet-spoken boy who is a newcomer to the class compares with the established residents. This is not a statistical matter. Statistics are planned to dispense with names and personalities.[1] The statistical interest of a score or recorded measurement is not in who gets it, but in how it compares with all the other scores and measurements. For example, a height of six feet two is significant because there are not very many instances of this height, and because a very large percentage of heights fall below it. The simplest statistical treatment consists in bringing out this significance clearly. How frequently have you found any given score, measurement, or level of performance actually occurring? Have there been ten others like it, or hundreds? Was it the only one? And secondly, what is its position? How often have lower scores occurred? Have higher scores been even rarer, and how much rarer?

A *frequency table* is exactly what one would expect, a statement of the frequency with which the various scores or measures have actually occurred in the present survey. On the left hand we make a list of all the *possible* values of our variable, as measured in the unit we have chosen, starting with the highest one likely and coming down, unit by unit, to the lowest one possible. It should be emphasized here that this column (usually called the X column) consists of every value of

---

[1] Although only for the time being. Statistical calculations aim at establishing an objective standard against which an individual performance can be evaluated. The end-purpose is highly personal!

the variable which *could* occur, irrespective of whether or not it has happened to appear among the results of the present investigation. In theory the X column could be made out without referring to the results at all, although in practice it usually begins with the highest *observed* value and goes down to the lowest observed. This would certainly be the procedure of a class teacher with a sample of perhaps forty-one test results. With very big samples, the human memory being what it is, especially after a long spell of hard work, it is usually better to begin a step or two above the highest score one remembers and take it down a step or two below the lowest one, leaving room for possible forgotten extremes (Figure 1, page 61).

Each value in the X column appears, of course, only once. It is the business of the frequency (or *f*) column to record the actual observed number of examples of each value that have occurred in the survey. Where overall numbers are small there will be some blanks, which may turn out to be quite significant blanks and will be duly reckoned with when calculations are made.

The easiest way to enter the frequencies is to take each case just as it comes and enter a tick or *tally* for it against the appropriate value, then add the ticks for each value at the end of the entering. This saves the trouble of sorting out a big bundle of examination scripts, for example, into order of merit. A machine can be induced to do the same work by sorting into slots cards with the results punched on them (Figure 2a). A less spectacular time-saver, if the survey is big and results cover a wide range, is to squeeze the X column into a smaller number of categories, or *class intervals*. For example, any score of 30, 31, 32, 33, 34 is entered against the X value 30–34. The class interval above would be 35–39, the one just below 25–29. There are various ways of indicating the limits of a class interval but there must be no ambiguity. We must never, for example, invent an X column which runs 40–45, 35–40, 30–35.

Results arranged in a *frequency distribution* are said to be *grouped* and grouping makes it easier to see the trend of our survey. A graph almost draws itself, as you may observe by turning the page sideways and looking at the clusters of tallies in Figure 1a. A regulation *histogram* or column graph appears in Figure 2b and a 'perfect' curve of normal probability in Figure 2e. The reader is reminded that it is the total *area* of all the columns, and the total area enclosed within the curve which represents the collected information.

A familiar way of summarizing results is to state the average, which in ungrouped data means laborious adding up of all the separate scores before dividing the total by the number of individuals. From a frequency table the first step can be shortened by multiplying across, that is, each X value by its frequency in the f column. If the class-intervals contain several values of X we take the middle one as our multiplier, which would, for instance be 32 in the interval 30–34. This will give us a very close approximation to the figure we should have got by totalling all the individual scores and will save an enormous amount of tedium. (Note that the product of our multiplying across will be zero if the X value has a blank against it in the f column).

There are other and more sophisticated time-savers in the calculation of the average or *arithmetic mean*, but it remains pretty cumbrous and may not serve classroom purposes any better than simpler devices. The *mean* can be misleading as a summary of the performance of a limited group. One or two exceptionally high scores may push it up, so that more than half the group have scores *below* the average; conversely, one or two very low ones will reduce it with contrary effects. For these reasons, the *median*, or midmost, score can be better. It is very easily arrived at for ordinary purposes by simply counting up our tallies from the bottom until we arrive at the middle one (the 25th in Figure 1) and then reading across to the X value where this middle tally falls. This is our *median* or middle score. If the number in our group or sample is even, then we take the X value at the tally which is just above half-way, since the median is defined as that score or value below which *half* the cases in our sample are to be found. The median, like the mean, may be taken as representative of the whole group's performance.

We must, of course, make some adjustments in this pleasantly simple process where there are class intervals containing several values of X. A *rough median*, good enough for many purposes, is simply to take the middle value of X in the interval known to contain the median because the identifying tally falls there. Or we can be more precise, basing our adjustment on the exact number of tallies we need from this category to make up our half-way total. When our mathematics have been of the more conscientious sort, the median is entitled to be called the *fiftieth percentile*, which means that score, or measure, or value of X below which there are 50 per cent of the cases in our survey, and above which are the other, or upper, 50 per cent. It must be emphasized that the *median* itself is a *score* or level of performance, but what it separates off is, so to speak, one half of the *performers*, the inferior 50 per cent, from the upper, or superior, half.

By counting up to our quarter-way, instead of to our half-way tally, we can identify the score which slices off the lowest quarter, or lowest 25 per cent, of our performers. This is consequently known as Q_1 (for first or lowest quartile) or else as the *twenty-fifth percentile*. Similarly there is a *seventy-fifth percentile* or Q_3.[1]

Between Q_1 and Q_3 there fall the two middle quarters or middle fifty per cent of our performers, which may be taken as the solid core, highly representative of the group as a whole, since they will be more thickly clustered between these two points than above Q_3 and below Q_1. The tighter they are packed (that is, the more their performances resemble each other), the narrower will be the little range of scores enclosing the central group. We can measure its limits exactly by using Q_1 and Q_3 like a pair of compasses. The distance between these two points on the X column (which is 5 in the table in Figure 1)[2] is called the inter-quartile range. It may be halved (which gives the average of the distance between Q_3 and the median and the distance between Q_1 and the median) and then is known as Q. The size of Q depends directly on how close to the centre of the frequency distribution are the middle 50 per cent of our performers. A small Q means that they are closely packed, a larger one that they are spread out further up and down the range of scores, or, as is usually said, they are more scattered. Q is a measure of *scatter* or *dispersion* (Figure 1b).

We now can present quite an informative summary of our group's total performance by stating the *median* as an index of its central tendency, Q as an index of whether the scores are close together or strung out more widely, and the actual values of the 75th and 25th percentiles if we wish to indicate where the score begins to taper off more thinly in the approximate shape of normal distribution.

Furthermore, if we know the respective values of Q in two tests or examinations we can combine their results with more fairness. Obviously an examination which has a range of scores from 30 to 100 is going to swamp the effects of another one with a much narrower range, where the highest score is perhaps 75 and the lowest 44. Suppose we want them to have equal influence or weight, then the influence of the first will be too great if we simply add them together to give a combined or aggregate score. But if we know that Q in the first distribution is 6 and in the second 3, we can adjust the scores proportionately. This is a simple case, to be sure, with our first Q just twice the size of our second, so that we need only halve all the scores in the first examination, thus reducing its total range and therefore its influence upon the

[1] Q_2 is the median itself. [2] Page 61.

aggregate score; or, conversely, we may double the scores in the second. Be it noted, in case any reader suspects some lurking injustice in all this manipulation, that when we make exactly the same adjustment to *all* the scores in any one examination, we do not interfere with the order of merit which is the thing that matters. It will, of course, make differences in the rank order of the *combined* scores, but that is the whole object of the adjustment!

The *percentile* technique can be extended as we wish, for cutting off any percentage of our sample of performers. The tenth percentile is that score below which are the poorest ten per cent of them. There is an 87th percentile, which is exceeded by the scores of only the best 13 per cent, and so on. Similarly, we can identify the *percentile rank* of anybody's score, though there is a little difficulty with the highest one of all. Strictly speaking, there is *no* 100th percentile score, as a percentile is always taken as the top limit of a class interval, and the very highest score of all is *inside* this category, so to speak, and not on the uppermost edge of it! In practice, however, this objection tends to be ignored when we are working with class examinations. The highest score is often called the 100th percentile and the lowest the zero percentile.

The statistical devices just described, though among the simplest, are very useful if we wish to combine examination scores more fairly, or even compare performances in two very different fields of study. This is an important matter in testing and assessment and we must return to it in a later chapter.

There remains to be defined one important statistical term (or *parameter*) although for various reasons, among them the awkwardness of calculation, it is not likely to be so useful a tool for the class teacher. But the results of large surveys and of educational research of all kinds make very little sense unless it is thoroughly understood.

The reader must now have a pretty good idea that the amount of 'spread-out-ness' or *scatter* in the scores obtained is just about the most important feature any test or examination can have—or for that matter any other kind of measuring procedure. The best-known index of all for this is called the *standard deviation*, which has for its algebraic sign the Greek letter for s, called sigma and written σ. It is calculated from the *mean* or average score, which acts as a base or departing point. Every score above or below the mean departs from its stated value, the scores which are close to it by small amounts, scores well above and well below by very much more. The closer packed all the scores are the less they will in general differ or *deviate* from the mean score.

We could summarize all the deviations in the usual way by simply averaging them[1] but for certain mathematical reasons this is less useful and less informative than the standard deviation. The calculation of this famous parameter, like that of the mean, is much quicker with grouped than with ungrouped scores, but even so it remains somewhat unattractive and its advantages are not apparent at first. To get it, we must square the deviation of each score from the mean score, add these squared deviations, take their average, and then extract its square root, which brings us back to something not unlike the *average* deviation, but with important properties the latter does not have.

For one thing, the squaring gets rid of the awkward fact that the deviations of scores *below* the mean are *minus* quantities, while those above are *plus*. Strictly speaking, then, they cannot be 'added' to get their simple average, since the minus and plus signs would cancel each other. But the really important property of the standard deviation is its relationship with normal distribution, which is the reason why its use is chiefly in grand-scale surveys, whose results have a reasonable chance of taking this form.

Normal distribution, when graphed, forms a curve whose shape is exactly defined. It can be drawn like any graph, from an algebraic equation which expresses the exact way in which the curve declines from the high central 'bulge' down to the base line at the two extremes, giving it the typical 'bell' shape (see Figure 1e and Figure 3).[2] The *area* inside this curve is the sum-total of the variable we are measuring. It represents the share each value has of this total, which is a large share at the middle where the curve is high, and a minute share where it comes down almost to the base line at the two extremes.

In normal distribution we can find out what exact percentage of our cases will fill up any part, or 'slice' of the total area that we like to indicate by drawing two vertical lines between the base-line (or X axis) and the curve. Suppose we draw one of our verticals (or co-ordinates) at the point of the average or mean score, which for convenience we may imagine to be 60. (Any other number would do equally well, as an illustration.) This vertical exactly halves our total area, and 50 per cent of our cases fill up each half. Likewise, let us imagine that the standard deviation has worked out at 10. (Again, our choice is for simplicity's sake alone, since σ like any other algebraic term can have any arithmetical value, just as x can equal 2 or 5 or 17.)

[1] Suppose the mean score is 50 and the next three above it are 51, 56, and 58, their respective deviations are 1, 6, and 8, giving an *average* difference from the mean of 5.   [2] Pages 61 and 63.

Then, if we count ten points along the base-line from 60 to 70 we have covered a distance of 'one times' sigma, and similarly if we count along from 60 to 50, except that this is in a negative direction. Suppose we draw two further verticals at these two sigma distances from the mean, which we can shortly refer to as +1 and −1; then, because of the fixed relationship between the standard deviation and the curve of normal distribution, we know that between our two verticals we have enclosed an area containing slightly over 68 per cent of all our cases, 34 per cent on each side of the vertical at the mean. That is to say, in any human trait or ability which is normally distributed throughout the population (which means a great many) over two-thirds of the individuals will have scores or ratings ranging from one standard deviation below the mean to one standard deviation above it.

Between the two uprights at $+1\sigma$ and $+2\sigma$ (in our example this would be at 80) the space is much smaller. It contributes a little under 13 per cent to the total area, or number of cases. The addition made by the next 'slice', between $+2\sigma$ and $+3\sigma$ is about 2 per cent, and by the next again (between $+3\sigma$ and $+4\sigma$) it is so minute that we may say, in effect, the whole population is enclosed between -3σ on the 'deficit' side of the average and $+3\sigma$ on the bonus side. So we have a good idea of what our highest level of achievement is likely to be in any measurable characteristic of the human race—and an excellent insight into why it is so scarce! (See Figure 3.)

The two statistical procedures so far described have the same purpose, which is to summarize results in a psychological enquiry, like a school or college examination on the one hand, or a large-scale educational survey on the other. The first uses the *median* score to represent the general level of performance, the distances between the quartiles to measure spread or *scatter*, and *percentile* ranks to pinpoint the value of individual scores. Because of its comparative ease in calculation, and because it can be applied quite usefully without too much insistence on mathematical precision, this method is one which a class teacher might use, especially when comparing attainments in different examinations.

The other method uses the *mean* to summarize the central tendency of the results and the *standard deviation* as a measure of scatter. This latter is a most important statistic in all large-scale surveys, chiefly because it has a fixed mathematical relationship with that particular kind of spread or dispersion which we call *normal distribution*, the pattern into which most measurable human characteristics tend to fall over the whole population, and in any sample large enough to represent the whole. Informal use of this measure, therefore, is not really desirable, as samples the size of a school class are not big enough to give it its full meaning. But it is well worth knowing about for the insight it gives into the results of educational and psychological surveys and investigations.

2

Educational Assessment

1 *Some surveys*

Psychological measurement is far from new. It has been going on in various forms for over a hundred years, and the value of its contribution to educational progress was realized very promptly. At the beginning of this century Binet in France and Spearman in England had both begun their enquiries into the nature of human ability, and on Binet's part more particularly into the curious inequalities in the way it is shared out. Meantime Pavlov, starting a series of experiments on the physiology of digestion, found that he had stumbled on an important set of psychological learning principles, which to this very day show no sign of being fully worked out and done with. Cattell moved about the same time from Britain to America, where he fostered the national enthusiasm for individual differences by urging Thorndike to adapt his animal learning experiments to human situations. Not that systematic study of human learning was an innovation even then, for it dated at least as far back as the brilliant work of Ebbinghaus on memorizing. During this period, too, interest in the growth of children began to find informal anecdotal methods unsatisfactory and to look for evidence systematically collected and set down, so that the progress of behavioural development could be charted with confidence. These, then, were three main lines of enquiry for which psychological measurement was found to supply reliable information for educators; individual differences in ability and performance, the nature and conditions of learning and the growth and development of young people. It would be hard to say which has the greatest share of educational importance, and in any case the question is hardly needed. Ideas have passed freely from one area of research to another, and, as usual in psychology, although it is convenient to treat them under separate headings, they are best understood as the same matter looked at from different approaches.

An interesting point to be taken note of here is that most of the discoveries made in those earlier days are still acceptable. Three generations of twentieth-century students have grinned (or groaned) at

38

Ebbinghaus's nonsense syllables, but his recommendations for good memorizing are still as useful a bit of modern classroom equipment as a teaching machine streamlined in perfect accord with Skinner's reinforcement theory. Likewise, the prognostic value of Gesell's tests of infant intelligence may be doubted (there are plenty of similar doubts about the more recently perfected *eleven-plus* machinery) but his conscientious assembling of almost endless examples of child behaviour before he ventured to identify the *norm*, is still the basic method in any developmental survey, although Gesell's early work is forty years old. Again, by the beginning of the nineteen-twenties Ballard was vigorously stating the case for 'new type' examinations, and many of his handy 'one-minute' tests have justified his claim for their reliability by being still in use. It was during the twenties that Burt collected his material for his two immense London surveys of delinquency and backwardness (1) (although the second was not published until 1937) and many modern surveys, like the one carried out some years ago over a complete population of fourteen-year-olds in the schools of greater Manchester (2) admit their debt to his methods and to the leads he offered for further investigations. The history of educational research since the war has been the development of psychological ideas already very active, and gradual refinement of the three great principles of measurement discussed in the last chapter—analysing the subject-matter of the enquiry into variables that can be measured and compared, building up an adequate sample of cases, and handling the results so as to make them give up all their information.

Sometimes the important thing is to break down the subject-matter. Burt, for example, had to define backwardness by some criterion that could be stated numerically and still remain a valid way of defining backwardness. Then he was able to map the London boroughs by the percentage of backward pupils found in each. In the Manchester survey, Wiseman describes how socio-economic conditions were analysed into twelve measurable factors which could then be correlated with the test-scores of fourteen-year-olds in each ward of the city. Thus the relationship, whatever it was, between social conditions and school performance could be established.

Sometimes the sampling is important. For example, if the difficulty level of a new test is to mean anything it must be *standardized* (see below) on a large enough number of children from the same *age* and *educational* group as it is going to be used on. An obvious example are the eleven-plus tests of Verbal Reasoning issued by Moray House College of Education in Scotland and the National Foundation for

Educational Research in England, in which it is critically important to find the value of any score in terms of the percentage of children in the age-group who fall below it, a process which clearly depends on a reliable try-out.

In theory sampling is not difficult to do, and most samples turn out fairly representative, although miscalculations have occurred. In 1932, for instance, the year of the first national survey of all Scottish eleven-year-olds by a group intelligence test, a representative sample was wanted from among them of about a thousand children who were to be tested individually as a kind of check on the results of the group test (3). In spite of its elaborate composition, this sample turned out to be slightly biassed in the direction of superiority, and corrections had to be applied before it could be used for comparison. On the other hand when the whole investigation was repeated in 1947 the special sample, chosen straightforwardly by date of birth and called the Six-day sample, turned out like a miniature of the whole year group. Their intelligence quotients had a distribution very near to normal (see page 35) and all the other factors studied in the enquiry, like the size of family they belonged to and the income group of their parents, were so well represented that they were dubbed a Scotland in miniature (4).

Sampling is also important when a new teaching method is being tried out by the 'control group' technique. This means that one sample of children are taught by the new method (such as the Initial Teaching Alphabet in reading) while a control group, matched child for child to the other one, are taught for the same period by traditional methods. Then any significant difference in tested performance must be due to the one remaining variable in the situation, all the others having been fixed or equalized between the two groups; intelligence, age, sex, socio-economic status, and educational background. Obviously the selection of two special matched samples like these is a skilled and lengthy business.

Sometimes, however, a special sample is easier to arrive at than a general representative one. Yet when Terman and his collaborators followed up the life-histories of a highly gifted group of children, he made up his sample by more than one criterion so as to avoid bias towards any one kind of giftedness (5).

In all present-day surveys and investigations, special efforts are made to refine the measuring instruments themselves, and at least to make sure what it is they are measuring. In his preface to the comparative accounts of the 1932 and 1947 Scottish surveys, Maxwell remarks that attempting to 'measure' the intelligence level of a whole national year group by one single pencil-and-paper test would nowadays be regarded as rather naive (4). Intelligence would seldom be spoken of by psychologists now as something that can be exactly measured by a single score or performance, but as a complex of many abilities and skills which need to be separately identified so that the examiner has a better idea what his present test is actually designed to measure.

Analysing results is another technique which has been undergoing refinement over the last twenty years. This is partly because educational surveys have so many different purposes, since most of them are undertaken to supply an answer for some particular problem or enquiry. Many surveys are comparative, and this of course means a pair of investigations matched as far as possible. For instance, one of the chief objects of the 1947 survey was to compare the test-scores of eleven-year-olds with the pre-war results, since there was a good deal of interest just after the war in a possible falling off in ability among schoolchildren (which, incidentally, was not confirmed). Again, the Ministry of Education national reading survey in 1948 was followed by another eight years later, which established significant improvements in standards of reading during the interval (6).

A perennially interesting educational enquiry is the relationship between school performance and environmental factors, particularly the social and economic conditions in the school's neighbourhood. This gives rise to surveys of the 'cause and effect' type, which may be very large, like Burt's classic exploration of backwardness, or limited to a sample where the influence of one factor only, such as home conditions, is singled out and estimated. Cause-and-effect surveys make particular use of the important device called *correlation* which will be considered in this chapter.

Studies of the *follow-up* type trace the progress of the same group or sample of children over a period. Terman's mammoth scheme for observing the characteristics of highly intelligent children and tracing their life-histories up to the middle years was begun in California in 1921, and has dealt one crushing blow after another to the many traditional misconceptions about the highly gifted. It is not true that their mental superiority is offset by physical inferiority; that early promise inevitably peters out; nor that the gifted are handicapped in their adjustment to ordinary life. This survey is a good example of the difference between vague popular assumption and evidence scientifically collected and presented.

Long-term investigations are, of course, expensive and difficult.

In this country they are mostly carried out to serve some definite educational need, such as the problem of transfer from primary to secondary school. For the best part of three decades this has been thought of chiefly as a problem of selection, although in many areas where comprehensive schools are replacing the old tripartite or bipartite arrangement a change of policy is now well under way. But whether one regards the sorting out and streaming of children by ability and attainment a good thing or not, the promotion policy of the forties and fifties gave a great impetus to research in psychological measurement. The tests and assessments have reached a high level of reliability and much useful information has been gathered.

The crucial requirement was that assessment of pupils at the point of transfer should forecast their secondary school performance three, or five, or even six years hence. The only way to find out what type of test, or battery of tests, would give the most dependable prediction, was to institute an elaborate follow-up programme, by trying out a variety of assessments on a sample year-group of primary school leavers, follow them through their secondary school career and compare their promotion test scores with their actual successes in secondary education. 'Success' was such things as their performance in school examinations and creditable passes at the G.C.E. or equivalent level. Whichever combination of tests proved by this method to have given the best prediction, would then be recommended for future selections.

Two of the best-known of these follow-up surveys are McClelland's *Selection for Secondary Education*, published in Scotland in 1942, and *Admission to Grammar School*, produced by Yates and Pidgeon in 1957 as the third part of an investigation by the National Foundation for Educational Research (7). Many of the experimental tests and assessments were very similar in the two studies; each arrived at a helpful working criterion of secondary school 'success'; the recommendations they offered on reliable predictors had certain differences of detail, but were again on the whole much alike. They agreed upon the principle that no *single* test or measure would adequately predict future performance and that some well-balanced combined score must be worked out. Both significantly concluded with a sober warning that no scheme of allocation can be perfect, since individual development does not conform to pattern.

However, allocation of some kind or another, either to separate schools or to separate instruction courses, will probably always be necessary, so that some form of comparison between child and child will have to be undertaken. This placing of an individual's performance or ability within the context of the general level in the group he belongs to, is the essential process of all psychological tests and measurements. The techniques are particularly clearly illustrated by the eleven-plus examinations, which therefore make a good starting point for a discussion of the principles of assessment which have developed during the present educational era, and of the kind of tests that are constructed on these principles.

We may go on, then, from this very brief account of the kind of enquiries that educational surveys have undertaken to the measuring instruments they actually use.

2 Tests and examinations

The typical form of the 'eleven-plus' is probably familiar to most readers. It consisted, characteristically, of the kind of test where the pupil needs nothing (apart from his brains!) but a sharp pencil for underlining, filling a blank space with a number or a letter, putting a cross against one of several alternatives, and so on. Not all promotion examinations were quite so austere as this, but it has been the basic form, even though it might be supplemented by something in the nature of a more creative effort, like a short written composition. Besides this, the teacher's personal impression of the pupil would certainly be included in the final count, although this would not be left in the form of a simple expression of opinion, but would be scaled and tailored to fit the other estimates.

What are the arguments for this kind of examination, and why has the traditional type been either discarded, or retained only with a number of limiting precautions? We shall consider this question in the present chapter only as it affects scholastic tests and assessment, leaving the special case of intelligence testing to be discussed on its own.

The substitution of *objective* test questions for the traditional kind was advocated long ago by psychologists like Ballard, so it is perhaps time we stopped talking about New Type examinations! The form of question which is answered by a tick or a letter of the alphabet is just as familiar to every reader of magazine quizzes as the old friends he remembers from his schooldays which ran something like these:

Discuss the importance of the events leading up to the outbreak of war in 1914.

What evidence is there for the assumption that matter is discrete and not continuous?

Compare the characters of Macbeth and Lady Macbeth.

These have been called *open* questions since it is open to the pupil to give the best account he can of himself. The question gives no guidance, or rather, imposes no limits and the writer can say anything he thinks relevant and in any form of words that seem to him effective. Is there anything wrong with this as a sample of insight into the logic of events, or his grasp of the chemistry teacher's demonstrations, or his appreciation of Shakespeare's genius? Probably not. Whenever behaviour is in the nature of a *whole performance*, the most valid index of ability that can be offered is a sample of the performance itself. The only way to find out how someone plays the piano is to let him play it. Items of musical theory correctly answered, along with a few correct identifications of pitch and rhythm, and a higher degree of accuracy in finger movement, will not add up to the same thing. Similarly, if we want to know whether a young child can write something of his own invention we had better let him write it. Thus: *Make up a sentence telling how Tom felt when he unwrapped his present* is an open type of question. Its *closed* or *objective* counterpart would be to ask our small examinee to draw a line beneath the one word out of three which tells how Tom felt. But this would not be quite the same thing.

Common sense leaves us in no doubt that the most *valid* criterion of someone's ability to perform some complex bit of behaviour is a sample of his performance. The criticisms that have come so thick and fast about this kind of test situation have not been aimed at its *validity*. They simply say that such a performance is not *measurable* and that it is unrealistic to stick a numbered score on it. The fact is, of course, that answers in an examination of the creative type (as traditional examinations are sometimes called) have the kind of value discussed on page 23. It is a *qualitative* value and cannot be stated as the sum total of anything, or indeed as a quantity at all.

The assessment which examiners employ for this kind of answer is based on overall impression, and this in itself is reasonable enough. *Impression* marking, as it is usually called, is the only way for it in the end, though teachers do sometimes 'break down' the performance into so many points of information plus points for vocabulary, punctuation, spelling, and so on. But there are constantly recurring dilemmas. How do you choose between a sensitive, enthusiastic, and ill-spelt appreciation on the one hand, and a brief, faultless, and un-interesting one on the other? If an imaginative child writes *Tom was fild with deligt when he saw his pressent* are you going to prefer the blunt and unexceptionable *Tom was glad*. There is nothing for it but a personal decision and the trouble is that no two teachers would make exactly the same one.

Impression scores vary from teacher to teacher, and there have been many experiments, goodness knows, to hammer home the fact. When experienced teachers are given the same set of written compositions to score, or even simply to arrange in order, the degree of agreement will be very low. If numerical marks are asked for, the discrepancies will not be trifling. This makes comparison between two children from different schools, or even different classrooms, completely unreliable and therefore unjust, because a numerical mark has the effect of *seeming* to be accurate and dependable, whereas in fact it is quite meaningless except in one very limited context.

But impression scores are not consistently awarded even by the *same* teacher on different occasions. This also has been proved by experiment again and again. Teachers have been asked to re-score the same essays after an interval and the correspondence of the second set of scores with the first has turned out far from perfect.

It is not, of course, the care and conscientiousness of the marking that is called in question. The complexity of what is being scored makes it impossible to concentrate on every aspect of it all the time; and no teacher, nor any human being for that matter, can carry in his head the idea of one hundred separate levels of performance, so that when he calls one essay 67 and another 71 he can guarantee that they are precisely four steps apart! In fact it is perfectly understandable why, in something so critical as selection for grammar school, examiners have felt inclined to exclude written composition altogether as having little reliability either in selection or prediction.

Nevertheless, long ago in 1942 McClelland found that of all the tests and measures tried out in his particular follow-up enquiry, the old type of promotion examination traditionally used in Scottish schools gave the best *single* prediction of secondary-school success. He pointed out that it contained some test questions which were objective in effect though not in actual form, along with the freely written material. Similarly, Yates and Pidgeon tried out what they called a more 'creative' type of English test, evolved by the National Foundation on less rigid lines than the out-and-out objective form, and found it no worse a predictor, but even in certain combinations with other test scores actually superior (7). Evidence, however, is unlikely ever to be final. School performance is something that is hard to compare between one area and another, so many factors can affect it almost overnight. Teachers, and for that matter anyone interested in education, are naturally unwilling to dismiss creative effort as an unreliable index of present ability and promise for the future. The answer probably lies in two devices; devising new types of test which make the best of both worlds, as the new National Foundation tests are trying to do; and arriving at more consistent scoring systems for written work.

The most obvious line of attack is to break the composition down and score it analytically. But surprisingly enough, experiments carried out in the nineteen-fifties, when the selection examination was a burning topic, showed very little improvement either in consistency or in agreement between teachers when uniform analytic marking schedules were tried. It appears that the overall impression is no worse than any other, especially (and this has been on the whole more successful) when helped out by a *scale*, that is to say a graded set, of sample essays.

This is an old technique. A scale of perhaps ten compositions ranging in merit from very poor to very good can be treated as ten fixing points against which each composition read by the marker can be tried and then have assigned to it the grade of its nearest counterpart in the scale. A well-known example of this is supplied by Schonell in his *Diagnostic and Attainment Testing*. Schonell's scale is made up on an *age* basis, and consists of what he calls median samples. He provides, that is, a specimen composition of average or median merit, at each age level from $7\frac{1}{2}$ to $13\frac{1}{2}$, which means that any individual essay can be given an age-grading, if the marker is so minded, or a simple numerical score according to the actual age of the writer. An eight-year-old would get a higher credit for a composition of ten-year level than a nine-year-old (8).

There are, of course, objections to the age-grading technique, but this method at least has the merit of limiting the number of categories to which essays can be allocated. It avoids the unfairness of very fine grading, which impression-type scoring simply does not justify. On the other hand, *few* and *wide* merit categories mean that free composition, or indeed an open-type task of any kind, is necessarily rather a coarse measuring instrument. In particular the discrimination is poor about the middle of the range where the majority of scripts will fall, and this may very well be the critical point, since in all selection programmes one of the biggest problems are the borderline cases.

Of course numerical differences may be avoided and the scripts arranged simply in rank order. This gets rid of the misleading idea of measurement, though not of marking inconsistencies, even when the marker pins himself down to a long laborious process of paired comparison. It is not unheard-of for judges to prefer A to B, and B to C, then some time later, to prefer C to A, presumably on some shift of criterion! On the other hand, any kind of systematic procedure will have the effect of drawing the marker's attention to his own inconsistencies, and there is a strong case for finding some way of retaining impression scoring, since for so many skills and abilities open-type performance seems the most valid sort of test.

We come now to the alternative. *Attainment* tests are so called to distinguish them from the other sort of objective tests which deal with native wit rather than information. Readers who have worked their way through the thorny material of this and the last chapter will have anticipated most of the principles on which they are constructed. They are a typical case of the kind of psychological measurement described in the first section of Chapter 1. The pupil's performance, from being a complex whole and difficult to assess except by general quality, is turned into a quantitative variable, consisting of a large number of fixed single items, which can be added up to a sum total like any other kind of unit—inches, or pounds, or seconds on a stop-watch. These units are of course the individual test questions, which are all designed on the *either/or* principle, just like the penny which has to come down either head or tail. The answer to the question is *either* right *or* it is not right; there are no degrees of rightness and no alternatives. Now we have already seen what a large number of arrangements of heads and tails we get by throwing so many pennies a great many times. In just the same way, set so many test questions to a great many children and you will get every *possible* assortment of right and wrong answers. You will also get something approximately like our old friend *normal distribution*, so finely graded that the results of our widely administered test can be represented by a smooth curve. (The graph of the essay type of examination is a simple histogram consisting of a few wide rectangles.)

Of course, although this is the basic principle, no test question is exactly like our penny. It will probably be a little weighted in one or other direction. Most questions will have a slight tendency to 'come down' right, meaning that they will be correctly answered by just over half the testees. Easy ones will show nearly 100 per cent successes, and there will certainly be one or two more difficult ones with the balance the other way. But the overall effect of most attainment tests is to favour the median type of performance and minimize the occurrences of the very poor or the very brilliant one. When tests are being constructed, far more single items are made up than will be needed in the end; they are all tried out on large samples of children, and included or discarded by what they contribute to the total effectiveness.

The first step in making up an objective examination of a school subject is to break the subject-matter down into single points which can be stated in a clear-cut way. Next comes the phrasing of the questions, and most students will be familiar with the characteristic idiom, having done their own share of ticking and underlining. In *multiple choice* the correct answer is offered along with several alternatives, all of which are wrong, although there are carefully planned differences in the various ways they are wrong! One will be obviously wrong (to anyone who knows better), one will be 'nearly' right, one may even be a pun! *Multiple choice* is a tried favourite, because it is a good way of sorting out the really well-informed, but the items are bulky, and need a lot of inventiveness if the 'wrong' alternatives are to be worth putting in.

The same effect can be got more simply by the *true/false* question. This is a statement, and the student may either agree or disagree with it. The examiner of course mixes up the correct and incorrect statements about the subject-matter in random order. It is usual to have the same number of each, and care must be taken to make the falsifications just as lengthy and impressive looking as the truths. On the whole, this is an easy kind of test to make up, but it has disadvantages, the most obvious being its vulnerability to guessing. Moreover, a candidate might prudently mark *all* the statements true, which would be bound to win half-credit, unless a guessing correction is applied, like subtracting all the wrong choices from the right choices, which would leave our shrewd logician with zero! *True/false* examinations are one way of finding out if pupils have read a prescribed book, and read the whole of it. Like all objective tests they can be made to cover the whole area of the subject-matter.

Another question form which suits narrative subject-matter is the *completion* type. The significant word or phrase in the statement is left blank, to be filled in sometimes at the discretion of the pupil, but more usually from a string of alternatives, which makes it just like *multiple choice*, or from one long list from which *all* the blanks are to be filled, which makes it like a *matching* test. In a *matching* test proper, items in one column are to be correctly paired off with items in the other. Like multiple choice, it picks out the well-informed, but it penalizes errors doubly, since one mis-placing means two.

The more 'creative' test is usually of the *completion* type, the pupil drawing on his own vocabulary. The length and form of wording, however, is shaped by the question asked, so that responses remain uniform enough to be reliably compared.

Reliability of scoring means one thing and one thing only, that the total score achieved by the pupil's performance will always come out the same, no matter who does the scoring. The scorer cannot award or withdraw points to suit his own taste or judgement; as in any other kind of measurement, he only observes and records what is there, and, with the exception of the last type of test mentioned, scoring has all the ease and dependability of any automatic action.

Advantages are obvious. Comparison between pupils becomes fair and reasonable, being based on known numerical differences. The discrimination can be as fine as one chooses to make it, more test items increasing the range of possible scores and so spreading the performances more thinly. The subject-matter is better sampled by a large number of small items than by one or two open-type essay topics. A student preparing for a comprehensive objective examination would have to make sure of every scrap of information, instead of taking a chance on a lucky guess as to what might 'turn up' this time. For the teacher, too, there are other gains from the objective test than ease of scoring. It is a good teaching device, resembling in some ways the 'programmed' arrangement of subject-matter. It brings a lesson down to precise details, and the results always show up the weak points of the instruction, so setting a longish objective class test would be a good preliminary in revision of class work. This is the well-known *diagnostic* effect of objective examinations. A typical arithmetic test, for example, consisting of a large number of single calculations, brings out very clearly exactly which number combinations (the sevens with the eights, for instance) are the root cause of the pupil's failures. In a large, complex bit of problem arithmetic they are embedded in the whole and cannot be spotted as the culprits. Indeed, thoroughgoing *diagnostic* tests are a useful variant of the objective examination, and have been in existence since long before the war.

It is not the purpose of the present book to multiply descriptions of attainment tests, or catalogue examples. Many excellent tests have been published in all the elementary school skills. The student is referred to the classical work of Burt, Ballard, and Sehonell; to Vernon's admirable surveys of available material (9); and to the highly standardized tests in English and Arithmetic which have been perfected in the service of the eleven-plus selection schemes.

The objective test has its traditional list of merits; criticism of it is equally traditional. Itemizing of material is thought of as demolishing all the constructiveness of the pupil's effort, and turning it into a set of passive, push-button responses, which cannot possibly be a *valid* way of measuring it. There is, in fact, little positive evidence one way or the other. Children who write good compositions score high in objective tests of English, but this of course does not go to the true heart of the protest.

There is some justification for the fears that exist of the famous 'backwash' effect, which is that in coaching for the new-type examinations teachers may be tempted to neglect *constructive* writing so that pupils can go up to secondary school without having learned the art of making connected, let alone original, written statements. But this is a criticism of the educational policy of selection, not of the psychological *methods* which were invented to carry it out to the degree of exactness demanded. The student would do well to keep the distinction in mind between the *form* of an examination and the *purpose* of it. If fine differences between pupils are wanted, scientific psychological measurement can produce differences which will be real and reliable. If the object of the examiner, then, is to draw a failure line at some point on the measuring scale, then he is at liberty to draw it wherever he pleases, and so cut off the exact percentage of candidates required. All this is one thing. The *validity* of an examination is another question altogether.

What in fact are we trying to measure and what is a valid sample of it? There is no direct measure of reasoning, imagination, and insight into the use of words. Free composition is thought to represent these well enough and very probably does. It is also possible that a comprehensive assortment of closed questions exercises the pupil's wits equally effectively, though the result of all the thinking may be no more than a single word at a time.

Responsibility for assessment must be placed somewhere; in the open type of examination it lies heavily upon the personal judgement of the scorer; in the objective type it depends on how the examiner chooses to analyse the performance. With one last point we may leave the difficult matter of validity. The usual way to estimate the validity of a new test is to correlate it with some other criterion of excellence in the skill in question. But there is no direct proof that the criterion itself is a valid test. If, on the other hand, two kinds of test both correlate well with some third kind of performance (such as future success in the secondary school) then we may choose either method, with suitable safeguards against its limitations.

3 Evaluating and predicting individual performance

There remain to be discussed two very important statistical devices, without which educational tests would lose much of their value and any kind of selection or guidance would have very little point. The first is concerned with evaluating the performance of any one individual; the second with predicting the likely degree of success he will have in some future performance from the one being assessed at present. Our right to make these two pronouncements depends in the first case on the standardization of test results, and in the second upon the *correlation* between human performances.

The reader must be well aware by now that the essential feature of all assessment is comparison between persons in respect of whatever variable is being measured. This is true of the simplest form of assessment, that of baldly ranking individuals one below the other; it is still true whatever units or grades of difference we are able to distinguish. A three-year-old is 'backward' in implicit comparison with other three-year-olds. When we call an adolescent 'tall' or 'gifted' we mean that many others are less so. We may go on from there to state exactly how many others—either in this particular group we are dealing with, or in a biggish *sample* which allows us to generalize in terms of percentages of the whole population. Standardization is just this process of comparison made exact and applied to large numbers.

In the prolific era of psychological measurement between the wars, the classic way of standardizing test results was to set up *age norms* of attainment. If you give a large sample of children a graded silent reading test you will of course get a wide variation in success over the primary school age-range, and even within a single year group the spread will be considerable. Some sevens will so far outrank the other sevens as to surpass all but the very best readers among the eights and also a large percentage of the nines. Nevertheless there will be an appreciable difference between the overall performance of two adjacent year groups. There will also be in each age group a standard, average, or median level of performance, which can be accepted as the *norm* for the age. It was customary in those days to translate the score made by a child on an attainment test into a Reading Age, an Arithmetic Age, and so on, which might or might not be the same as his age in birthdays. If his reading score was the same as the median type of performance for eight-year-old children, then his assigned Reading Age was eight, whether he himself was eight, or ten, or six and a half.

The obvious next step was to summarize his reading progress by the ratio of his attainment age to his actual age, which last can be taken to represent, in a sense, the *expected* level of his attainment. A child of nine could be expected, in default of any other information, to have a score entitling him to a Reading Age of nine. Normal progress, then, would be in a 1:1 ratio, one year's betterment in reading for every year of instruction. Dividing attainment age by chronological age would give an ordinary arithmetical quotient, in this particular example without any fractions or decimals. Where the attainment and chronological ages were not the same, dividing the first by the second would give a clumsier result. For this reason the now time-honoured convention of multiplying the quotient by 100 was first adopted. Thus a child of eight with a reading age of ten would have a Reading Quotient of 125. So, of course, would a six-year-old with the reading ability of a seven and a half. The reference of an attainment, or scholastic, or educational quotient (all three terms were in common use) was to the rate of *progress* as observed so far.

This practice of evaluating the individual child's score by allocating it to an age level is now going out of favour for various reasons. One of them undoubtedly is this. An *age norm* is really only meaningful for the educational area in which it has been established at the try-out of the test. Yet many teachers would use a test of reading pronunciation standardized by age in London upon children in the north-west who probably had different reading experience and would make different errors, so that the norms would be different. It is now pretty well appreciated that Reading Age as a measure can have no national significance but only a regional one at best, and usually only a temporary one. Secondly, age 'norms' in school attainment go up or down with the educational and social conditions in the neighbourhood, which is not surprising, since ability to read is an acquired characteristic and therefore subject to considerable fluctuation. During his school history a child's attainment level will vary with reference to the average of his age group. There is absolutely no guarantee therefore that his Reading Quotient of 125 will stay with him indefinitely.

It is rather surprising that the term *quotient* has been retained at all. Nevertheless it has, which is confusing as well, since nowadays it is not a quotient at all but is arrived at by another device altogether. If an eleven-plus pupil had his attainment test scores translated into an English Quotient and an Arithmetic Quotient, it would not be done by comparison with other age-group performances, but on the following principle.

The value of an individual score is worked out by internal comparison within an age-group. This has come about partly because the much-discussed elevens within an educational area *were* a year group and the critical distinctions were to be made among themselves. It is partly due to a shift of opinion about the meaningfulness of age units in mental measurement, as we shall see in the next chapter, and partly to the growing realization that one should be wary of applying attainment standards outside an area, or even outside the present investigation, whatever it is.[1]

The first step in evaluating a score is to find its percentile rank. This, as the reader may remember, refers to the percentage of other scores which this particular score surpasses. It is then translated into a quantity based on units of sigma or standard deviation. When scores are *normally distributed* the percentage of scores which fall between the mean score and the various sigma distances from the mean is a fixed and known percentage. Between the mean and one unit of sigma above it there must be just over 34 per cent of all the scores. Similarly, since in normal distribution the median and mean are the same, with 50 per cent of all scores falling below (and the other 50 per cent above) it follows that a score at the 84th percentile (that is, a better score than the scores of 84 per cent of the performers) must be placed at a distance of one sigma $(+1\sigma)$ above the mean. Its *numerical* value will be the numerical value of the mean score *plus* the numerical value of sigma. The traditional mean in mental testing has been 100 since very soon after the days of Binet and the most acceptable value for sigma is 15. Consequently, our original score, no matter what its original amount to start with, now becomes 115, that is 100 (the mean score) plus 15, which is the value of the score almost corresponding to the 84th percentile. (See Figure 3.)

With a little thought, the reader may realize that the relative values of the scores are now *what they would have been* if the results of the test had taken the form of perfect normal distribution. In actual practice this perfection never happens, but in any large survey the result is

[1] A standardized test must be used exactly according to the original instructions; otherwise no reliable scores can be obtained. But it is just as misleading to apply it blindly without considering local educational differences. Strictly speaking, a score that has been standardized in the manner described on this page gets its standard value only because a certain percentage of the scores *in this particular survey sample* fall below it. We cannot assume that it would occupy the same position and have the same value on a nation-wide survey.

near enough to it for us to assume that we are merely giving it the form it would have had *if there had been no accidents of sampling*. But for those who find no comfort in mathematical explanation, it is quite enough to keep in mind that *deviation quotients* are reached by way of the standard deviation, are not *educational quotients* in the old sense at all, and would be better described as highly precise *standard scores*.

We may now consider a simplified process which teachers can use to compare results in two examinations or in two subjects. To turn an ordinary examination score into a rough standard score we simply say how many standard deviations it is away from the average. A pupil may have 64 in English and 64 in French, which looks as though he has done equally well in both until we apply a little of our statistical knowledge. The average or mean in English is 52, the highest is 71, and the standard deviation works out at 6. The corresponding figures in the French examination are 60, 93, and 10. His superiority in English is five times as great as it is in French, where it is only ·48 above the mean as against 2σ. This is another useful trick of the trade for a classroom teacher who wants to find out if someone's perform-ance is as good (or as mediocre) as it looks, and performs much the same sort of function as the simplified versions of the median and semi-inter-quartile range described on pages 32 and 33 ff. It is one of several techniques for comparing two or more marking systems which are, in effect, using utterly different units of measurement. The grades of difference in our French test were more numerous and therefore smaller in size. To say that 64 is the *same* mark in both examinations, is like calling two things the same size because one is six centimetres and the other six inches.

When there are only two scoring systems to be equalized, one can easily translate one into the units of the other by reducing or stretching as required (see page 33). But this would be clumsy with a large number of assessment systems, and it is neater to bring them all on to one common, or standard, scale. This is always done when teachers in the various schools are asked to submit estimates of their pupils at the time of the eleven-plus, or its equivalent. Such estimates, when scientifically *scaled*, become just as *reliable* or *comparable* as any other kind of assessment, and many authorities regard them as more *valid*, since they are based on many different observations of pupils and their performances, of which the best examination in the world can never give more than a sample.

From what has been said so far, it appears that the uses of an examination can vary all the way from the highly competitive entrance examination, which acts as a barrier, to the weekly classroom quiz, in which the teacher would like nothing better than to see everybody letter perfect! Questions in the first case will (some of them) be too difficult even for the very best candidate, which will give very fine discrimination at the top of the range; in the second, questions will be within the scope of all but the dullest pupils, and if they turn out not to be, then some of the lesson needs re-teaching. The two extremes summarize the two chief reasons for having examinations at all; measuring progress so far, and selection for future instruction.

The first sort of purpose tends to be more satisfactory and to cause less heart-burning. Reliable assessment is never easy but measuring what has been done is easier than using it to predict the future, although there is really no other index that we *can* use. But when examinations are to predict as well as to assess, their results must be handled in a special way and their design may seem strange to parents and even to teachers. Generally speaking, a good selection examination is a group or *battery* of measurements whose *combined* result makes the best known predictor of success in some future activity; hence some of the separate tests may seem rather a peculiar way of assessing what someone has done with his time so far, but they may be quite good at assessing how he can use it most profitably four years from now. The best way to find out how well someone can understand trigonometry or Greek verbs is to ask questions about trigonometry and Greek verbs; but if our pupil knows nothing about either, and someone is anxious that he should know something, we must fall back upon some present skill which he does know about and which correlates highly with those others.

This is where correlation, in fact, comes in. Its function is to let us argue from one state of affairs to another state of affairs, because we know there is a relationship between them, as we have measured its extent.

As the day lengthens, the cold strengthens.

Like father, like son.

A wife, a dog, and a hazel-tree, the more you beat 'em, the better they be. The idea of correlation is obviously nothing new. Human beings have observed that certain pairs of events appear to happen in step and have naturally wanted to establish the amount of the correspondence. The third proverb looks like an early, but one hopes, imaginary learning experiment. The middle one had the honour of attracting the attention of Galton, a cousin of Darwin's and a sort of psychological Leonardo da Vinci. His was the pioneer enquiry from which the whole concept of correlation has developed.

That tall fathers have, in general, tall sons Galton did not find so interesting as the recurrent exceptions. Tallness in the father was not a guarantee of tallness in the son, and other factors must therefore be modifying the simple cause-and-effect relationship. Galton called this effect *regression*, because of the tendency for sons to be slightly less tall on the whole, or to *regress* back to the average in their heights, so that the best prediction you could give of what a son's height would turn out was something *between* the father's height and the average height of the male population. The correlation, that is, was not perfect.

Galton was equally interested in the nature of the connection between different mental abilities, but the credit of inventing an actual measure of it belongs to Karl Pearson. It is called the *coefficient of correlation* and to this day is symbolized by the letter r to commemorate Galton's early work on regression, although correlation and regression are not quite the same thing.[1] The correlation coefficient can be understood as stating the difference between certainty and probability, in this case in predicting from one variable what the size of another is going to be. When two variables are perfectly correlated then we can predict with certainty, since any increase or decrease in the units of one of them will be accompanied by a corresponding increase or decrease in the units of the other. Some common factor (which we may or may not know something about) is affecting them in this step-for-step manner. The changes in one variable may be the direct cause of the changes in the other, as rising temperature lengthens the mercury in a thermometer. Or the same thing may be affecting both simultaneously. There are many reasons for the phenomenon of correlation, but we are not for the moment concerned with these, or indeed with anything but this extreme form of it, this perfect one-to-one correspondence between the two variables, which consequently is expressed as $=1$.

Now such perfect correlations are unusual, and really only occur when the state of affairs is obvious anyhow without calculating the correlation; for instance selling-price and cost-price increases will be perfectly correlated if one is always half as much again as the other, and when the cost price goes up we can predict with certainty what

[1] The regression of the son's heights back to average height was part of the fact that the correlation of heights to fathers and sons was not perfect, and the extent of the regression could be calculated from the correlation.

the rise in selling price will be. We are assuming here that only one factor is at work: increased charges on goods to the shopkeeper. But if other factors enter, such as a change in his overheads and the selling price is adjusted also to meet them, then its perfect correlation with cost price will be disturbed. Our *certainty* about the size of the increase is now reduced to *probability*. The correspondence is no longer a perfect one-to-one ratio and must therefore express itself as only a *fraction* of the total certainty; that is why when the coefficient of correlation between two partially inter-dependent variables is calculated, it works out as a decimal fraction. The higher this decimal, the nearer it is to unity, the more do the changes in the two variables reflect each other and the better is our chance of predicting from the present amount of one of them what the amount of the other is going to be. Conversely, when the correlation coefficient is low, we cannot venture to predict very much, because it means that the two variables are affected by many other factors than the common one. Nevertheless, it can be quite low and yet indicate something significant, since this is a diverse and crowded universe and any connection at all between two apparently unrelated things may be worth following up.

It is time we looked at a few correlations. If you take the heights and weights of a group of young people you will probably find a correlation of about ·4. This means there is a small, but marked tendency for tallness and heaviness to go together. A young adult an inch or two taller than another one is likely to be a little heavier—though not inevitably. This is where the complicating 'other factors' come in, such as bone formation and slimming campaigns! If we turn to family resemblances we get a much higher crop of correlations, just because in members of the same family, several factors affecting height, or intelligence, or whatever it is you are measuring will combine to work together and so increase the correlations instead of reducing them. Thus the correlation of heights between fathers and daughters might be as high as ·6 or ·7. If we narrow our field still further and take our measurements as between pairs of twins we get correlations in both physical and mental characteristics of the order of ·8 and ·9. And so on.

Some of the highest of all obtained correlations are in educational assessment. Between scores on a carefully combined test *battery* at the eleven-plus stage and secondary school performance by the same pupils four or five years later, the correlation could be as high as ·9 or even slightly higher. This means that as predictors of future performance such selection programmes have been highly reliable. It does not mean that every child did exactly as well, or exactly as badly in secondary school as his selection examination score indicated. *Perfect* correlations are nowhere to be found in human measurement.

Other conclusions can be drawn from correlation techniques than the prediction of future performance. We shall come to some of them in due course. Meantime, as a working rule, it will do to bear in mind that, in educational psychology, correlation often means the amount of overlap between two human performances and how far we can count on skill in one being accompanied, or followed, by skill in the other. Many of these paired performances would seem rather alike to the eye of common sense alone; what the psychometrists have succeeded in inventing is a reliable measure of the degree of resemblance.

There are various mathematical techniques for working out correlation coefficients, but they are all based on the way two related sets of measurements are spread out, or scattered. 'Spread-out-ness' or *scatter* is summarized by the standard deviation, and the only way, you remember, to find out whether a pupil's two scores are equally high is to express them as so many standard deviations away from the average. So before calculating the correlation between two sets of scores, we must turn them all into standard scores. We then go on to consider how many children come out about equally well (or badly!) in both performances. Thus child A, with a standard score of $+2 \cdot 75$ in English and $+2 \cdot 75$ in Arithmetic has an identical place in both, while child Z is three deviations below the mean in both. In other words, the same hapless name is at the bottom of both lists! The chances are that the same name will also be at the top of both, but it is also certain that other children will be higher in one examination than in the other, so that the correlation may work out at about $\cdot 8$, leaving a fraction of unpredictable difference in the two performances of any one child.

High correlations are the rule, in the primary-school stage at least, before specialization widens the difference between a beloved and chosen subject and a hated and neglected one. A class teacher can easily make use of a simplified method of calculating r as between two subjects.[1] He may also care to amuse himself by working out the correlation between the two sets of marks he has awarded the same pupils on two different occasions. He will probably find that it is not as high as he would like, thus indicating some inconsistencies in his own scoring system, as well as fluctuations in the performance of individual pupils.

[1] See end-note and Figure 4.

But *interpreting* a correlation, that is to say, trying to work out the reasons for it, is not the same as simply calculating it, and this is something to be considered in the next chapter. The present one has taken a look at some of the vast literature on educational assessment, and it has not been by any means comprehensive, although it has taken a pretty lengthy chapter to do it. Mention was made of some of the different types of educational survey which have been undertaken in the present century, with special note of how their scope and methods have changed to suit new lines of enquiry. The 'follow-up' type of survey led to an account of some of the principles on which selection examinations were developed during the years just after the war when transfer from primary to secondary school became an urgent problem in educational policy. Whatever the policy for classification of pupils may be in the future, the transfer programmes gave a great impetus to research into reliable methods of assessment, and some of the findings of this research have been mentioned, in particular the relative advantages and disadvantages of assessing performance objectively and by general impression. Some of this information can be put into practice by a classroom teacher who is interested in making his own system of testing and scoring more valid and reliable. It is also useful for a teacher to understand the main techniques of the standardized attainment tests which have been such a characteristic feature of the whole period.

The general theme of the chapter has been that assessment of any individual's performance always means comparing it with other performances in the same group or population. To make such a comparison fair it is necessary to bring all the measuring and scoring systems on to one common scale where the units are standard and have a recognized value. When this has been done it is also possible to make comparisons between two different performances by the same pupil and establish the likelihood of there being some factor common to them both. With this very important idea in mind we may go on to the subject of the next chapter.

NOTE: Figure 4 presents an example of the correlation of *r* by the rank order method which is suitable for small groups such as a school class. With bigger numbers the arithmetic becomes clumsy and it has of course the disadvantage of ignoring the size of score differences. This does not matter where the scoring system itself is not a precise one but for bigger surveys and for research purposes the Karl Pearson product-moment formula should be used:

$$r = \frac{\Sigma X_1 X_2}{N\sigma_1\sigma_2}$$

This is the same as taking the product of each individual's two scores expressed as so many standard deviation units away from the average of mid-score point, and then finding the average of all these products. It will tend to be positive and large through such conditions as the following: if there are a good many people with both scores on the same *side* of the mean score (e.g. $+2\cdot3$ and $+1\cdot8$ or else $-\cdot75$ and $-1\cdot2$) because this will make the product a *plus* quantity, and if most individual pairs of scores are about the same distance from the mean, since this will maximize the number who have *both* scores very high, or very low, giving large products. This formula, like the rank order formula, is arbitrarily designed to produce no values of r beyond 1. For a complete description of the calculation, which is mathematically complex, readers should look up a textbook on statistics and measurement such as P. E. Vernon's *Measurement of Abilities*, U.L.P., 1956 or H. E. Garrett's *Statistics in Psychology and Education*, Longmans Green & Co., 1951.

REFERENCES

(1) Burt, Cyril, *The Young Delinquent*, U.L.P., 1925; and *The Backward Child* U.L.P., 1937.

(2) Wiseman, Stephen, *Education and Environment*, Manchester University Press, 1964.

(3) Scottish Council for Research in Education, *The Intelligence of Scottish Children*, U.L.P. (the 1932 Mental Survey).

(4) Scottish Council for Research in Education, *The Trend of Scottish Intelligence*, U.L.P., 1949. (A comparison of the 1932 and 1947 survey results. A simpler account was written by James Maxwell in 1961 in the same series.)

(5) Terman, L. M. and others, *Mental and Physical Traits of a Thousand Gifted Children*, Stanford University Press, 1926; and *The Gifted Child Grows Up*, Stanford University Press, 1948.

(6) Ministry of Education, *Reading Ability*, H.M.S.O., 1950; and *Standards of Reading 1948 to 1956*, H.M.S.O., 1957.

(7) McClelland, W., *Selection for Secondary Education*, U.L.P., 1942.
    Yates, A. and Pidgeon, D. R., *Admission to Grammar Schools*, Newnes, 1957.

(8) Schonell, Fred. J. and Eleanor F., *Diagnostic and Attainment Testing*, Oliver and Boyd, 1950.

(9) Vernon, P. E., *Intelligence and Attainment Tests*, U.L.P., 1960.

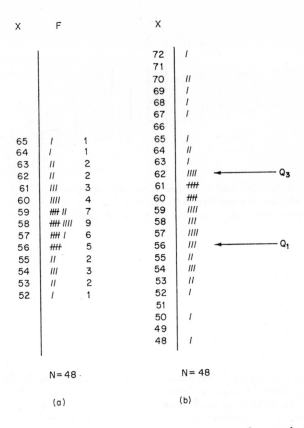

X	F			X	
				72	/
				71	
				70	//
				69	/
				68	/
				67	/
				66	
65	/	1		65	/
64	/	1		64	//
63	//	2		63	/
62	//	2		62	//// ← Q₃
61	///	3		61	##+
60	////	4		60	##+
59	##+ //	7		59	////
58	##+ ////	9		58	///
57	##+ /	6		57	////
56	##+	5		56	/// ← Q₁
55	//	2		55	//
54	///	3		54	///
53	//	2		53	//
52	/	1		52	/
				51	
				50	/
				49	
				48	/

N = 48

N = 48

(a)

(b)

Figure 1. A simple statistical treatment to demonstrate the spread of marks in a school examination. The X column lists the total range of scores obtained; the ticks or tallies, one for each pupil, show the frequency of occurrence of each score, which is summed in the F column. The frequencies add up the total number of examinees. (Table a.)

Table b could represent either an examination with (say) more and shorter questions to allow finer grading, or the same examination scored by a different system, such as by separate points instead of by overall impression. The F column is omitted to show more clearly that the twelfth pupil (counting up from the bottom of the tallies) falls in opposite score 56, which is therefore Q_1 or the first quartile, slicing off the lowest quarter or 25 per cent of the group. The thirty-sixth comes at 62, which as Q_3 or the 75th percentile, marks the level below which fall three-quarters of the group. Between Q_1 and Q_3 are enclosed the middle 50 per cent of the examinees, spread over a range from 56 to 62. Half this difference, called Q, is 3. Readers can calculate that it is smaller in Table a, representing a corresponding difference in the spread of the two distributions.

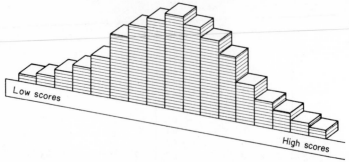

(a) Cards punched with individual scores and sorted by machine into a set number of piles or categories, with the biggest pile-up at the middle values and the piles diminishing symmetrically in each direction.

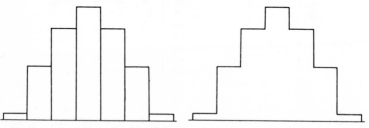

(b) We may represent the pile-up in each category by a 'perpendicular' rectangle. Its width is the width of the category or class interval.

(c) By removing the dividing line we show the total number of individual scores as the total area of all the rectangles.

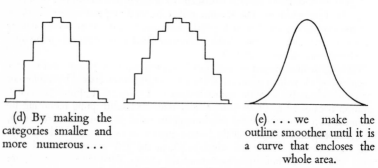

(d) By making the categories smaller and more numerous . . .

(e) . . . we make the outline smoother until it is a curve that encloses the whole area.

Figure 2. Graphs showing 'normal' distribution.

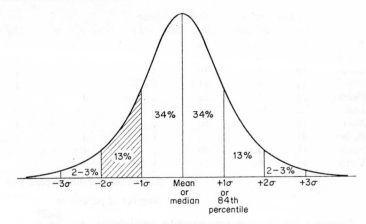

Figure 3. How to express scores as standard scores with a large sample which can be represented as normally distributed.

The horizontal axis or base line represents the range of scores. At any point along it the height (Y-axis) of the normal curve is known from its equation and the area can be calculated that is cut off by any vertical or enclosed between a pair of verticals, and bounded at the top by the segment of the curve and at the bottom by the distance marked out on the base line. That is, we can tell what percentage of the sample is bound to be contained in this division of the total area enclosed by the curve. It is 13 per cent in the shaded section of the diagram. (Note: the percentages have been rounded off for simplicity.)

Example. Suppose a score has a percentile value of 84 (i.e. better than 84 per cent of the sample). Fifty per cent of the cases are packed into the low value side of the central Y-axis, which rests on the mid-score point. We need another 34 per cent, which brings us almost exactly to one standard deviation above the average ($+1\sigma$) the base line being marked out in standard deviation distances

We may now give our score any conventional denomination by choosing a numerical value for the average and for the standard deviation—say 100 and 15 respectively. The intelligence quotient 115 in fact comes very close to the point indicated.

A number of separate tests can have their scores brought on to this common scales of values and compared (see pp. 54 ff).

	Story-writing Score	Story-writing Rank order	Problem-solving Score	Problem-solving Rank order	Rank difference	Diff.²
Ann	18	4.5	12	7	2.5	6.25
Carol	17	6	17	4	2	4
Chris	19	3	16	5	2	4
Don	14	8	13	6	2	4
Helen	23	1	24	2	1	1
Leslie	12	10	8	10	—	—
Matt	15	7	10	9	2	4
Robert	21	2	25	1	1	1
Susan	18	4.5	20	3	1·5	2·25
Victor	13	9	11	8	1	1

Sum of squared differences $= 7\cdot25$

Number of pupils $= 10$

According to the formula for rank-order correlation: $r = 1 - \dfrac{6\,\Sigma d^2}{N(N-1)}$

the correlation between these two performances may be calculated as follows:

$$r = 1 - \frac{6 \times 27\cdot5}{10 \times (100 - 1)}$$
$$= 1 - \cdot13$$
$$= \cdot87$$

Procedure. 1. Enter against each pupil's name his two scores. Assign each score a rank order. For example Matt's score of 15 for story-writing comes seventh, Helen's score for problem-solving (the second highest) gets a rank order of 2. Where there is a tie give both scores the average of two ranks (see Ann and Susan).

2. Enter in the next column the difference between each pair of rank orders. For example in Chris's case it is 2, in Victor's it is 1. Square these differences and sum them (column sixth).

3. Subtract from 1 (the symbol of perfect correlation) a fraction arrived at by the formula $\dfrac{6\,\Sigma d^2}{N(N^2-1)}$ where $\Sigma d^2 =$ the sum of the squared rank differences and $N =$ the number in the sample group. The 6 is a constant.

Note. If two performance were perfectly correlated each pupil would do equally well in both, i.e., would occupy the same position in his group; therefore we may use the combined *differences* in rank as a measure of how far an actual correlation is short of perfect. When differences are small the fraction deducted from 1 is small and the correlation coefficient will be high, as in our example. A large deduction will reduce it to near zero, indicating little or no relationship between the two performances. (We need not concern ourselves in this context with those instances where *r* is a minus quantity, indicating that the relationship is an inverted one. They have little practical significance for human performances.)

Figure 4. Calculating correlation by the rank-order method.

3

Intelligence and Intelligence Tests

1 Measurement on an age-scale

Curiously enough, it is not necessary to open a chapter on intelligence and intelligence testing by defining intelligence. We can leave this difficult matter till later and content ourselves, for the moment, with acknowledging that all intelligence tests are made up of performances which are supposed to distinguish individuals by their intelligence, as another sort of test might distinguish them by their long-sightedness or their strength of handgrip. Considering how hard it would be for even two people to agree about what intelligence is, there has been a surprising amount of agreement about the kind of performances which seem to sample intelligence well—that is, performances in which the individual differences are primarily caused by intelligence and in which these differences can be directly measured. Obviously, the choice of test items has rested on a very broad basis of common observation. We call some sorts of behaviour intelligent or stupid, and other sorts of behaviour, like the ability to digest food or lift weights, we think of as neither one nor the other, but as belonging to some other scale of values. A great many things which human beings can do, and in which their performances differ quite considerably, are easy enough to exclude from intelligence tests in this common-sense way. What to include, out of all the variety that is left, is the real problem.

One thing about the measurement of human behaviour is very clear indeed. We can never measure more than a sample of it, and how can we be sure that the sample chosen is adequate and representative? Well, of course, we cannot. We have come across this difficulty already more than once in educational assessment, and yet that is a comparatively narrow field of behaviour we are trying to measure, with the different performances pretty well defined. With intelligence the range of behaviour is far wider, as psychologists are only too well aware. It is just one more case of the common psychological problem, that human behaviour can take innumerable forms; and although in considering intelligence particularly we have the doubtful privilege of being able to ignore strongly emotional reactions like aggression or awareness of pain, it does not really help us much. For one thing there are emotionally toned elements in all intelligent behaviour, such as interest and determination. But even if we could omit them from our estimate of ability (and it would not be wise) it would not reduce the range of behaviour at all. In fact, *variety* itself is one of the characteristic marks of intelligent behaviour.

We find that human intelligence adapts to different cultures. Undoubtedly it channels itself into different skills in Borneo and Birmingham. It adapts to different life-styles. Undoubtedly a trained mathematician is exercising intelligence, but there are also more, and less, intelligent ways of providing for old age, designing furniture, and driving a bus. An intelligent cook is more inventive with her recipes—and this very habit of inventiveness and divergent thinking, so very hard to assess objectively, is now becoming a matter of concern to the makers of tests. It would be a very lifeless (and highly misleading) definition of intelligence which left it out, just because it is not easy to invent ways of measuring it.

From all this multitude of activities, then, an intelligence test can only select samples. One of the earliest to identify the problem was Galton, whom we have met before in just this capacity. He called the practice of giving mental tests 'sinking shafts' like miners prospecting underground workings in the hope of striking on tell-tale information. Now there is really only one way to do this and that is to match variety with variety, by giving as many and as heterogeneous tests as can possibly be devised—in which case a fair proportion of abilities will get an airing. Obviously there is no single performance which varies exactly along with the level of intelligence, as the length of a column of mercury faithfully counts off the changes in temperature that are pushing it up or down. We know that intelligence is a complex factor that 'pushes up' the levels of many performances, and there is no perfect index for it. Performances which are supposed to be 'pure' intelligence have a way of turning out as complex as intelligence itself, so that we have to fall back on the same old device of setting a variety of test situations, and hoping that we get an off-print of the general ability which is reasonably complete.

This was exactly Binet's method. He put children into test situations where their responses could be of the open and unrestricted type and they might employ, at choice, any kind of 'higher order' behaviour—remembering, reasoning, perceiving, imagining—which happened to be in their repertoire. This type of test posed, as usual, one great problem, how to assess the performance. Binet did solve it, and his solution was one of brilliant simplicity. He put to systematic use a bit of ordinary information available to anyone—only no psychologist, racking his invention for the perfect test, had ever thought of it as a measure of the intelligence level of a child's performance. And yet it is a simple and obvious fact, which is true of every child who has ever been born, and there is hardly any performance by children to which it does not apply.

Children's powers increase as they get older. We say that they improve, become more capable, better organized in their responses, better judges and so on. You would hesitate, perhaps, to send a four-year-old on an errand which a six-year-old will manage competently, so any four-year-old who does the same certainly qualifies for a place among the sixes in respect of this one thing. His birthday age is four, his competence-in-doing-an-errand age is six. And it is, of course, likely that his competence in a few other tasks is six-year-old level as well.

These two principles, of setting a great variety of tasks and assessing the complex responses on an age-scale, between them compose the traditional Binet-type test of intelligence. Its advantages are clear. Its inspired simplicity fits in with the ordinary ideas about children and education which thinking parents, for example, are likely to have, as well as with specialized psychological knowledge. It allows tests to tap almost any form of behaviour, and to use almost any kind of material, provided they conform to certain broad criteria which we shall be discussing in a moment. It makes the unrewarding task of defining and analysing intelligence quite unnecessary, except as the examiner's idea of it affects the choice of test problems. And above all, it gives the child freedom to use his own judgement and his own inventiveness in solving the problem. Some of the tests, for example repeating numbers from memory after one hearing and reciting the days of the week, require an accurate answer and allow no second chances, but in others, such as building a sentence from three key words or explaining why a statement is absurd, great latitude of idea and phrasing is allowed. It is the examiner who gets the detailed instructions as to how he must phrase the questions and evaluate the answers.

Binet's technique was not perfected at once. He himself would undoubtedly have said that it never was, since he was constantly revising his scale up to the time of his death. The idea of *mental age* seems to have evolved gradually but some of his other ideas about intelligence seem to have been his criteria for test-making from the start. As all the psychological world knows, his discoveries, like so many others we have come across, were made as the result of a direct request for help in the framing of an educational policy. The Parisian Minister of Public Instruction had set up a committee of enquiry into the education of mental defectives, and it was in connection with this that Binet and his collaborator, Simon, drew up their first series of test questions in 1905. Basic to the construction of these early tests of ability was the distinction drawn between sheer native wit and acquired information. Ability is not just knowledge. An ignorant person is not necessarily stupid—he may have been unlucky in his environment; and a glib recital of facts can go along with a woeful lack of common sense. That native ability is independent of acquired knowledge and ought to be estimated separately from it, as far as possible, is probably part of everyone's idea of intelligence. Binet's aim was to keep this distinction clear and to purify his test material of *specialized* schoolbook information. Of course, he could not do away with factual information altogether, but it must be the kind of information which is open to any child living an ordinary life among normal people—for example, the names of the days of the week. Failure to acquire common knowledge of this kind will be significant. Not knowing the name of the capital of Peru will not. This principle, that the test questions must be relatively free of special knowledge, continued to operate in all the modernizations of Binet's work which have appeared since his death, down to the third Stanford revision of 1960. It is not, however, a universal principle of mental testing and we must return to it later.

Binet's other criterion was that the test questions must discriminate, must really sort the children into clearly marked mental categories. His interpretation of the standardizing procedure was to assign each task a difficulty value according to the age at which it was done successfully by about 60 to 70 per cent of children. By 1908 he had shifted his tests around and into an order which satisfied this requirement to a great extent. The 1911 revision (published in his sole name) refined still more upon his standardizing techniques. At each level from 3 to 15 were five tests of the same age difficulty and showing a steady increase in the percentage of children who could pass them in later years. Thus any child who could do all the nine-year-old tests could be reliably assigned a mental age of nine, since the level of performance at age nine had been reliably demonstrated when the tests were being tried out. This was infinitely superior to previous estimates of what children of a certain age could be expected to do, most of which were based on vague and unfounded generalizations.

When Binet had established the idea of normal ability, the very important matter of individual departures from the normal was high-lighted automatically. For the first time, there was numerical proof of the counterbalancing percentage of superior children whose ability was as far removed from the average on one side as that of the feeble-minded on the other. Three children may have a mental age of eight, and if one of them has just had his eighth birthday there is nothing remarkable in his performance. But there is a mighty difference between the other two, of whom one is nearly ten and the other six and a half. Clearly, there was one crucial ratio, between the child's age level in test performance and his age in years. Within two years of Binet's death there emerged the famous formula of the intelligence quotient.

Normality in intelligence presents a one-to-one ratio between mental age and age in years. For every year the child has been alive he has been one year the better in mental progress (leaving aside for the moment the teasing question of whether he has profited from his cultural environment to this extent, or Topsy-fashion 'just growed'). In his case the quotient would be a neat and perfect unity, and would not need to have the decimals tidied up by the usual method of multiplying by 100. However, across the street there is a better-endowed youngster whose mental progress outruns his earthly years to the tune of three extra months per annum, giving a ratio of $1\frac{1}{4}:1$ or the more familiar I.Q. 125. Meantime a less fortunate child does not reach a mental age score of VIII[1] until he is nearly ten years old. His intelligence quotient is 80, or, putting it in the other idiom, his yearly gains on an average must have been just 20 per cent short of normal.

Is the ratio constant? Does our 100-I.Q. child always gain exactly one year of mental growth between birthday and birthday? Does our bright one always have a yearly three months' bonus, so that when he is four his cumulative gains will give him a mental age of five and we can predict for him a mental age of ten about the time of his eighth birthday? More important perhaps, is our backward one con-demned to a steady shortage of 20 per cent per annum, so that by the time he is ten he will have fallen two whole years behind his age-group in mental performance? No psychological controversy has ever raged more fiercely than this one about the constancy of the I.Q. And with good reason; for the educational implications of the matter, whichever way it goes, are endless. But before we consider it, we should perhaps complete our brief account of the Binet intelligence scale and its revisions.

[1] The Roman numbers are conventional.

There have been many translations and adaptations of the original set of tests. Early translators, like Burt in England in 1921 (1) and Terman in America in 1916 (2), of course found that literal translation would not do. To take the simple example of naming the nine most common coins—which British and American coins are in fact equivalent for familiarity? The only way to find out is by a fresh standardization procedure. Instead of hit-or-miss substitutions it was necessary to try out different coins on the nine-year-old and discover, in accordance with Binet's procedure, exactly which coins in fact the normal nine-year-old can recognize. Similarly with the 'Look at this picture and tell me about it' question. A typical French scene will present quite a different difficulty level to British and American children. And so on. Revision of Binet's tests have continued to apply and even to refine his basic principles but have had to contain many minor adjustments of material and wording in order to do that very thing.

A Binet-type test is a standardized interview. The instructions to the examiner (what he is to say and how he is to say it, whether a second chance is to be allowed or explicitly disallowed, whether there is a time-limit, and so on) must be adhered to literally, else the difficulty value of the problem is altered and an age-score would be meaningless. If new material is introduced, its difficulty must be fixed by previous trying-out. The same applies to evaluating the child's responses—many pages of the Stanford revision are devoted to scoring and assessing the kind of responses which children will give, since these have been found to occur in actual research among children.

It is interesting to note how in spite of essential alterations, some problems have gone on being used in their original form, as Binet invented them. There is, for example, the pleasantly named *Patience* test, where the child is asked to re-assemble a dissected triangle. Binet did not favour this manipulative type of test so much as the verbal question and answer; yet it is a good illustration of his own conception of the nature of intelligence—behaviour directed by a purpose and judged successful or unsuccessful by the individual's own power of self-criticism. The same ability to size up a situation and respond appropriately is tested by the sort of question which begins 'What ought you to do if ——?' Binet used this kind of problem twice, presenting what he calls 'easy' decisions to the eights and 'difficult' to the elevens. The same kind of judgement is required by the fourteen queries listed under *Comprehension* in the Wechsler Intelligence Scale for Children, which departed so emphatically from the Binet tradition in some respects. And fifty years later, children are still being asked to copy a diamond or draw from memory those two linear designs which must be as familiar to every educationsl psychologist as the 007 to readers of espionage novels.

Manipulative-, or performance-type tests, however, were in the minority, and have remained so, except for the younger ages, for whom the second Stanford revision by Terman and Merrill introduced a collection of attractive miniature objects to be named and manipulated (3). This 1937 revision (popularly called the Terman-Merrill to distinguish it from the original Stanford) has remained in constant use owing to the care with which it was standardized on larger and more representative samples of children. It contains two alternative versions of the scale, so that the same child may be tested twice, if necessary, which are of course to be regarded as being of parallel difficulty at corresponding age-levels. There are six tests to the year between five and fourteen, and credit is given for each test passed at the rate of two months of mental age, so that the final age-score is a straightforward addition sum, beginning with the age for which the child passes all six tests and adding on two months for each success beyond this to the point where he fails all six. Thus a child of eight might pass all the eight-year-old tests, four at age IX, one at age X, and none at age XI, giving a total of VIII.9, or eight years and nine months of mental age. Conversion to an intelligence quotient can be done by the old familiar calculation, but in practice a reference table saves this trouble.

Age groups below five have six tests to the half-year, each giving a month of mental age, and there are adult-level tests where, for reasons to be mentioned in a moment, the mental age units cease to have the same meaning as they do for children.

The 1960 Stanford revision, which Terman did not live to see completed, is known in educational circles as Form L–M, since it is an amalgam of the two 1937 versions. Little positively new material was added because it was thought desirable to be able to compare present-day performance with records of performance on the 1937 scales, and this could not be done if the content was substantially altered. Some of the old-fashioned material was dropped, and still enough remained to allow a further selection so that L–M could rank as having all the test items which had proved most efficient over the years (4).

Certain test items had higher correlations with the total score than others—that is to say, the children who did best in those were the children who ended up with the highest overall intelligence scores. Those 'best' tests were all verbal, with Vocabulary, the backbone of the scale, coming first and followed by such things as Sentence-building, Drawing Analogies, and explaining the exact nature of an Absurdity. From this we are entitled to draw two conclusions, the first being pretty obvious. The general ability measured by the Binet scale, both in the original and all the revised forms, is highly verbal or at least abstract. The child is asked to manipulate words and numbers rather than things; and even when, instead of answering questions, he is to *do* something (like sketching the opened-out appearance of cuts made in a folded paper) he has to be quick at understanding instructions. There are practical reasons for this. Grading the difficulty of *performance-* or manipulation-type tests is a problem not always convincingly solved. There is, also, the awkward bulk of material, building blocks, wooden boards with missing pieces, dissected puzzles, and so on. Besides, a performance test is rather specific and limited, whereas words can pose problems about all sorts of things. Verbal-type intelligence tests have a very high correlation with school success, which may only mean that they are two ways of measuring the same thing; but nevertheless have their value, if the prediction of educational success is what we happen to be looking for. But most ability tests, as they stand, do favour the child who has had plenty of language experience; in its upper reaches especially, such a test simply could not be done at all by a child who was not literate. We shall see presently how substantially language development is affected by environment, and what has just been said is one aspect of this. Non-verbal problems tend to appear most often as tests of special aptitudes, which is probably their most important function. Yates and Pidgeon, in their *Admission to Grammar Schools* (5) quote markedly lower correlations with school success for their two *Space-relationship* tests, and on the whole performance, and non-verbal tests generally, do tend to show lower correlations with other criteria of ability. Be it noted, however, that this may be no argument against including them in an assessment battery.[1] It really means that such tests are measuring something *different* from the ability measured by other sorts of assessment, which do inter-correlate highly; and it is no bad thing to collect as many indexes to ability as possible.

This brings us to the second conclusion that we may reasonably draw. By calling those tests 'the best' which fit in most closely with the overall score, the authors of the Stanford revisions make it quite plain that they take the prime concern of the intelligence scale to be *general* ability, and not subsidiary particular abilities which may be

[1] *Battery* is the name used for a group of tests designed to function together.

more independent of each other, and not so exactly in line with the total performance. In this respect they are quite in the Binet tradition. Binet did sometimes write as if he believed that 'general' intelligence might contain a number of separate abilities, but it was not an idea he chose to develop. Although he invented such a variety of task situations, he continued to be primarily interested in the overall level of the child's performance, and that was why he needed a general measure like Mental Age.

Even at the time of the 1937 revision, however, several new ideas about the nature of intelligence were making their appearance, and this led to a critical appraisal of the current ways of measuring it. Some concessions to the new techniques were made in the 1960 revision, and in the interval there had appeared a new scale for measuring intelligence, constructed on lines which sometimes departed quite sharply from those laid down by Binet.

2 Nature and nurture in intelligence

Brilliant though it was, the concept of Mental Age was open to misuse. After all, it represents only a test score, and it is misleading to think of the same mental age rating as necessarily meaning the same state of affairs in two different children. At one time, for example, it was even suggested that it would be more realistic to classify children in school by *mental* instead of by *chronological* age—which, carried to its logical extreme, would give a physical age range in the same classroom of at least four years! Apart from the undesirability, on social and emotional grounds, of mixing bright sevens, for example, with slow-witted tens and elevens, such children would not even remain at the 'same' mental age for very long, since the young, bright children would get on at their characteristically faster pace. Even the less drastic remedy of retarding backward children by a year or so has never thoroughly satisfied insightful teachers, and with good reason.

It is possible, then, to over-interpret a mental age score—to take it as in some way meaning an absolute, overall developmental level. But a dull nine with a score equivalent to the seven-year norm is not in any sense to be treated as a seven-year-old. He is a nine whose performance falls measurably below the average performance of the nine age-group, and this is the most significant thing about his performance.

Another serious disadvantage of age-units was that they became less valid for calculating intelligence quotients in the age-groups above middle childhood, and broke down altogether at the adult level. It would be absurd to persist with the formula $\dfrac{\text{M.A.}}{\text{C.A.}} \times 100$ into adult life. The *score* cannot increase beyond the scope of the test, so that even the most able of young adults would probably do no better at thirty-four than he did at seventeen, and therefore by the formula his I.Q. would exactly halve itself, which seems rather a premature estimate of declining mental powers! The earliest device for avoiding this obvious piece of nonsense was to call all adults the same age, and use this as the divisor, whether the testee was sixteen or sixty. But this ran into further trouble. Although it was perfectly true that the average adult performance on the Stanford-Binet scale was about the level of the age fourteen tests, this is not to say that the average adult is an intellectual fourteen-year-old any more than he is a physical fourteen -year-old. At fourteen most people have a good deal of their bodily growing still to do. We have little reason to assume that their mental growth is finished either. In fact we do not know when intelligence stops developing, or what age should act as the basis of our calculation.

These and other ideas led to the adoption of the deviation method of working our intelligence quotients in most modern ability tests. A similar change of practice, the reader may remember, took place in connection with attainment tests in school subjects (page 52). The average score *within any one given age-group* is dubbed I.Q. 100, and higher and lower scores are scaled by the distance they depart from this mean score turned into units of *standard deviation*. Just as, for traditional reasons, the average score is called 100, so the standard deviation on most intelligence tests is arbitrarily fixed as 15, simply because educationists had got into the habit of thinking of intelligence quotients as being spread over such a numerical range. The reader should perhaps glance back to the pages in chapter 1 in which the properties of the curve of normal distribution were discussed, in order to remind himself of how within the range -3 to $+3$ sigma *almost* 100 per cent of a population will be contained. Translated, this means that the I.Q.s of a large representative sample will range from 55 to 145, with a negligibly minute percentage above and below this. Likewise approximately 68 per cent of all I.Q.s fall between 85 and 115, one standard deviation below average and one standard deviation above average respectively. As I.Q.s go up beyond 115 the percentages of them in the population become very rapidly smaller. In this, as in other human performances, the value of very high levels is a scarcity value!

Mathematically inclined readers will have realized, of course, that by changing the raw scores on intelligence tests into deviation-type I.Q.s, we are taking it for granted that the *true* pattern of such scores is the curve of normal distribution; furthermore by inference, since intelligence-test problems are supposed to offer a representative sample of general intelligence, we are also assuming that *general intelligence itself* is normally distributed in the whole population. It should be acknowledged that this is a reasonable assumption and nothing more. 'Intelligence' cannot be directly measured like height and weight, nor directly observed like certain skills. It only seems likely that the percentages of human beings who have the various degrees of intelligence correspond to the percentages we find in successive 'slices' of the area enclosed by the normal curve (page 63) since it is true of almost all the other measurable characteristics of human beings. Therefore intelligence tests are designed to produce this overall pattern of results. We also assume (but again we cannot absolutely know) that a similar spread of intelligence is to be found among all the members of any one age-group, whether the fives, the fifteens, or the fifties, and therefore that we are not falsifying the true facts by *always* calling the average I.Q. 100 and by fixing the size of the standard deviation so that the upper and lower limits of the I.Q.s remain the same at all ages. (If the standard deviation came out with even slightly different values at different ages, as indeed it did in the two earlier Stanford revisions, then the 'cleverest' child in a year-group could have a higher I.Q. if tested on one birthday than if tested on another, say a few years later. That is, we should be giving the same 'best' performance two different values, which there seems no good reason for doing.) Now, it is possible, if rather unlikely, that the range of intelligence 'spreads out' at some ages and 'shrinks' at others, or, putting it in another way, that children pass through certain developmental stages when their individual differences in ability are wider, and other stages when their performances are all a little closer to the average. It has been suggested that something of the first kind may happen during the growth spurt of the early teens; but we have no clear way of finding out, however interesting and educationally important a discovery it would be.

Now, many children do get different intelligence quotients when tested at different ages, but this is another matter (see below, pp. 79 ff). A child's performance on an intelligence test, as on any kind of test, is subject to variation, and this will be considered in a moment.

The Wechsler Intelligence Scales made use of deviation I.Q.s at first for assessing adults, but later in the nineteen-forties applied the same principles to the now very well-known Wechsler Intelligence Scale for Children, popularly called the WISC (6). Since the Mental Age unit was discarded, items did not have to be arranged in rigid year-groupings, and they are therefore classified by type of test, which is more informative in some ways. The rather haphazard assembly of skills found in any one year of the Stanford scales sometimes blurred distinctions in the *kind* of successes two different children might have, although they reached the same Mental Age level eventually. Thus WISC straightforwardly divides tasks into verbal on the one hand and manipulative on the other, with five sets of each, and a Verbal I.Q. and a Performance I.Q. which can be kept independent or lumped into a general one, this being completely in keeping with the present view of intelligence as a complex of many abilities, some of which may even be relatively independent of the others. On the same principle, each separate set of tests was independently scaled, a fixed number of points being awarded to every score in accordance with the child's age. Thus for the same raw (original) score of 18 correct in Vocabulary, the *scaled* score for a five-year-old is 12, for a seven-year-old, 9, and for a nine-year-old, 6. Then ten scaled credits are then totted up and converted to I.Q.s, which only needs a simple two-column table, the age-correction having already been made.

It will be seen that the WISC results present their information very clearly. One can see, for instance, what type of task has contributed most to the child's total intelligence rating—what is the characteristic 'flavour' of his ability, so to speak. This technique stresses the composite nature of the measuring unit used in any test of general intelligence, and the diversity of tasks collected into this one process. WISC does not, of course, claim to do a thorough job of measuring each special ability—the separate sub-tests are not long nor comprehensive enough —nor even to have picked out a perfect sample of the abilities consituting 'intelligence'. The items in WISC as in any other 'intelligence' test are in the last resort the choice of the examiner. This is especially the case with the 'performance' half, which breaks some new ground, the language tests being more traditional and in some cases modelled direct on Binet's original favourites. On the other hand, the WISC *norms* were carefully established from a sample of 200 children for each age from five to fifteen, making a total of 2200, evenly divided between boys and girls. The sample was also stratified, that is to say, different population groups were represented in as near as possible the same proportions as in the general population of the U.S.A., the sample containing for instance the right proportion of children from urban and from rural areas and from the different social and occupaional levels.

Rather unfortunately, perhaps, these norms cannot be accepted for British children with as little modification as was possible with the Stanford-Binet norms. Indeed, the Scottish Council for Research in Education found it advisable, not long ago, to do a thorough restandardization of the Wechsler material upon Scottish children, which for some test items meant a complete change of content. This brings us to the second of Wechsler's departures from the Binet tradition.

Binet, you will remember, set himself from the very beginning to distinguish intelligence from information, ability from knowledge, 'nature' from 'nurture'. For him an intelligence test should be purified as far as possible from what has been called the *cultural* element, the accidents of upbringing and education. These last undoubtedly create differences between individuals of all ages, children among them, but they are not of the same kind as the differences in natural ability and an intelligence test should minimize their effects by keeping them as equal as possible. A test of 'pure' intelligence would pre- sumably be 'culture-free'. Now this remains, I suppose, a basic feature of most people's idea of intelligence and intelligence tests, but in practice a culture-free test is an impossible ideal; if indeed it even is an ideal. We have seen that Binet and his successors, did make use of information—after all, the problems must be about *something*—and we have seen also that the information was supposed to be of a general kind and available to any child capable of ordinary human contacts. But some children may be deprived by circumstances of even this generalized information; their social contacts may be limited, like those of deaf children, or their cultural inheritance may have profound national, or even racial differences from that of the children on whom the test was standardized.

In practice, intelligence tests always make this assumption of a roughly common background of experience, otherwise the problems could not be of equal difficulty for every child, and the further up the age-scale we go, the greater must be the ratio of experience to ability in the child's answer. We have seen that school-age children are expected to have common knowledge in the form of the three R's at least, and this matter of common knowledge brings us to another aspect of the culture problem. Among older adolescents and still more among adults there is so much specialization that it is hard to find enough common ground on which to compare them adequately. (The truly gifted adults, one is forced to admit, can never have their own best efforts measured comparatively against the whole population, but this, luckily, is not an urgent problem!)

Wechsler decided, therefore, in making up his intelligence scale for adults to ignore the 'culture-free' criterion when necessary, and make use of special information. In his opening test, the questions come from science, literature, history, and so on, at about the high-school educational level, so of course adjustments would be needed as between American and British subjects. So with the corresponding items in the children's scale, where the variations in difficulty could not be corrected by the occasional substitution of one word for another, or by tinkering a little with the order of difficulty. WISC was therefore completely restandardized, as has been mentioned, on a large sample of Scottish children, which is something that has not yet been done in Britain for any of the Stanford revisions.

The practice of altering a word or two in these carefully standardized tests has never been recommended by psychologists. As we have seen, until the change has been tried out on a sample of children we cannot truly tell how it has affected the difficulty level of the question. This is why individual tests like the Stanford or Wechsler scales can only be administered by a skilled practitioner. Teachers who would like to be able to do this must undertake special training in the way the interview is to be conducted and the response scored.

Most teachers, however, and many pupils too, are familiar enough with the pencil-and-paper type of intelligence test which can be conducted like any other examination, allowing for the special instructions and (usually) for the very exact timing. Some of these group tests (so-called) are done a page at a time, the testees having to turn to the next page and to stop work strictly in unison. The eleven-year-old tests, however, are of the omnibus variety, being worked straight through for forty-five minutes, as a rule. Questions, of course, are of the closed, not open type, to allow uniformity of scoring, and nearly everyone who reads this book will remember 'Calf is to cow as lamb is to ——' and 'Write the letter of the alphabet which occurs most often in the word *absolutely*'.

Naturally a child's performance on a group test is hardly a valid a sample of what he can do as it would be in an individual interview where he had the sole attention of a skilled examiner for upwards of an hour. Yet well-constructed group tests give reliable results for large surveys, which is their principal use. They show very high correlations with other measures of ability and are often found, in follow-up investigations, to have given the best single predictions of future success (although the reader must remember that a composite assessment will always give a better prognosis than any single one). They stand up well to the criterion of re-testing, that is to say, children on the whole get similar 'intelligence' scores on successive testings, whether on the same test twice with an interval between, or on two different but equally well made tests. This, on the whole, is true. But not always.

No question is more familiar to educational psychologists than the one which goes something like this: 'Does the I.Q. never change? Can a child not turn out more intelligent than the test says? What about the slow developer? What about the teacher who coaches children—can the scores be boosted this way?' And so on.

Well, of course, a child would be unlikely to get an identical score on a second testing. It would probably improve very slightly, if the two tests were of the same pattern, thanks to his better acquaintance with the rather queer idiom of intelligence-test questions. There might be a small but appreciable difference caused by incidentals like his own degree of interest or the time of day. But a few points' difference in the I.Q. rating is neither here nor there. Serious fluctuations are more disturbing, and they do occur.

Let us deal briefly with the matter of coaching. Children can acquire the knack of answering a kind of question, or rather, they get better at spotting what they are supposed to do. But scores cannot be pushed up beyond a certain point by this kind of familiarity, and there is a maximum effect from coaching which is reached quite quickly and will not be exceeded however long it goes on. What coaching cannot do is supply the ability to see the actual answer. The best-trained candidate is on his own in the end.

But what our anxious questioner really wants to know is this. During childhood at least, the intelligence quotient is stating a development ratio. How does a child's mental development compare with what we should expect of him for the number of years he has been alive and in ordinary human company? How well has he profited from his own innate growth pattern and from his environmental opportunities? And, when we know this, do we also know that this is the rate at which he will continue to develop always, and in all circumstances? This is what is really meant by asking if the I.Q. is a stable once-and-for-all assessment.

Normally, anyone who has profited from his life-span up to the present will go on profiting from it at roughly the same rate—provided certain things remain constant. It is quite likely, though not certain, that every child has his own characteristic developmental potential, inherited along with his other constitutional idiosyncrasies. But this potential cannot be independent of environment. Children deprived of what they need will not develop as fast as they might. Beyond a shadow of doubt the I.Q. reflects the child's history, and just as intelligence-test questions cannot be culture-free, so intelligence itself cannot be independent of stimulation and nourishment.

If the environment ceases to stimulate, almost certainly performances of all kinds will suffer, intelligence-test scores among them. Even a mature adult who has let his powers fall into disuse will score worse than if he had kept them alive by fresh activity and new learning, even if the test itself contains nothing he does not actually know about. In the same way, the material in a school intelligence test may be ordinary but a deprived child may not be able to *deal* with it. Conversely, a child who has been kept on his toes by a variety of things to be done and thought about, whose parents talk to him, play with him, and take him on excursions, will give the best possible account of himself in any test of alertness.

Now it is only too easy to exaggerate these effects, and to make intelligence tests seem much more unjust than they are. One of their actual merits is that they are often better at diagnosing intelligence in an educationally handicapped pupil, who has perhaps been off school more than most. Again, the ordinary social life of an ordinary family is stimulation enough for the mental growth of a young child, and a large income is no guarantee of richness of environment. We must also keep in mind that the effect of environment is limited by a child's own intake. The environment will not make him bright; it can do no more than give him the chance of being as bright as he can.

We can sum up by saying that some of the variance in a child's intelligence scores, whether upwards or downwards, small or substantial, must reflect environmental variations in his life-history. Psychologists have long since abandoned the idea that the I.Q. measures native capacity pure and simple. It measures a sample of what that capacity has become during an individual's lifetime. Whether any of the variance in the intelligence-test score is due to an actual temporary change in the child's own rate of development is quite another matter, and one nearly impossible to settle. This is something which belongs under the general heading of development and is to be considered later in the book.

Meantime we should keep in mind the modest but useful service which Hebb did for the whole science of mental measurement, by distinguishing the three ways in which the word *intelligence* can be used. A writer may be talking about the native *potential* of the individual, which we have no means of measuring whatsoever, since all we can measure is performance, in which, as we have clearly seen, there must be environmental factors as well. We can only assume that human beings are born with different capacities for mental expansion and that this is something which the environment cannot positively alter. Or, secondly, by *intelligence* the writer may be meaning, for the moment, someone's characteristic way of running his own life, his overall powers and insight, his adaptableness, good judgement, excellent memory, social tact, and aesthetic taste! This we may evaluate in a general sort of way (and rather enjoy doing so!) but we cannot hope to measure it exactly. And obviously the third thing that the word can refer to is someone's performance on an intelligence test, which is something else again. It is a good *sample* of his 'lifemanship' but it cannot possibly include every aspect of it, even in miniature. There is no harm in any of the three uses, so long as we remember which one we are meaning for the moment. We can measure intelligence-test performance pretty exactly, we can evaluate but not measure general capability, and we can only guess at the existence of native capacity; but we must assume there is a good deal of common ground among them, or else it would not be worth while inventing intelligence tests at all.

3 The composition of intelligence

Readers must have a very good idea by now of why it is that attempts to define intelligence have been unsatisfactory. As was remarked at the beginning of the chapter intelligence is a typical quality of human behaviour in that it can take so many forms that they cannot possibly be all collected in one description. The only agreement reached has been that intelligence must be got at by a variety of performances, so intelligence tests have gone along quite usefully for half-a-century without any explicit definition of what they measure.

Anyone who makes up an intelligence test of course defines it by the kind of performances he chooses. If he discards hearing acuity as a test he is in effect saying that it has nothing to do with ability (and considering the conditions under which Beethoven composed the Choral symphony we had better agree) while by including comprehension of abstract words, he is saying that one index to intelligence is vocabulary. Some psychologists have been troubled by the rather unmethodical way in which test items have been chosen in the first place, since unimportant elements may be accidentally highlighted and significant ones left out altogether. Definitions also tend to show some bias towards the psychologist's own 'favourite' type of performance, although there have been some famous attempts.

Binet's own, you remember, contained the idea of behaviour directed to some result and guided by self-criticism, which seems sensible enough, considering that an intelligent person does censor his own responses to a situation, and that only very stupid people are incapable of realizing that they can go wrong. But it has been objected to on the grounds that self-criticism is a quality of character rather than intellect. Then there is Spearman's well-known analysis of ability into being able to perceive the relationship between things (*black* and *white* are *opposites*) and being able to deduce the *correlate* of something by way of the relationship between them (from *black* and *the opposite* we deduce the correlate *white*). Burt's strong plea for the central importance of *reasoning power* is based on much the same idea of intelligence as Spearman's. Both may appear to modern readers as rather austere. A well-rounded concept of intelligence must surely have room in it for creativity and inventiveness, and we have seen that attempts are being made to construct tests of these important abilities.

Then, since intelligence is no longer regarded as all 'nature' and no 'nurture', not only must the performances which sample it be wider and richer than any so-called test of native wit, but also any definition of ability must contain a reference to the way experience has been used. Which, at the present moment when ideas are changing about how tests should be selected and assembled, puts any satisfactory definition further off than ever.

The traditional type of intelligence scale was a miscellaneous collection of items, grouped by age-difficulty; any other arrangement was not thought to be important since any item could be taken as measuring intelligence in an overall general sort of way. We have seen how Wechsler abandoned this notion by arranging his tests so that the composite score can be clearly seen to consist of credits for separate types of performance. The fact that it is a composite score, however, means that in the end the purpose of the Wechsler scale was the same as Binet's was—to arrive at a general measure of intelligence from a variety of items. But it is possible, and many modern educational psychologists think it is desirable, to discard this idea of a general assessment of intelligence, and think of an intelligence scale as a number of separate measures of a number of separate abilities, which may not form a whole at all, but can be considered as quite distinct from each other.

The idea of there being not one fundamental, but many distinct abilities, has come about through the invention of a mathematical procedure called factorial analysis. This has certainly been the most determined and thoroughgoing attack to be made so far on the structure of intelligence, so a little must be said about it.

Factor analysis has grown out of Spearman's work on the correlation between human performances, which he began in this country at about the same time as Binet in France was working out his first tests (7). It is a nice study in contrasts, for Spearman's approach to intelligence was analytical, Binet's functional. Spearman wished to break down the complex structure of intelligence into its parts. Binet preferred to think of it as overall behaviour. Nevertheless, by present-day standards, Spearman's analysis did not go very far. Any performance, he believed, could be analysed as the combined effect of two factors, and two factors only, one of them general (this is Spearman's famous g) and the other specific, that is, effective in this particular performance but not in any other. Thus a score in any arithmetic test would be achieved partly by g and partly by a particular success with the numbers in this test alone, which would not, for example, have anything to say to the same individual's performance in a Greek test, where the g influence would be joined with another specific facility altogether. Now, how did Spearman locate this g factor, and what in any case are we to understand by a factor? This is where we come to grips with an aspect of correlation which so far has had to be taken on trust.

We have come across it as a state of inter-dependence between two performances, but it can be thought of in a slightly different way. A test-score, you remember, is a *variable*. It occurs in different amounts, and we can represent this by a straight line going from very little to maximum. The total *variance* of a test is made up by all the performances which are piled up, so to speak, on this base-line, to different heights, the highest pile of them being usually about the middle point of it. Now what is responsible for this *variance*? We can say flatly, of course, that the children are! The variance is the sum of A's performance, B's performance, C's performance; A's is one of many heaped up at the middle, C's heap has only three performances altogether; it is they which fill up the space based on the highest score of all. What is operating at full strength in C's contribution to the total variance and at average or ordinary strength in A's? Can we identify it more accurately than by lumping it under the general heading of 'intelligence'?

Not very easily if there is only one test with one total variance brought about by we do not know what. But supposing we give the same children a second test[1] and find that its variance has been filled up in a very similar fashion, that the performances of quite a large proportion of the children take up the same positions, make part of the same pile-up as in the first test. If we laid the second variance against the first, so to speak, we should find that they coincided to the extent of a large percentage of the performances. We say that the two tests have a large co-variance or correlation. What we really should be able to say is that the same factor, or ability, is at work on both tests and is mainly responsible for the variance in both, which is exactly what we mean by a factor. We could not say this if this were one isolated pair of tests and one particular group of children, but in practice something like this always happens. In other words, between any two human performances, there is always some degree of positive correlation. As Spearman found, any one child tended to contribute about the same share to the variance of all kinds of tests. His performance would help to fill up much the same space, even in skills as diverse as Latin grammar and knitting loops. Of course the correlation was never perfect, since at least one other factor was at work in each skill; some pairs of test had higher correlations than others, which meant that the influence of their common factor was less disturbed by the intrusion of something else. But some degree of correlation there always was (see footnote to chapter 2).

From all this, Spearman deduced a *general factor* of human performance, which varied in amount from individual to individual. Its effects were to be seen in every skill and activity, so that someone 'good' at any one tended to be 'good-ish' in them all.[2] In some skills

[1] For the purpose of factorial analysis, quite large surveys are usually carried out and group or written tests are used instead of the individual type of test interview associated with Binet's idea of intelligence as one overall function.

[2] There is, of course, an occurrence known as negative correlation, which is the tendency for two sets of measures to be in inverse ratio. The more there is of one variable, the less of the other. But this, in the writer's opinion, need not be considered in the present context. Negative correlations between human performances are practically non-existent. Nobody does something badly *because* he does something else well.

this general factor of ability had most room to operate, and we might call them *g-saturated*. An individual's score in a test of a *g*-saturated performance gave an index to all his other performances. The extent of the correlation with any of them would depend on the amount of *g* in it. Conversely, a skill or activity which was less affected by *g*, such as having an ear for musical pitch, could tell us very little about any performance except itself.

Spearman never actually equated *g* with intelligence, but having accounted for the part of a test's variance wich was brought about by individual differences in *g*, he was not much concerned to analyse the remaining influences at work. For him, the area not covered by *g* was entirely specific to that one performance and could tell us nothing about any other performance. Performances had only their *g* factor in common, and nothing else.

Latterly, Spearman began to admit that this might not be so, and that two or three tests might be jointly influenced by a common factor other than the general one. Any student, offhand, would probably agree that tests in Latin syntax, French irregular verbs, and English vocabulary, would show higher correlations with each other than with, say, drawing a plan to scale. But drawing a plan to scale would probably hive off with geometry, memory for design, and so on. A readily identifiable factor of this kind is the verbal one, which almost certainly is responsible for the very high correlations that appear between pencil-and-paper tests and school success. This is the factor which Vernon would prefer to call not the *v* factor pure and simple but the *v : ed* (for verbal: educational) factor (8). Another distinct ability is for number; another for mechanical skill, which, in particular, would not necessarily correlate very highly with language skills.

Thurstone in America (9), by using different mathematical devices from Spearman, not only satisfied himself that tests correlate with each other in groups (meaning that such a group is testing a common ability) but also that they correlate hardly at all with tests outside the group, which implies that abilities, or factors, are more or less in-dependent. That is, he explained correlations without the help of *g*. For him intelligence is not a power that operates in every performance but an assembly of quite separate abilities. A Thurstone type of in-telligence scale would not state its findings as a composite score repre-senting the general quantity of someone's intellect but as a *profile chart* or graph joining up points, each point representing the level of one type of performance. And in Thurstone's view it would be quite possible for the graph to be irregular in shape since he thinks of his

Primary Mental Abilities (or group factors) as independent and distinct.

An elaborate analysis of what he calls the structure of intellect is proposed by J. P. Guilford under whose guidance a so-called Aptitude Project has been going on for many years in the University of Southern California. Guilford claims that through the Thurstone procedure of setting a large variety of tests to large numbers of students, and analysing the correlations, there are already known to exist about fifty distinct abilities, or, as he says in a typical article (10) fifty different ways of being intelligent! He predicts that at least 120 are to be located to fill up the total structure. Guilford postulates five main kinds of mental function, each with many different sub-functions. His most famous distinction is between convergent and divergent thinking; it will be considered more fully in the section on original thinking in Part Three (page 224). Meantime it should be noted that his theory gains support from the fact that high scorers on conventional intelligence tests do not necessarily score highly on tests of creativity. In other words, one kind of assessment of ability is not enough.

Thurstone's influence showed in Wechsler's plan for distinguishing the Verbal I.Q. from the Performance I.Q. The tradition continues in the large number of tests of special aptitudes which American psychologists have produced. An *aptitude* test is designed to measure the ability that controls performances likely to be needed in a chosen career. An aptitude-testing programme is a prolonged diagnosis of a student's separate abilities and their strengths so that they can be matched with a suitable college course or professional training. For this a generalized ability estimate is assumed to have no practical use and little meaning since special ability of a high order may go along with mediocre performances in other zones. It is this assumption that British psychologists are most doubtful of, although they do admit that the old composite I.Q. has probably served its turn and is due for replacement by something more discriminating.[1] For an inventory of the various mental factors that have been more or less reliably identified on both sides of the Atlantic, and for an appraisal of their usefulness in vocational and educational guidance, readers should consult the last chapter of P. E. Vernon's *Intelligence and Attainment Tests* (11).

Theoretically it should be possible to construct for each Primary Ability a test purified so as to measure that ability alone; and this has often been tried. But such 'single ability' tests show a fair degree of

[1] At the time of writing a new British intelligence test battery on these lines is under investigation.

inter-correlation, as Guilford himself admits even while stressing that it is the area of their *non*-correlation, so to speak, that is significant. On the other hand it may be reasonably taken that this confirms the existence of a fundamental g factor, which has the advantage of appealing to common sense as well. Highly gifted people do tend to show at least above-average success in most performances; a phenomenon apt to be obscured by the very brilliance of their specialized achievements. (It is noted elsewhere that the high 'creatives' have I.Q. ratings, when tested, of at least 120, which is a long way from mediocrity.) Furthermore, without a fair general average, outstanding special achievement is unlikely. Bright children in primary school are little worse at number concepts, for example, than at writing imaginative short stories; though in the teens and twenties specialization will have made a bigger difference of it. The point is that doing something very well does not in itself cause something else to be done badly. As a well-known professor of educational psychology was once heard to remark: 'In the Himalayas the valleys also are high.'

On this pleasant note the chapter may conclude. Its subject has been intelligence as a measurable thing. One way of measuring it is to treat it as a whole, complex behaviour which can reach certain known levels of performance, each carrying an age-tag. What we do here is to set up a linear scale marked off in years and months, and measure the performance as it were against this scale. This method avoids analysing the performance itself except by admitting the presence of both 'nature' and 'nurture' elements. Another device is to break general intelligence down into distinct types of performance which can be separately and more scientifically measured. This is the analytic as opposed to the developmental approach. Whether by analysis we also define intelligence is another matter. The most useful definition so far has been by the kind of performances which psychologists have chosen as sampling intelligent behaviour, and this, like so many psychological procedures, comes back in the end to personal judgement and common observation.

This chapter has dealt with the development of intelligence chiefly as supplying a measuring device. It is, however, an important matter in its own right, and is to be considered in the next section of the book, along with other aspects of developmental psychology.

NOTE: A short commentary on vocational and educational guidance will be found in Appendix I at the end of the book.

REFERENCES

(1) Burt, Cyril, *Mental and Scholastic Tests*, King & Son, 1922.

(2) Terman, L. M., *The Measurement of Intelligence*, Boston, 1916. (First Stanford revision.)

(3) Terman, Lewis M. and Merrill, Maud A., *Measuring Intelligence*, Harrap 1937. (Second Stanford revision.)

(4) Terman, Lewis M. and Merrill, Maud A., *The Stanford-Binet Intelligence Scale*, Harrap, 1961. (Third Stanford revision.)

(5) Yates, A. and Pidgeon, D. R., *Admission to Grammar Schools*, Newnes, 1957.

(6) Wechsler, David, *Wechsler Intelligence Scale for Children*, The Psychological Corporation, New York, 1949.

(7) Spearman, C., 'General Intelligence', *American Journal of Psychology*, 1904, Vol. 15, pp. 201–293.

(8) Vernon, P. E., *The Structure of Human Abilities*, Methuen, 1950.

(9) Thurstone, L. L., *The Vectors of Mind*, Chicago, 1935.

(10) Guilford, J. P., 'Three Faces of Intellect', reprinted from *American Psychologist*, Vol. 14 (1959) in *Human Learning in the School* (ed. de Cecco), Holt, Rinehart and Winston, U.S.A., 1963.

(11) Vernon, P. E., *Intelligence and Attainment Tests*, U.L.P., 1960.

4

The Psychology of Growth

1 What development means

One of the great problems of psychology is how to subdivide its subject-matter without creating false impressions. There are no natural, clear-cut boundaries in the personality of a human being, nor in his life-history. If an action or experience is taken out of its setting of the whole behaviour, then we cannot say all there is to be said about it, and sometimes we may even find that it has not been understood at all, because we have omitted the very factor that affects it most.

Human learning, for example, will have a separate chapter heading in every textbook on educational psychology, and one might think that from this topic certain considerations, valuable enough in themselves, may be excluded without doing harm to our understanding of the actual learning process. Surely someone's devotion to mathematics and his devotion to someone else's welfare can be safely treated as separate psychological matters. This may well be the case. Yet there is good reason to believe that the learning of children in school will not go on so well if they have not previously learned the habit of dependence upon the goodwill of adults. Children are prone to imitate, for which master-stroke on nature's part all educators count themselves lucky. What motivates a child's enthusiasm for imitating is by no means completely understood; but it is significant that deprived children are often listless as imitators. You will have a much more satisfactory game of blowing invisible bubbles with a secure and well-loved baby, and by the same token he will more readily learn the delight of pleasing you by articulating his early syllables.

Readers will remember that children who get a generous share of parental attention make a better showing in intelligence tests and some psychologists who have made a special study of children's language development are convinced that an indispensable condition of progress for a child is contact with a deeply interested adult. This is especially so in the early years when the division between mental and emotional experience (never quite complete at any human age) simply does not exist at all. Older children may sometimes acquire a simple bit of new activity with little excitement; it is just not in the nature of a young child to do this. He will rehearse his brand-new skill over and over again with shouts of laughter, and will love above all to have someone to share it with. Further on in life it may be possible for a remarkably bookish and determined adolescent to get over his dislike of a teacher and positively learn something from the man; but it will not be easily done. Most people who read this book can remember, too, a class of thirteen-year-olds sullenly refusing to see sense or interest in a demonstration, because the teacher, perhaps out of nothing worse than nervousness, has touched off their hostility.

In discussing children's behaviour in particular, psychologists must be cautious how they make their subdivisions. The same thing applies to the useful chronological 'age-and-stage' plan of dealing with development. Of course there is no clear-cut boundary for a child to cross between 'early' and 'middle' childhood, and though certain physical changes may be accepted as marking the start of adolescence, there is no agreement about what determines its upper limit. To fix this we must draw upon a different set of determinants altogether and these will vary with the social structure of the community. It is not a *developmental* but a *cultural* decision when an adolescent becomes an adult, indeed he does not begin to be an adult but, by imperceptible degrees usually, begins to be treated like one.

It is not always possible to distinguish developmental from cultural differences when we compare one time of life with another, but it is important to try, since very often a certain kind of behaviour may be taken as typical of a certain age-group, when in fact it is cultural in origin—that is, it is a way of life imposed on these individuals by the people round about them. All human beings who live in communities have social roles to perform; they must live up to certain expectations and stop short of certain limits. Children are very early made aware of this and a reaction taken as 'age-typical' may be no more than their way of obliging (or resisting!). For instance young children make almost universal use of double-syllable jingles like bow-wow and puff-puff, but it cannot be categorically accepted as a stage in language growth, for who is going to deny that they are encouraged by friendly adults who enjoy the word-play almost as much as they do? Commonly accepted as an example of resistance to a difficult social role is the behaviour of some adolescent boys and girls. It is a long time since adolescence in itself was thought of as a state of un-avoidable disturbance.[1] What we rather see today is the adolescent

[1] Except in a rather special sense which will be mentioned later.

worried by the ambiguous demands of the environment and, like a human being of any age, struggling to adjust to them somehow, and to escape when they become impossible.

These are only two examples of 'age-and-stage' behaviour for which the social explanation seems to be sounder than the developmental one; and there can hardly be a developmental problem in which it is not worth while to take cultural and environmental causes into consideration. This has the advantage of implying that something positive can be done, whereas a developmental phase by its very nature could only be left to work itself out! But in fact, one of the important trends in present-day psychology is to study any given kind of behaviour in its social setting, and not in isolation. The significance in particular of human relationships is taken more seriously with the increase of psychological knowledge, and it is quite difficult to find a behavioural pattern from which their effects can be safely counted out. Perhaps some of an infant's earliest needs, like sleep and excretion, may be quite simply organic and self-regulating, and may or may not have psychological importance for later life; but there are others just as early, like the food-need, which depend for satisfaction upon the exertions of another human being, and of the psychological importance of these there is no doubt at all. Many famous studies, like those of Goldfarb in America and Bowlby in this country have stressed the persistent effect of early human contacts and their associated emotions upon later personality patterns. (See below, page 134.)

This matter will appear again; meantime it is well to keep the personal-social environment in mind for all those aspects of a child's development which are psychological, rather than physical. We shall see that this does not exclude so very much. The strands in a human being's development are as intricately interwoven as in his personality and though only a sample of their connections can be traced, it must be remembered that they exist. Obviously, a baby cannot enjoy the *function* of walking till the bodily *structure* for walking is matured in his nerve tracks; just as obviously his happiness in achievement will ensure adequate practice of the new skill till it no longer needs his immediate attention and another is ready to succeed. At every stage he will be provided with the best of motives both for exercising his own powers and taking the measure of his environment.

This is the process of *adjustment* which means adapting oneself to the environmental conditions on the one hand and on the other manipulating the environment to one's needs. This is a very bald summary of a very complex psychological idea. The environment contains more factors than can be conveniently reckoned and by adapting himself an individual does not only make the best use of his abilities but makes his wishes and needs more realistic.

It is interesting to watch a young child when baulked by lack of inches, or someone else's opposition, philosophically turning his attention elsewhere. A time will come when he can climb out of his play-pen and is no longer expected to stay in it; a ten-year-old girl may find herself, to her surprise and pleasure, admitted to the family councils instead of being fobbed off with the discouraging 'Run away and play, dear; we're busy.' A whole new set of behaviour patterns becomes available and therefore worth mastering. Substitute for the emancipated two-year-old and the girl learning her first lessons in womanliness, a man of thirty-five realizing, with the death of a reliable older person, that he now represents the responsible generation on whom the very old and very young are going to depend for many years. The age of privilege, of living mainly for his own concerns, is over for him and his personality must accommodate itself to suit; it may be enriched but it cannot be the same.

Development can be seen as a continuous series of adjustments between changing self and changing environment and of course does not stop abruptly when bodily growth ends. Adults, like children, are constantly altering and the problem at any time of life is how to achieve satisfaction of needs typical of the present level of development. Children's behaviour is not basically different from adolescent behaviour or the behaviour of young adults. Children and adults are active strivers, reinforced by success and depressed by frustrations. Neither child nor adult can stay the same for very long; each will be a slightly different human being a week from now and noticeably different in a year or two.

We see that to understand almost any single aspect of a child's behavioural development we must relate it to other aspects of his personality. Very little of his progress, bodily or mental, is independent of emotional experiences like satisfaction. It is also believed by many modern psychologists that among the most significant emotional experiences for children are those which have to do with personal-social relationships. There is a marked trend in psychology to look for explanations in the social environment for many developmental changes in behaviour. Warm human contacts are thought to be not just desirable but a positive condition of full development and self-realization. Secondly, there are behavioural patterns which are cultural rather than genetic or developmental.

The reader has been reminded that there are no sharp boundaries between one age-and-stage and the next, and that human development is a life-long history of adjustment between self and environment which does not end with the period of growth. There are developmental tasks for every time of life.

The psychology of development can have this wider meaning, which is sometimes useful. It can, of course, be used in the traditional sense for the period between birth (or in some contexts, conception) and the early twenties during which all the changes take place which turn a baby into a young adult. To the special features of this developmental period proper we may now turn, and to the psychological methods of studying them.

2 Methods and sources

Like children and adolescents, adults change, but the changes are slower and less dramatic. This is partly because there are more repetitions of old tasks in adult life and fewer first occasions; and partly because changes in an adult are often simply alterative, one kind of behaviour displacing another, whereas during growth the changes are expansive upon the whole and so more stimulating. Another difference is that children are put in a dependent position by being, for example, small in an oversized world and ignorant of even common knowledge. Neither they nor the fairest minded adult can do away with this difference. It is not culturally imposed and must be recognized in any educational policy.

All this means that a child's adjustment tasks are different and it accounts for the psychological impact of development. Children are bound to grow; they start with neither knowledge nor skill and are to acquire both; they are bound also to outgrow their social dependency. These special features of adjustment in childhood and youth are interrelated but they are not the same. They justify, to this extent, the familiar arrangement of developmental psychology under the three headings of physical, mental, and social, although the amount of available information is very unequally divided among them.

By far the best documented of the three is physical maturation. It is much easier to establish the facts, of which there has been an accumulation over the last forty years and more, and it benefits as well from all the research in the neighbouring sciences of biology and medicine. Of course the hereditary factor in intelligence is partly explained by what we know of genetics, the science of heredity; and recent theories about the development of thinking are supported by neurology, especially as it concerns the structure and function of the brain. But these are only hints for the mapping of mental development, which is still at the tentative stage. Likewise, there are kindred sciences from which something can be learnt about social development, or at least about its cultural elements. From anthropology come studies of tribal customs in child-rearing and their apparent effects, from sociology surveys of the more sophisticated differences of attitude between the classes of the same society. But again, these findings can do no more than guide our observations of children's progress towards emotional and social maturity. They cannot be applied in a hard-and-fast manner. The use made of other sciences is different in the study of mental and social growth on the one hand, and physical on the other. The psychological methods used are different also. The facts about bodily growth and many bodily skills can be assembled by the usual techniques of measurement and survey; these investigations have usually been normative as we shall see in a moment, and their object has been to provide a basis of certainty for educators. The foundations of this familiar method were laid long ago by people like Gesell, and the idea of a generalized maturational pattern has not been substantially altered. But details have been filled in, and a few refinements in method have shown up some misconceptions. The pattern of increase in standing height, for example, comes out differently when measures are taken *longitudinally*, that is on the same group of children over a period of years, instead of by a quicker *cross-sectional* study, where average heights of all the year-groups are taken on one single occasion and then put together to form a graph. The reader will see that this graph is an artifact, useful in some way, but not presenting the actual growth progress of any one group of children, let alone of an individual child however 'normal' or 'average'. But normative studies are still helpful, not least because they highlight cultural and individual variations. We have already seen this in connection with intelligence testing.

It would be wrong to give readers who are new to the subject the impression that all psychologists in the early years of the normative studies were solely concerned with norms and generalizations. Their work is enriched by the kind of description and commentary which is only possible through the so-called *clinical* methods of child-study.

This method views a child as a unique whole, not as representing one measurable trait or performance, or even a constellation of them. It implies observation over a period, and at least some informality in the interviews, so that behaviour is free, not structured by tasks and questions. In developmental studies it works best along with other, more controlled kinds of observation and measurement which discipline its tendency to become loose and vague, while at the same time it gives life and meaning to the quantitative results.

The encyclopedic three-volume studies of Arnold Gesell and his collaborators at Yale, while impossible to summarize, show clearly the complementary advantages of both methods. We find many of the techniques of psychological measurement: adequate sampling of children (for instance, for the ages ten to sixteen, a core group of 115 boys and girls were observed longitudinally and an additional normative group at some ages), standardized tests of development and observation of single traits, and statistical records of results. The most famous of these last are the development schedules for the pre-school years with age-norms for performances like 'Walks; seldom falls' and 'Makes a tower of six cubes'. Nevertheless, Gesell repeatedly states that his methods and interests are clinical and he always emphasises the individuality of behavioural development and the usefulness of descriptive as well as statistical statements. His age-portraits, notably *Five Years Old*, are educational folklore. A short appraisal of his findings will come in a later chapter.

Something was said a moment ago about adequate sampling. If a developmental survey is to have real depth it cannot always be done on a very wide scale, since it may involve careful following up of the same children, or careful analysis of the behaviour. So samples may be small. Piaget's conclusions about the sensori-motor stage of thinking were based on the activity and talk of his own children. There were never more than twenty-three children at the Malting House school long ago, where Susan Isaacs experimented with activity teaching methods. Validity of observations made on such small and special groups must be achieved by careful control of the observation itself and the records kept. Informal anecdotes and generalization can be quite valueless. For example, to say 'The children acted aggressively at times' tells us nothing useful. Which children; all or only some? How often and at what times of day? In what circumstances; as a group or in pairs? How is 'aggression' defined; by words or blows? Obviously some attempt must be made to fix the conditions so that the significance of an act can be measured. This can sometimes be done by the technique of *time-sampling*. The observer notes down the incidence of a certain type of behaviour during ten minutes in every hour, which gives the children the same length of opportunity for committing aggressive acts, or whatever it may be. You might otherwise note five to Alex's discredit and only one to William, but Alex was under your eye most of the time and William had the good luck to be elsewhere. Time-sampling also allows for a variety of background conditions and one can compare afternoon aggressiveness when the children are tired, with morning aggressiveness when they are frisky.

Controlled observation also means defining what we are estimating. Observers exploring the important matter of home influence upon behavioural development in school must select explicit variables by which homes can be classified. To call a home satisfactory or indifferent is not informative; nor can we make use of the assessment 'fairly strict' till it has been placed somewhere along the range of a rating scale for the *strictness* variable, which might have five points running: *indulgent, permissive, firm, authoritarian, harsh*. A rating scale for family harmony might likewise extend from *serene* to *quarrelsome* and so on. If the school behaviour of the children were similarly itemized, it would be possible to calculate degrees of correspondence between home and behaviour variables. Admittedly interpretation of the correspondence would have to be cautious. It is reasonable to assume a relationship between the quality of home discipline and a child's responsiveness to a teacher, but the real common factor might be missed. Suppose frequency of punishment is one of the variables in the breakdown of quality of discipline, we might have two homes scoring about equal. But punishment may come from capricious, irritable parents or from parents affectionately concerned about their family's social well-being. An all-over difference of atmosphere may be lost by rigid analysis, or interpretation. This is a point made by Jersild in his account of the home studies carried out by Baldwin and others. Himself a confirmed believer in the all-importance to a child of warm relationships, Jersild goes on to say that a parent may measure up rather well on the established child-rearing practices in a social group and still be an unsatisfactory parent from this point of view (1). The real advantage of analytic rating devices, as we shall see in other contexts, is as a reminder to the investigator of the dangers of vagueness and inconsistency in case-study observations, even if scientific objectivity cannot always be achieved.

In contrast to the reliability of the measuring tape, or even of the mental test, techniques for assessing social development have always been hard to invent and are not always convincing. But the attempt is always interesting to psychologists, who have tried many devices, some adapted from other areas where they have worked well. The *control-group* technique has always been a favourite; we came across it already as a way of comparing two teaching methods. Two samples are matched for age, sex, ability, social class, or whatever else might affect results. The experimental group gets a special form of treatment and the two groups are given a common test or assessed behaviourally at the end of the experiment. The difference, if any, may be fairly called environmental in origin. The method is not foolproof, for reasons which apply to similar methods in other sciences but which make developmental investigations particularly difficult. Some factor not foreseen may be making hay of the results, and not all of these cases turn out so luckily as the one described by J. M. Tanner. The original object of enquiry was the effect of increased calories on the growth of an experimental group of orphanage children. In the outcome the expected results were reversed, the control group actually showing greater gains. It was the intervention of another factor altogether which had this effect, a changeover in the experimental group from friendly to hostile supervision at mealtimes. The records in this case had been so carefully kept that the factor could be identified and so a bit of medical research found its way into a psychological textbook (2).

The control-group method is often at its most useful as a pointer to further research with bigger samples. One idea which could only emerge from experiments of the control-group type was that of stimulus-induced maturation, which means the boosting of the developmental sequence itself by some environmental challenge. E. R. Hilgard was able to distinguish it some time ago from the learning process proper. It has been given support by reasearch like Hebb's into mental organization (see page 157) and fits in very well with modern views about the cultural factor in intelligence.

In some developmental studies, as we have seen, the sampling requirement may be abandoned and validity achieved some other way. The old-established technique of *co-twin control* started from the assumption that as between identical twins (or monozygotic twins as they are called now) all the complex hereditary factors have already been equalized by nature. So if one twin gets special training over a period, superiority in performance must logically be due to the learning factor. If, as quite often appeared, there was no permanent superiority, with the control, or untrained twin catching up quite quickly, then the innate maturational sequence could be taken as the dominant factor in this behavioural item. This was a favourite conclusion of Gesell's in his classical twin studies, and he was inclined to take this independence of environment as the characteristic of the genetic trend. (But see page 109 below.)

Psychologists nowadays, as the reader must have realized, hesitate to chalk up any kind of behaviour to the credit of either maturation or learning, or even to estimate their respective shares in it. But the general principle of an inborn tendency to mature, and to mature according to a sequential pattern has not of course, been questioned. Clinical studies have been supplemented by surveys of child-rearing practices like the much-quoted instance of the Hopi Indian papooses, whose mobility was so little the worse for rigid cradle-boarding.

It remains to mention *formal experiments* which social psychologists, particularly in America, have attempted to carry out, using group situations as their material and varying some factor. A favourite enquiry has been into the effect upon children's social responsiveness of different forms of adult control; the topic is a little like the classification of homes described above. For survey and observation only, the experimenter substitutes deliberate structuring of a group situation and notes specific reactions. Thus an adult club-leader will assume the authoritarian role in directing some hobby, the children will then be turned over to another kind of leadership (say *laissez-faire*). Efforts are made to equalize the conditions, for instance by varying the order of the two types of control, and by assigning different leadership roles on successive occasions to the same adult, to cancel the effect of the personality factor. The children's responses, needless to say, are specified as separate variables like the tendency to imitate, so that some measure can be taken of the amount of reinforcement of this tendency which results from (say) friendliness in the adult leader.

These experiments are probably as far removed as a psychological method can be from the normative surveys. The aims are different and the results cannot be applied in the same way, which summarizes the theme of the present account of the sources of information which developmental psychology draws upon. They range all the way from relevant data in the medical sciences, through anthropological and sociological field surveys, to such specifically psychological studies as an enquiry into mother-child relationships or pre-school language habits. Methods must vary with the purposes and as a correction to each other's deficiencies, and results will have different kinds of usefulness depending on the size of the survey and the complexity of the behaviour observed. Where there are many factors at work, development studies often act as pointers to further research; the main usefulness of Piaget's work may well turn out to be of this kind in the long run, as we must consider in a later chapter in the present group. Underlying the normative surveys was the concept of a general maturational sequence, which remains a useful first principle of developmental psychology and can be applied to mental, and perhaps to social, as well as to physical growth patterns. How it applies, and how it has been modified by recent psychological ideas is an important topic.

3 The maturational sequence

The process called maturation is the genetically determined tendency of a young creature to become an adult of its own species and to do so in a genetically determined sequence of growth and behavioural changes. It was this pattern which the normative studies of Gesell, Shirley and others made it their business to trace in the development of human children. Their observational methods might vary in detail but the essential principle of establishing a developmental *norm* was always the same. With a large enough sample of children, accidental differences of environment and individual departures from the common rule will cancel out, leaving us with the normal characteristic trend of maturation in the trait in question. Gross unsuitability of environment may deflect the pattern, but upon the whole the function of the environment in such an idea of maturation as this, was taken to be rather a neutral one, offering the growth pattern the chance to work itself out rather than stimulating it into something different. We have seen also that the *restrictive* power of the environment was believed to be limited. Children deprived of practice even at the moment of readiness would catch up on the early starters, provided it was not left too late; premature training did not hurry on a skill. The ability must be waited for. These were the days when 'reading readiness' was a common educational idea, and it is interesting to note how on this one point alone, educational opinion has shifted.

If maturation is regarded as a process which cannot be hurried, which is one way of putting it, nor yet stimulated by a favourable environment, which is a rather different way, then obviously the whole of education should be conducted on the 'readiness' principle and children should not be required to learn something until their power is ripe for it. The *structure* must emerge before the *function* can be performed. But in fact it is now believed that function (or activity) may have a good deal to do with actually bringing the structure into existence. Possibly without actually practising stepping movements a baby would still become able to walk during the genetically appointed month, or week. Perhaps he would be physically bound to make guttural sounds without the stimulus of comfort sensations from food and human contact. But, as will be discussed more fully in a later chapter, the organization of mental abilities is believed to come about at least in part through experience and activity. We may even go so far as to call such organization a product of the culture in which children happen to live. In some primitive societies, for example, adults cannot understand counting beyond 25, although in the ability to classify objects together, which is the basis of number ideas, primitive bush children have been found about equally competent with primary school children of the same age (3). There are many other examples of a psychological trend away from the belief in a genetically independent maturational sequence; and even from the tacit definition of maturation by distinguishing its effects in some way or other, from the effects of learning and the environment generally.

On the other hand, however, we have from modern biology the description of the original cell as carrying a blueprint of instructions determining the order of appearance of all the complex adult features. Yet it will improve our psychological understanding of this process if we think of the other meaning of determination. There is a very great appearance of determined purposefulness in the way a child moves beyond his helpless beginnings into greater and greater competence. Many psychologists today would be ready to accept just such a persistent, self-initiated activity as the inborn core of the developmental process. It is the guarantee that behaviour will develop in the only way it can, by vigorous interaction between the young creature and its environment. Furthermore, it is a progressive, expansive, and outgoing activity. Children do not normally creep backwards to the inertia of the pre-birth period, or to the security of what they were able to do a year ago. They are natural learners and adventurers; and this is the real importance of the maturation process for teachers.

The normative studies of course recognized this. The child's maturation was thought of as presenting a sequence of developmental needs which the environment must supply with the right tasks at the right time, or the ability whose turn it was might be by-passed. The phase during which some ability was ripe and ready for exercise was known by some such title as the *plastic* or *critical* period, the whole idea being an extension of the known facts of development before birth (see below, page 106). If something goes wrong with the intra-uterine environment at a given moment it is the physical feature due to ripen then which is impaired, and the damage cannot be made good once development moves into another phase. Developmental psychologists have by no means given up the old idea of there being similar critical phases in the growth of mind and personality. Indeed it has gained ground now that we are a little further on in our knowledge of the timing of some of these phases. It is suspected, for one thing, that even good subsequent relationships do not easily repair the emotional damage done by early mother-deprivation; and for another, that the foundations of our powers of symbolic thought are laid by the sensory and motor experience of the first years of life. What has been abandoned is the idea that readiness, the appointed start of the 'plastic' period, must always be waited for.

Potentiality may well be increased by favourable experience. Characteristics once accepted as part of the maturation pattern may turn out to be susceptible to cultural modification. For example a significant difference has usually been found in language development between the two sexes, girls being further advanced than boys of the same age, which was thought to be in accordance with their higher developmental rate (see below, page 110). But at least one recent study (4) shows evidence that this traditional difference is diminishing, and offers the suggestion that this may be due to more uniform treatment of girl and boy babies by present-day parents.

Again, psychologists have qualified their ideas about the value of norms. Gesell, of course, always allowed for the huge range of individual variations when he made his developmental statements. Yet his aim was essentially to tie each successive skill or *behaviour-syndrome*[1] to an age. They were fixed points for charting the standard course of development, which he elaborated finally into a cyclic or spiral form. Thus, as he sees it, a period of withdrawn behaviour at three will be followed by vigorous expansiveness at four and consolidation at five. Seven, eight, and ten, and then again thirteen, fifteen, and sixteen, are later versions of the same thing (see below, page 000). Now, as has been noted already, a graph based on age averages is not the true course of development of any one child. Even a child near the average

[1] A *syndrome* is a cluster of behavioural features typical of an individual in his present state.

for a trait, whether it is his standing height or his score on a vocabulary test, will vary a little in his relative position, being in one year a little below average, in another just above. These changes, as we have seen, are masked, since some other child in the sample is likely to show exactly contrary ones, so the two sets cancel and the graph remains smooth. This might be defended by calling these annual variations in an individual child's relative progress accidental, and the smoothed graph the 'true' progress. But the fact remains that such fluctuations really happen and smooth progress graphs do not. Individual development shows ups and downs in comparison with the whole year-group, and to this point we must return (see page 116).

Norms are the midpoints of a huge range of variations and one more example will not do any harm. The 'average' three-year-old knows and uses almost a thousand words; but what is more important is that among the threes there are many still at the stage of baby conversation who will talk quite competently when they enter school; and there is a large number advanced enough to have some command of the simple tenses of the verb and the social implications of the three persons of the pronoun. Such a variation not only makes word-counts hard to establish, but also takes away most of their developmental meaning. Language behaviour is a complex whose variance results from far more than the age-factor. Certainly, vocabulary increases and does not diminish with a child's birthdays, but many other things have been happening while he was getting older. Children grow up among people who talk to them, love them, encourage and restrain; among other children who compete and co-operate; among things which can be looked at, eaten, counted, pushed away, asked about.

Besides the environmental factor, there is another source of variation in the timing of the maturational sequence. Although the order may be almost universal to the human species, the age-placement of developmental events is not at a point of time but over a range of months, or even years, out of which every child selects his own moment. The human individual's maturation is unique, like everything else about him. J. M. Tanner inclines to the belief that there exists a general maturational factor in the individual make-up (5), so that his forwardness in any aspect of development would indicate a similar degree of forwardness in any other. The evidence at present is not conclusive, for example as to whether there is any significant relationship between early pubescence and the degree of mental maturity (see below, page 114). But at the moment, educational decisions (for example about the age of transfer to secondary education) are just as likely to be influenced by these considerations, as by the age-placement tables.

Upon the whole, a teacher is bound to be an environmentalist in practice, whatever his developmental theories may be. Even a firm believer in the basic importance of 'readiness' must recognize that choosing the right moment for an ability to be realized is an environmental responsibility. And while it seems common sense to think of the level of a pupil's 'structural' development as limiting his possible 'functions', there is a maturational principle of anticipation as well as readiness. The 'structure' is ready in very good time. In the recordings of infant vocalization there is evidence of every known human sound in the first two months of life, ready for stimulation, in due course, by the speech environment.

Maturation has social as well as educational importance. Not all the items listed in the age-placement tables are behavioural, and some simple motor abilities make their punctual appearance without having much predictive value in respect of later, more complex kinds of ability. But self-realization through the acquisition of new per-formances is psychologically important at any age. Besides, there is the child's own progress, the talking-point of the latest height-mark on the door-jamb and the bigger size of shoes, and above all there is the appealing blend of sturdiness and vulnerability, which gets a response from adults that has a great deal to do with his emotional well-being. The effects of maturation have psychological importance, then, for the upbringing of children in general, and in the individual experience of every child.

4 The beginnings of individuality

Individuality, as all biology students know, makes its appearance at the very start of life in the zygote, or first cell, which will be reduplicated billions of times over to make the mature child, and contains his unique set of genes. A gene carries in unimaginable minuteness its code of instruction for the special shape of the bodily feature it is concerned with. One gene, or gene cluster, predestines (let us say) small earlobes, curly hair, tone-deafness, a flexible thumb joint. Any single one of these peculiarities may be a faithful reflection of some ancestor's, recent or distant, but no one else in history except a twin has much chance of having exactly the same assortment of peculiarities.

From any human point of view, this is an interesting result. A simplified account follows of how it comes about.

Genes, the determinants of physical features, and possibly of many behavioural ones as well, cannot be seen in isolation by any present microscopic technique. They can however be located. It is known that they occupy positions like beads on a string, which is a common way of representing them. These strings of genes are called chromosomes[1] and they are to be found in the nucleus or core of the living cell. A human body has many millions, all reduplicated from the first cell. The human cell has forty-six chromosomes or strings of genes, and they are paired. In every pair the genes are matched, so that there are two genes working side by side, so to speak, to determine the form of the particular body-feature.

The chromosomes are paired because one member of each pair is contributed by the individual's father, the other by his mother, so that there are two complete sets of twenty-three chromosomes. After conception, the original cell begins to duplicate and reduplicate, so that theoretically every single cell carries copies of the original forty-six chromosomes, or two sets of twenty-three. You may therefore be said to possess a gene for (say) colour-vision in such an unlikely place as your big toe, where obviously it cannot do much to make its presence known—nor indeed anywhere except in those cells which have been dealt out to the retina of the eye. Once allocated, a cell begins to specialize according to its position, a point we must return to later.

Just as the cells of the eye specialize for the function of vision, so the cells composing the gonads or sex glands specialize for their own unique function. They become capable of releasing what are, in effect, half-cells with one set of twenty-three chromosomes. When body cells are duplicated, they remain connected as tissue, but the sex or 'half' cell is free-floating and independent. If conception occurs, it is united with a corresponding half-cell from the other parent, thus restoring the chromosome total to forty-six in the zygote, which is the name given to the first cell of the new individual. The zygote then proceeds to duplicate its forty-six chromosomes in the usual way. If this new individual becomes a parent in due course he will transmit twenty-three of them to the member of the next generation.

Now when the twenty-three are split off from the other set at the formation of the sex-cell, the selection of them is made at random.

[1] From Greek *soma*, meaning body, and *khroma* meaning colour, which signifies merely that they can be stained for observation.

Suppose we call the first member of each pair of chromosomes A
and the other B, then the twenty-three will not be all A's or all B's.
Of any pair, either A or B may hive off, creating a very large number
indeed of possible arrangements of these two alternatives. Thus a
parent will transmit a selection from the twenty-three he inherited
from his own mother (perhaps fifteen A's) and the remainder are
made up from the other, or paternal, twenty-three: in this case eight
B's. On another occasion of conception he may transmit, say, only
eleven A's and twelve B's so that his two children, though probably
sharing a fair overlap of genes, will differ considerably in their total
genetic make-up. One gets his father's broad hand with spatulate
fingers, the other gets one but not the other, and is the only one of the
family with his pleasantly lop-sided grin. Or, for that matter, his
grandfather's brilliant eyes. For this random selection of genes has
been going on in all the past generations. Obviously, a baby's chances
of inheriting even one gene-cluster diminish with the remoteness of an
ancestor. But a mother may be able to admire in her growing daughter
the elegant Roman nose which made its last appearance in the person
of her own long-dead great aunt. This legacy from one of the eight
great-grandparents has been unsuspected until now, because some
other ancestor's more dominant gene has had its own way with the
family nose!

When the chromosomes, and therefore the genes, are paired up
with their opposite numbers from the other parent, each gene pair
gets to work, as has been indicated, on the body feature concerned.
Sometimes one gene dominates the other, and takes over the whole
feature, though the suppressed or latent gene may perhaps be transmitted and get its chance in the next generation. Quite often there is
a blending of the effects of the two genes and we find children coming
half-way between their parents, perhaps for height, or hair-colour.
This produces a whole new crop of possibilities in the astronomical
range of human differences. Interested readers may amuse themselves
by working out an imaginary set of permutations. To get a fuller
story of genetic inheritance they should consult one of the many
excellent accounts in textbooks on developmental psychology;
enough has probably been said in the present context to show why
every human child, with the interesting exception of monozygotic
twins, which we shall come to in a moment, is bound to grow up
physically unique, and why his heredity may be held at least partly
accountable for the uniqueness of his behaviour patterns as well.

Behaviour, in the sense of function or activity, must simply be accepted as a built-in characteristic of living cells. It makes its appearance in the embryo astonishingly soon after conception when the heart begins to beat, followed by the beginnings of other elementary physiological functions. The muscles are mobile before the nerves link them up to the receptor cells in the sense organs, so that the earliest activity is not a response to the pre-natal environment, but is self-originating. There can be no awareness, however dim and amorphous, not even of primitive touch experiences.

But unborn babies do become capable, again miraculously early in the pre-birth period, of behaviour in the true psychological meaning of linked sensation and response. That is, there is an elementary kind of awareness and an attempt at accommodation, however generalized. Arrangements for the familiar reflex actions of the new-born are ready long before birth. Now what is true at the beginnings of maturation probably goes on being true, so that the capacity for certain behaviour is there before the behaviour itself, and the behaviour in its turn makes spasmodic early appearances before it is going to be seriously needed. It is one of the favourite topics in the nature/nurture argument, and both sides can find some support in embryology, the study of development before birth. Like all the life-sciences, and especially those concerned with *ontogeny*,[1] embryology has some findings which act as pointers to the nature of *behavioural* development. A good deal of use has been made of embryology, perhaps because much more is known about the progress of growth and of tissue specialization in the unborn than is known, for example, about the development of brain structure in later childhood. But although many years separate adolescent and intra-uterine growth patterns, it is assumed that the same principles continue to operate, and that structure and function are related in much the same way.

The principle of *anticipation* has been mentioned. Another interesting process is the specialization of the cells, as they increase in number and find themselves at different points of the expanding structure. A cell on the outer rim, so to speak, will be subject to different pressures from those at the core; and there materialize the three concentric systems of the ectoderm (skin and nerves), mesoderm (muscle and bone), and endoderm (internal organs). Now there is a period when a piece of tissue transferred elsewhere would proceed to grow according to its new situation, although it had already made a different sort of start. But this plastic or adaptive period is limited. A moment arrives when the tissue is committed to a particular growth pattern and could

[1] The history of the development of individual organisms.

neither be replaced from elsewhere nor itself develop upon any other lines. Readers no doubt have drawn the psychological inference for themselves. It is very likely that specialization in human development tends always to bring about this state of affairs. That is, there is probably a period during which someone's mental powers, for one thing, could take several forms, and his personality traits, for another, could bend this way or that, according to circumstances, but at some critical point the momentum of growth itself takes over and the course becomes fixed. This is a serious matter educationally, though not necessarily disturbing. Specialization and adaptation are what make behaviour meaningful and give it its individual stamp.

About the most interesting feature of pre-birth development is the elaboration of the structure which comes about through the specialization of the cells, and the differentiation of function which turns a featureless lump of protoplasm into a creature capable of organized behaviour. The process involves another important principle of development which is co-ordination, by which the variety of cells becomes harmonized into a working whole. The same important principle regulates the gene assembly which is, as we have seen, a motley inheritance. The astonishing thing is how seldom there is any serious disharmony, let alone abnormality. Father's determined upper lip settles down with grandmother's agreeably tip-tilted nose, and from one ancestor's stubbornness and the other's comic turn of mind comes a special blend of cheerful courage. This subordination of parts to the whole has been remarked in human history, but perhaps not so often as it should be in the psychology of development where it is sometimes taken for granted. Yet it is quite as important psychologically as the principles of specialization and anticipatory readiness. Learning, for example, even of the simplest skills, must be fitted into some general purpose. The dominance of one hand is co-ordinated with the subservience of the other. One holds the seam, the other plies the needle; one steadies the book, the other writes the sentence; if it were not for this integration of the two functions, the learner would hesitate about the use of either hand. Likewise, if a left-handed skill is called for, as in gear-shifting say, the dominance of the right hand can be subordinated to the total pattern. Co-ordination in fact is one of the most important links to be made between maturation and learning.

There may be a temporary failure of co-ordination caused by the countering effects of the *growth gradients*. Although all body areas eventually reach the goal of maturity, they do so at different rates and some, at birth, start with a bigger handicap. The newborn's head has got very much nearer adult size than his body has, and he is quite likely to be angry at his own lack of locomotion long before his legs can carry him where he wants to go. An adolescent can feel burningly conscious of his nose until the rest of his facial growth is allowed to catch up on the start nature gives to that distinctive feature of the human primate. On the other hand, there are growth periods like middle childhood when the co-ordinating principle is at its happy best. We must return to the growth gradients in another context. Some of them, like the advancement of the arm over the leg, have only minor interest; but others have important implications. Nature, as we have seen, hurries on the growth of the head before birth and just afterwards. By a baby's first birthday it is 50 per cent of its future adult size and it will be about 90 per cent by five years old. Whether similar gradients regulate the maturing of the different brain areas is not known for certain, but the possibility will have to be considered under the general heading of mental development where its significance can be better explained (see Chapter 6).

What the life sciences can do is give some guidance to the science of behaviour; they cannot settle behavioural questions. We have seen that embryology sustains the importance of both nature and nurture, and we may take as a particular example the phenomenon of monozygotic twinning. This produces the only known cases of genetic identity in two human beings, because when the zygote begins to multiply itself, the duplicate cells do not cohere but separate and start afresh in parallel, so to speak. Two individuals develop along genetically identical lines. A monozygotic twin must share the uniqueness of his gene assembly. It is a rarer occurrence than the other form of twinning in which two maternal egg-cells are separately fertilized, each by a different sperm cell. Hence dizygotic, or fraternal twins, need have no more genes in common than any other pair of children of the same parents.

Because of their dramatic resemblance twins have always figured largely in literature and they have had more than their share of statistical attention as well. The older twin studies tended to stress the hereditary factor. In one classical survey published in 1937 (6) the likeness in intelligence measured by the correlation coefficient was found to be greater between monozygotic twins separated early and reared in different homes than between dizygotics reared together. In other words, the hereditary trend absorbed the environmental differences with only marginal variation, whereas a common environment (and twins in a family do get greater similarity of treatment than the other members) did not noticeably undo the original genetic difference in the fraternal pairs. Co-twin training techniques (see page 98) tended to stress the same kind of conclusion. There was no lasting distinction between the trained and the untrained twin.

More recent twin surveys tend to stress the cultural factor, which is in keeping with the trend of the times. For one thing they take a broader view of individuality, involving social as well as mental assessments. For another, the object of enquiry is not whether differences between twins are minor but what makes differences occur in twins (and by analogy in other human beings). The environment in fact is regarded as an individualizing factor. The title page of the book *Monozygotic Twins* carries a significant sub-title. Its author describes it as an investigation of both genetic and environmental causes of personality differences (7). Although able to assemble case-histories of forty-four pairs of separated monozygotic twins (which is a large sample where both conditions are so exceptional) the researcher makes no claim to scientific conclusions in view of the complexity of factors. The sundering of twins, for instance, is apt to take place in circumstances that disturb normal upbringing.

However, the individualizing effect of social experience is a topic for a later chapter. Individuality is stamped into the development process by the gene inheritance in the first place and no doubt by the individual pattern of cell specialization soon after conception. Some localized regions may achieve a greater degree of their full growth potential than others, which will produce slight imbalances, such as the common difference between the left and right profiles. Sheldon's theory about the three physical human types is based on the possibility that one of the cell layers in the embryo (the ectoderm, mesoderm, and endoderm) develops more fully at the expense of the two others, so creating the slight, nervy ectomorph, the sturdy mesomorph, or the plump, easy-going endomorph. *Typology* is one way of trying to make some sort of order out of the range of individual differences. But whether differences in developmental patterns are inherent in the family genes or are brought about by differences in the pre-birth environment is another problem.

5 Childhood and youth

The index known as the percentage-of-adult-size is a useful way of taking stock at certain points in the growth period. It emphasizes those changes in proportion which, quite as much as size, make an adult look different from a child. Secondly, it indicates the amount of growing still to be expected in a given area, and thirdly it brings out individual differences in rate of maturation (8). Thus a child can be tall because he belongs to a tall family, or simply because he is nearer to his own ultimate height than the average child of his age. The first child has time in front of him to become a tall adult, the second child has completed most of his growing and therefore his present superiority may not continue. It is possible by other observations, such as an X-ray of the ossification process in the bone, to estimate how far on a child is in his maturation, and so to distinguish between bigness due to type and bigness due to the early maturation factor. Both characteristics, incidentally, may be innate. Children besides inheriting the family size may equally well inherit the tendency to get through their maturation early.

Now this particular difference may not matter very much in respect of bodily height (though it might console a gangling teenager to know that he is not always going to tower miserably above his companions). But we have no real way of distinguishing the absolute ability factor in a mental score from the early maturity factor. A child may be, for various reasons, less far along the road to his own intellectual maturity than is usual at his age and may therefore have much of his mental growing still to do. It would be unfair, therefore, to take his present achievement as the index for all time of his status in his peer group. There is a well-established difference in the maturity factor between the sexes, girls being further on than boys towards their own maximum. Consequently, well-meaning people could (and sometimes do) think of girls as being 'cleverer' than boys, which would of course be a most invalid conclusion! And there may well be individual differences in the maturity factor which makes comparisons between two children of the same sex and age misleading and perhaps unfair.

There is a great deal of interest just now in this question of whether the individual tendency to earlier or later maturing extends to the mental as well as the physical. Because menarche or first menstruation is a clear-cut event, the chronology of physical maturation is easier to establish in girls and consequently much of the research has girl pupils as subjects. Correlations between school success and age at first menstruation have not always been decisive but this could, of course, be due to clumsy measuring instruments. But there probably is a kind of general factor in maturing in an individual's make-up, which along with the co-ordinating influence, affects every aspect of his development, although the correlations between different aspects may not be very high. It is a more reasonable interpretation of the evidence with its wide scatter of age-scores and age-measurements than the idea of a classically 'normal' timing. From this point of view a child who is well and happy is neither advanced nor retarded, but punctually fulfilling his own maturational pattern.

As has been remarked, this particular individual trend may be transmitted to the genes, or gene-assembly rather. Or the pre-birth environment may be able to stamp in a development pattern which cannot be reversed afterwards. And part of a child's developmental individuality after birth may be his absorption rate. Some children may be able to absorb and use more environmental stimulations than others. There is nothing educationally unjust in this view. Quite the contrary, since it allows scope for variation and avoids making demands on a pupil which he cannot possibly satisfy. To be an athlete requires environmental opportunity and motivation but it also requires a rather special type of body-build, as an interesting little survey of Tanner's has demonstrated, with Sheldon's somatotyping as its basis (9). What the environment can be expected to do is stretch innate potentialities to its fullest. A compact, small-built child is just as able to grow to his own full height as a lanky one. There is a difference between smallness and stuntedness. What the environment cannot do is change the type and make a musician, for example, out of a tone-deaf person.

There is one observed fact in surveys of physical maturation for which it is difficult to find a purely genetic explanation. Children are now bigger, age for age, than they were in former generations and the onset of puberty is becoming earlier (see below, page 119). It is tempting to look for a cause in the improved environment and perhaps to go a step further and suggest that mental and social acceleration may be keeping pace with the physical. Readers may remember previous hints that the environment may be able to meddle more effectively with those aspects of maturation—an important question which we must return to. Meantime it can be conceded that the concepts of modern human beings must be more complex than the concepts of ordinary men and women in the simpler cultures of the past. Many educators would regard a sixth-form grammar school boy of today as better equipped intellectually than (say) his Victorian counterpart. But whether it is all acquisition, or a real alternative in quality environmentally caused, it is still much too early to say.

Returning now to the other things brought out by the percentage-of-adult-size index, we find that they help to divide the growth period into three phases. They are the changes in proportion and the relative amount of growing still to be done in various regions. It is differences in proportion that distinguish the toddler's round head, fat wrists, and short limbs from the slim legginess of his nine-year-old sister, and the 'grown-up' jawline of sixteen from the chubby features of middle childhood when the brow and eyes still take up a bigger share of the face area than they will do later. Not, of course, that they subsequently get smaller, although it is tempting to picture proportional changes in this convenient way! There is no real pause in growth, let alone a decrease, in any zone (with minor special exceptions like the baby fat which dissipates itself in the upsurge of toddler energy). What does happen is a slowing down of a spectacular early rate of increase in some zone whose growth is nearly complete, and an equally spectacular acceleration in one which has been biding its time. Thus early childhood, middle childhood, and puberty are each the special season of growth in one or other of these bodily zones. If this were not the case we should finish up looking very odd indeed by human standards—immobile top-heavy computers, for example, if the brain volume went on doubling itself as it does at the beginning of life.

Although mothers, endlessly letting down hems and lengthening cuffs, would find it hard to believe, growth is a decelerating process, much faster at the start than it ever will be again. Calculated as a percentage of his total body length an increase of an inch in a baby's size is a great deal more than in a fifteen-year-old's. But the pattern of deceleration also distinguishes the three growth phases one from another. Although the greatest gain in all-over weight is in the first year of life it is not much less in the second, and it is not till after five that the child enters the period of modest annual gains which last throughout the primary school years. During early childhood too, the development of muscular activity and control is exceedingly rapid, as anyone knows who has watched age three at his back-pedalling stunts and four's horrific competence in indoor mountaineering. Skill in manipulation, though of a slap-dash variety, quickly distinguishes the dominant hand. Every kind of tool, from food-pusher to crayon is purposefully subdued. Even without reference to the human masterpiece of language, of which a working acquisition is crammed into the same few years, it is impossible not to perceive this as the greatest season of getting ready in the whole course of life. Psychologists have noted the *finished* quality which there is about age five, giving him both poise and friendliness. The first great forward surge is achieved, and ahead lies the long, sunny interval of middle childhood for the gains to be consolidated and put into use.

It is justifiable to think of middle childhood as an interval. As we have seen, growth slows down between five and ten, at which latter age, or a little short of it, gains are the lowest they will ever be. Development is not the headlong adventure it was, nor yet disturbing as it can be in the teens. The progress of maturation, as such, is steady and unobtrusive, with no characteristic emphasis on any single bodily aspect, except such minor ones as the shedding of baby roundness and the gradual lengthening of legs. Girls, being that step nearer puberty in accordance with their higher development ratio, are the leggier sex, though only by a little. Which brings us to a special feature of the primary school child's development, its relative sexlessness. Up to age five the reproductive system shares in the general rapid growth; after five there is the same slowing down as the rest of the body and the secondary sex characteristics are not due to make their appearance for several years. Dress them alike and it would often be hard to tell boy from girl; most of us have come across at least one young lady for whom it is an uproarious joke when her cropped hair and denims bamboozle strangers. Girls of this age are not self-consciously feminine nor boys aggressively masculine. They are primarily children, equally energetic, vigorous, and lively. The community of course is hard at work prescribing the social roles and tending, on the whole, to favour segregation of interests. Girls are discouraged from too much tomboyishness and boys, with more success, from sedentary games. But both sexes whiz about on bicycles, read books, watch television serials, and amass collections with not a pin's difference of gusto, and with this we come to the real characteristic of the age.

In almost any textbook which is specifically developmental middle childhood will naturally get a shorter chapter than the pre-school years or adolescence. It is hard to crowd in all the physical effects of puberty but the bodily history of the middle years can be summarized in a few sentences and there is no great psychological interest in an inch and a half's gain between the eight and ninth birthdays. There is however a great deal of psychological significance in the rapidly widening choice of activities, the absence of distraction by the developmental process itself allowing the maximum possible amount of outward-going activity. It is a phase when learning rather than maturation directs the course of development; it is, traditionally, the opportunity for education, and this temporary postponement of full maturity is probably one of the greatest natural privileges of the human race. With the trend to earlier puberty, middle childhood is shorter than it was. Time will tell whether the educational gain is greater than the loss.

There is some reason to believe that mental and social habits formed in these years are of importance for maturity of personality in the modern world and there is no proof, as yet, that earlier sex maturity brings any corresponding leap ahead in these two other psychologically more important aspects.[1] Very early menstruation, for example, can confer no advantage on a little girl and certainly entails some loss of physical liberty. Early-maturing boys sometimes become leaders in their social group, but this may be a concomitant less of the earliness itself than of the kind of build which the early maturing boy is likely to have, sturdy and athletic with a temperament to match, as Sheldon would believe. The combination, as teachers well know, always makes a favourable impression on the twelve to fourteen age-group.

Middle childhood will be considered more completely in the next chapter. We can only infer that this is the crucial phase for the acquisition of mental structures. On the debit side we have little or no idea in what order different regions of the higher brain come to functioning maturity, or if there is such an order. On the credit side we do know that a baby at birth has almost all the nerve cells he will ever have and therefore that much of the brain's increase must be due to the forming of connecting tissue, which links them into intricate working organizations. Common sense would suggest that with the range of experience open to primary school children, great strides must be made in mental organization and by the criterion of per-centage of adult structure achieved, it is in this area that middle child-hood must make its greatest headway.

This is also the period when personality traits get a chance to form. When human beings are going through common developmental changes of major importance, as in early childhood and at puberty, they tend to have prominent behaviour patterns in common as well, which is why it is often easier to generalize about kindergarten children and adolescents than it is about the eights, nines, and tens, who are often individualists in their tastes and hobbies, accomplishments and skills, loyalties and affections, much as they will be again

---

[1] Any superiority shown by the early maturers operates *throughout* the primary school period, not suddenly at the time of menarche. This appears to be the finding of recent studies. See particularly Chapter X of *The Home and the School* by J. W. B. Douglas, which attrbutes the superiority of early maturing girls to social rather than genetic factors.

when they are young adults. This again must be considered in a later chapter.

But it should be noticed that the effects of learning are more evident than the effects of maturation in the sensory and muscular development areas as well, although a little less so in the second case. From observations of his behaviour we can conclude that the sense organs of a year-old child are fully functional and that what still remains to be achieved is discrimination of the sense impressions received. The world comes to be recognized right way up very early in life although the retinal image is an inverted one, and likewise depth and distance begin to be perceived and (about age two) colours to be distinguished. Fierce argument goes on about the actual amount of *learning* involved, but that experience plays its part is obvious even in the early years. Clearly this part must increase in the middle period of growth when language and symbolic thought give pattern and meaning to sense impressions. Similarly, although full muscular co-ordination, both postural (involving the large muscles) and manipulative (involving the small muscles) takes the first ten years of life to achieve, progress must be due less and less to maturation and more and more to the exercise of skills. What is added to the muscular abilities by the fresh maturational surge of puberty is adult size and strength. Readers with an interest in physical education will find convenient tables of motor progress in Gesell's surveys, particularly in *Five to Ten* (10) but significantly he refers far more to what the middle-school child *chooses* to do than to what he merely becomes able to do.

As children reach the end of their time in primary school there are signs that the end of this middle phase of growth is also approaching. The most apparent is that very well documented phenomenon, the pre-pubertal height spurt. Over a short interval standing height increases by a noticeable amount, often several inches in a single year. The long bones of the limbs are most obviously affected, hence the typical 'all arms and legs' appearance, but the whole skeletal and muscular system is involved in it, and so girth, weight, and strength all increase as well. The growth of the lower jaw, which has been gradually catching up on the skull and brow, now shares in this final speeding up and the face acquires its adult proportions also over a fairly short period.

The existence of the growth spurt could only be confirmed by long-term or longitudinal surveys. The *average* height of eleven-year-old girls, for example, in a large sample would show an unspectacular increase over the ten-year-old average and would not reveal the existence of a small minority who are *suddenly* a great deal taller than they were a year ago. The growth spurt is one of those noticeable changes in the developmental ratio which were referred to early in this chapter, and which cause the same child to occupy somewhat different positions in his age-group from one year to the next. These positional differences may be minor, like the variation by a few points in someone's I.Q. on successive testings. But when the shift is substantial it poses a number of questions.

Long-term, or longitudinal, studies have their drawbacks apart from their laboriousness. Results are so long in appearing that many conditions may have changed, making comparisons difficult. Children may drop out over the years and the composition of the end sample will not be the same as in the original one. For instance, in one of the earliest of these long-term programmes, the Harvard growth studies, the sample began as 3,500 children, the intake of the kindergartens of all the schools in certain districts of Boston, Massachusetts in the year 1922. Twelve yearly testings and measurements followed as the children moved up through the schools, but records were completed for only about half the number, so that the sample though still very large had become in a sense a selected one. The fact that it consisted of children in more stable families who had remained within the compass of the survey was itself a developmental variable. For this kind of reason a longitudinal study, although it is a record of living histories, is not necessarily able to settle arguments.

On the other hand one of the objects of a longitudinal follow-up is to emphasize those very variables which are bound to affect the course of development and create differences between children of the same chronological age-level. An important British survey of children all born in the first week of March 1946 has traced them to the end of their secondary schooling and has managed to keep continuous records of a large percentage of them—admittedly a more feasible proposition in Britain than in a population area the size of the United States. In the third volume of a series of published reports of the survey (11) the author, Dr J. W. B. Douglas, analyses the history of the wastage and expresses his belief that the sample is not seriously distorted but remains representative of the year-group as a whole. Reliable conclusions can therefore be drawn about the effect on children's development of certain environmental and educational conditions which have been found to make differences among the children of the sample.

Significantly enough, when some of the Harvard results were

published in 1941 it was under the title, *Predicting the Child's Development* (12). More recently, we find the same preoccupation with the individual pattern in an article by Nancy Bayley setting out some findings of the Berkeley long-term growth study (13). Now, short-term positional changes are a marked feature of individual growth patterns, and the pre-pubertal growth spurt is a substantial one.

Briefly, what is psychologically interesting is not the growth-spurt itself but its wide age-range. At any time between ten and sixteen, an adolescent child may pass through the relatively brief period of peak velocity in growth. And if the age-range is wide for this simple index of the adolescent process, then surely it must be wide for those other aspects too complex for quantitative measurement and of much greater psychological significance. The pre-pubertal growth spurt has important educational implications.

Long ago the famous Hadow Report recommended that all children aged eleven should be removed from the kind of education typical of the primary school classroom, with its 'family' atmosphere and highly personal teacher-pupil relationships, to one or other type of secondary school where the educational role could be more varied and challenging. This educational policy implied two things, both deriving from the traditional view of adolescence associated with Stanley Hall's classic on the subject (14). The first was that childhood and youth were sharply divided phases with few needs in common, and the other that most children began to be adolescent at much about the same time, or near enough for practical administrative purposes. The age of transfer is still a burning topic to which has been added more recently the problem of fixing a minimum leaving age, so that between the two the adolescent process can be comfortably contained, and even taken as roughly contemporaneous with secondary education. Now no developmental psychologist can nowadays give any reassurance that this is so even in respect of physical maturation. An adolescent may have his growth spurt at any time in the teens; the same is true of the maturation of the sex functions which in some cases is nearly complete by twelve or thirteen and in others not till four or five years later. Nor is pubescence itself a sudden event. Like all the other aspects of development it is a process of gradual transition.

At a given time near the end of middle childhood the pituitary gland is stimulated by some kind of releasing mechanism in a part of the brain called the hypothalamus (which regulates the functioning of certain internal organs). The pituitary in its turn prods into activity the glands concerned with the production of the sex hormones.

Greatly increased amounts of these in the bloodstream cause a girl to acquire the characteristics of a woman and a boy the corresponding male characteristics. These include the specifically reproductive, as signalled for example by the onset of menstruation, and all the secondary features like the deeper voice and stronger shoulder muscles of the boy, and the girl's softer facial contours and rounded hips.

Now it is perhaps the case, although this is not known, that the release action of the hypothalamus operates on a 'time stat' which is part of the child's individual development mechanism and clicks on at the exact moment when the delay period of middle childhood is set to terminate. It is certainly the case that the sequence of the pubertal process thereafter is fairly uniform for adolescents, just like the creeping crawling-standing-walking sequence in the first years of their lives. But though some of the alterations appear like single events, they are actually the outcome of quite lengthy preliminaries and are not themselves finished occurrences. There is in every young girl's life a first menstruation just as there is a first time when a baby holds on to its cot bars and scrambles unsteadily to its feet. But the baby stands differently and better on later trials, and it takes a year or two for menstruation to settle down to its adult rhythm, nor is it always a sign of full reproductive ability at first. Many other adolescent changes like the boy's genital growth are transitional like the whole of development.

Because of this and the wide range of variability adolescence cannot be narrowly age-tied. Even supposing we accept its beginnings as physiologically laid down, these beginnings are not sudden, and its ending, as we saw at the start of this chapter, being behavioural and social, is an even more gradual and individual process. Sexual maturing may be completed by sixteen for the vast majority of school-leavers and in many cases well before; but maturity of personality will show a wider scatter of variation and will be a great way off for many. This comment appears in Chapter Eleven of recommendations by the Central Advisory Council for Education made in response to a government request for guidance on the educational policy to be adopted for the fifteen-to-eighteen-year-olds (15). The raising of the school-leaving age will allow some of the educational needs of the teens to be better fulfilled for those pupils who normally will not go on to higher education, but does not remove the problems of differences in maturation rate while the adolescents are all in school together.

The fact is of course that physical maturing is not a good criterion for educational planning unless we cease to insist on a narrowly age-based administrative plan. Transfer from primary to secondary, for example (if we think of the primary schoolroom as being 'good' for children and the larger, more stirring comprehensive school as being 'good' for teenagers) would be better to take place over a span of years, especially if a relationship should ever be proved between developmental advancement and mental advancement. Supposing, on the other hand we ignore the child's level of physical maturity and group pupils by ability or vocational goals, there may be difficulties of a social or disciplinary kind. In spite of the *secular trend*, as the trend towards earlier maturing is rather curiously described, there are many girls and more boys who are still children at twelve, but some girls of twelve are women, or nearly so, as many teachers are well aware.

The genetic difference in maturity rate between girls and boys starts before birth and can be traced by all the techniques for ascertaining the developmental distance that has been covered. Long ago it made separate standards necessary for giving age-scores to boys and girls in basic school subjects. On a one-minute reading check, for example, girls would be expected to pronounce a larger number of words correctly to get the same reading age as boys of the same birthday age. Readers may have noted that environment may be partly responsible for so-called innate differences, and our measuring criterions are still not good enough to establish how big these are. It is common to speak of a two-year separation between the onset of pubescence in girls and boys, which even J. M. Tanner with his insistence on the individuality of maturation is prepared to accept as a useful generalization. The earlier, and shorter, age-range of the height spurt in girls was one of the first discoveries of the long-term growth studies and ordinary observation shows girls in the upper primary school classes and the first two years of secondary to be bigger and heavier on the whole than the boys. The growth acceleration tapers off after first menstruation so that early (sexually) maturing girls are often not so tall or long-legged as late maturers, and girls generally are shorter than boys and do not increase their muscular strength greatly, as boys do in the later teens.

Nevertheless the 'average' two-year gap may be an over-estimate. The beginnings or the first instances of the intimate bodily changes in boys are hard to place even in medical surveys, most of them being well under way by the time the voice breaks or hair appears on cheeks and upper lip. But one result of the wide age-range of the adolescent sequence may be that parents and teachers need to reassure worried or embarrassed young people that their individual timing is well within the bounds of normality, whether they do it by actually saying so or just by matter-of-fact acceptance. There are good, medically based accounts in developmental textbooks, and teachers can familiarize themselves with those changes which are likely to have behavioural impact. This means, upon the whole, the changes that adolescents themselves are conscious of. The glandular ones, on the other hand, may upset the hormonal balance for a little while, but we do not positively know that this has a directly disturbing effect upon the emotions of the young. As a speculation, it is a little too near the old 'storm and stress' idea of adolescence.

Physical growth has a right to a chapter in a psychological textbook only by its relationship to behaviour, and any account of it must contain many comments of a behavioural kind. This brings us back to something mentioned at the beginning of this chapter, the indivisibility of psychology's subject-matter. An item of behaviour cannot be fully understood out of its context of behaviour in general. In the same way development is a whole process with all its aspects related and the social environment can often explain its course better than the age-and-stage principle. Development itself is part of a life-long adjustment between self and environment, and there are no sharp boundary lines in an individual's history. But there are natural differences between the behavioural adjustments of adults and the developmental adjustments of children. The changes in children are expansive, because they are maturing, because they have much to learn and because in doing these two things they outgrow their special dependency. These three differences may be taken as identifying the three aspects of development, physical, mental, and social. By far the largest stock of information has been accumulated about the first. This is because, being directly observable it can use material and methods from related sciences, whereas special methods have had to be invented for the study of behavioural development and samples are often small.

Early maturational surveys established developmental norms and invented the principle of readiness. Both concepts have been modified. Readiness may be as much the product of education as its basic condition, and although there is a normal maturational sequence, it is not strictly age-tied in individual cases and real-life progress curves are not smooth but show variations.

The individuality of development is in great part the result of the uniqueness of the selection of genes which is transmitted at the moment of conception. Brothers and sisters, who draw from a common stock of available genes, are naturally likely to resemble each other in some particulars, but genetic identity only occurs in monozygotic twins. The individual zygote proceeds to multiply itself according to a standard sequence which gives clues to the nature of development after birth. Of particular significance is the specialization of different body cells, the co-ordinating effect of general development, and growth gradients, by which is meant the relative maturity of different body areas and functions at a given moment.

The percentage of adult size differentiates one body area from another at any age but the percentage of total growth achieved by individuals of the same chronological age has a wide variance. There is a broad sex-linked difference in rate of maturing but individual differences in both boys and girls are equally influential. If this were proved true of mental development it would be educationally very important.

Different kinds of developmental gain distinguish the three main phases of growth, early childhood, the primary school years and adolescence. Although generally growth is a decelerating process, being never again so rapid as in infancy, there is a bigger percentage of total height still to be achieved after five than of adult head size. There are indications that the characteristic achievement of middle childhood is in the mental structures, though lengthening legs bring adult head-body proportions much nearer. Characteristic of the teens is the almost total completion of sex maturity and adult size, though a little remains to be added in the early adult years, at least in some cases. The timing of the pubertal sequence is highly individual and that this is true of the whole maturational history has been the main theme of the chapter.

REFERENCES

(1) Jersild, Arthur, *Child Psychology*, 5th Edn, Staples, 1960.
(2) Tanner, J. M., *Education and Physical Growth*, U.L.P., 1961. Chapter 6.
(3) (a) Mead, Margaret, in *Discussions on Child Development*, Tavistock, 1958.
   (b) Price-Williams, D., *British Journal of Educational Psychology*, Vol. 32, 1962.
(4) Templin, M. C., *Certain Language Skills in Children*, Minneapolis, 1957.
(5) Tanner, J. M., op. cit. Chapter 3.
(6) Newman, H. H., Freeman, F. N. and Holzinger, *Twins, a study of Heredity and Environment*, Chicago, 1937.
(7) Shields, James, *Monozygotic Twins*, London, 1962.
(8) Tanner, J. M., op. cit. Chapter 3.
(9) Tanner, J. M., *The Physique of the Olympic Athlete*, Allen & Unwin, 1960.

(10) Gesell, Arnold and Ilg, Frances, *The Child from Five to Ten*, Hamish
     Hamilton, London, 1946.
(11) Douglas, J. W. B., *The Home and the School*, MacGibbon and Kee, 1964.
(12) Dearborn, W. F. and Rothney, J., *Predicting the Child's Development*,
     Cambridge, Mass., 1941.
(13) Bayley, N., *Individual patterns of development in Child Development*, 1956.
     Vol. 27.
(14) Hall, G. S., *Adolescence—its Psychology*, New York, 1904.
(15) Central Advisory Council for Education, *15-18*, H.M.S.O., 1959.

5

The Maturation of Behaviour

1 Developmental sequence

With behavioural development we are dealing with the functional rather than the structural aspect of maturation, although, as was evident in the last chapter, they cannot always be considered apart. We may assume for every structural gain a functional one to match. On the other hand we cannot chart the behavioural items with confidence in their order and age-placement, and during the long first phase of developmental psychology's existence as a science, it has been necessary to rely heavily for guidance upon the known features of physical growth. It may be that one day behavioural development will be studied in a new context and there are signs that it may be a social one. But the physiological sequence of development is still extremely useful, especially as we become better able to sort out the significant from the trivial, and there can be no doubt that a great deal of significant material is still to come. For instance we do not know nearly enough about how a human brain grows and works although much has been discovered in recent years with very interesting consequences for psychology. Meantime psychologists work in the belief that a future generation of educationists will have the benefit of a complete explanation of behavioural development, although no one would venture to predict what influence will be found to be the dominant one. It may be the physiological or it may be the social factor. When this is decided some educational disputes will come to a natural end, but we do not know how.

We may consider now some of the developmental sequences which psychologists have traced in behaviour, fitting them into the maturational pattern on the one hand and the social environment upon the other. Some of them are well established because they are limited to specific items like the acquisition of motor habits, whose order and age-timing can be checked. But anything more complex, like the growth of logical thinking, cannot be conclusively age-tied. That is, although the *sequence* of the development stages may sometimes be confirmed by different researchers for a performance, as has happened with many of Piaget's findings about children's thought, the locating of them within an age-range is not always agreed upon. When the context is a social rather than a maturational one, the 'normal' progress of development is even harder to establish, for obvious reasons. Emotional maturing is an example, which we must return to later in the chapter.

Nobody doubts that behavioural development must be—like physical development—progressive. There must be *increase*, a wider repertory of actions, and there must be greater *complexity*, more intricate organization. The difficulty is in measuring this progress. We do not really know when behavioural advance is gradual or accelerated.

Some time was spent on this point in Chapter 3 in relation to intellectual development. It applies more forcibly to the kind of behaviour for which we use words like mature, controlled, socialized on the one hand, and childish, irresponsible, and egocentric on the other. Like test scores these judgements contain the idea of progress, but about its nature we are agreed only in a general sort of way. When children's behaviour is ordinary and improving, they are making progress, but readers need not be reminded that any attempt at defining either will run into trouble sooner or later.

Unluckily for psychologists there is no escaping the obligation. Sometimes they must come out boldly on the side of one kind of behaviour and call it better just because it is that bit further removed from the most primitive level of all by the child's own efforts, or the efforts of someone concerned, or both more likely. And we must not always be restricting our idea of *normality* to a catalogue of age-typical goings-on. This might console anxious mothers of the fours and fourteens, but would not do much to help them contrive the next foothold in the dogged upward struggle. But in any case to draw up a behavioural sequence at all, with hardly any comment, would still imply the concept of betterment. Most age fives, for example, and almost all age tens will agree that telling lies is wrong. But we assume that given ordinary social experience age ten's idea of the wrong will be a more stable, more realistic, more comprehensive idea altogether. We assume that socialization, although it is a function of environmental events, and would not come about without some deliberate manipulation, still follows the same course as the genetic process in development.

Of the psychologists who prefer to describe behavioural development in maturational terms because they believe that it is the genetic trend which gives the cultural features their turn towards expansion and improvement, the best known is probably Gesell, whose normative studies were referred to in Chapter 4. Gesell does not hesitate to apply the concept of genetic sequence even to language development, and the great variance caused by the learning factor does not in his opinion cancel the maturational order of acquisition. We shall find much the same idea contained in Piaget's stereotypes of the developmental stages in children's thinking. Gesell states his results so that allowance for individual differences does not blur the normal age-sequence in any given sort of behaviour, which he calls a growth gradient in a very different sense from the use we have already come across for this term (see page 108). In keeping with his purpose in general, Gesell's growth gradients are not mathematical but descriptive. He uses quantitative methods to establish majority performances. Then he draws up against the list of ages a list of typical behaviours and performances. You will find a few examples of these gradients in the early pages of *Five to Ten* (1) and while they are only illustrative and therefore simplified, they are quite a fair statement of his approach to development.

The behavioural stages may cover a brief age-range with typical behaviour items at intervals of months, in which case it probably belongs to the very early years and is a very simple activity like prehension. Thus 24 weeks 'Looks and crudely grasps with one hand' while 36 weeks 'Looks and deftly grasps with fingers'. Or the trend of behaviour may be boldly sketched over the whole period of childhood and youth. Then it will be behaviour of a global type, a complex from which selected items represent the kind of thing to be expected at each yearly interval. The shape of the development of the acquisitive tendency is defined by Six's collection of odds and ends, Ten's organized collecting hobbies, and the deliberate saving up of the teens for planned purchasing. With such varied items measured assessments do not enter. We cannot *score* the progress and graph it mathematically. But breaking down behaviour into measurable units was not really Gesell's main object. His interest was in the forward surge of the whole individual towards maturity. For him an age-stage was not only the point reached so far by this, that, and the other sort of behaviour, but a level on which the young creature's whole personality and life-style is to be surveyed—activities, abilities, socialization, and all their inter-relationships.

Now this is a necessary service to developmental psychology and Gesell has brought together many different forms of behaviour; some of them may seem to have little psychological importance but for Gesell nothing in a child's equipment, from the number of his teeth and his food-preferences to his use of words and his willingness to bargain, is too trivial to add to the all-over picture. It is easy to criticize the age-comparison technique as unscientific when the successive stages are described informally and with a hotch-potch of items; the reader may remember that the Binet-type intelligence tests were similarly criticized. But it allows exploration of any and every sort of behaviour and reduces the risk of missing out a significant factor. Few psychologists have attempted anything so comprehensive as Gesell's succession of age-portraits. They are not all equally successful in distinguishing one year from another especially in later childhood and the upper half of adolescence, but it has to be admitted that he often hits the exact tone of an age-level, the peculiar behavioural quality. Five is famous but Gesell has drawn attention also to the transitional phase between five and middle childhood, the tensions caused by the backward pull to home and babyhood and the forward pull to the outside world and the wider circle of school friendships, which has been a neglected area apart from Gesell's work. Children of six and seven are often lumped along with the early or middle years according to the behaviour under observation.

Gesell of course explains why this is a transitional period by his usual reference to the growth cycle theory. There is no need here for a formal account of all the alternatives between stable and transitional or 'bi-polar' ages—between withdrawn and exuberant phases. The rotation of behaviours as Gesell sees it takes a little longer at each repetition but the pattern holds. A new growth period begins ($2\frac{1}{2}$, 6, and 11), gives rise to anxieties and the need for reassurance (3, 7, and 13), then to boisterousness (4, 8, and 14), and finally to equilibrium and the coming to terms with life on the new level. A full appraisal of the Gesell cycles can be found in John Gabriel's *Children Growing Up* (2) though parents and teachers can often appreciate for themselves the stable periods which make age five helpful and realistic, the nines and tens well adjusted and confident, and the fifteens and sixteens pleasant mannered and reasonable upon the whole.

Common observation cannot quarrel with many of Gesell's generalizations and much is due to his contribution in the modern view of the essential normality of developmental phases, with the wiser handling of children which follows. But we may wish to modify the maturational emphasis of his explanations and look for more detailed evidence of the growth and learning processes respectively. His diagrams, for example, are not graphs but symbols—

pictures of his idea of the growth trend. Besides believing it to be
genetically controlled he even leans a little towards the old idea of
recapitulation—that the stages of behavioural development repeat the
stages the human race went through in its ancient evolutionary past.
Hence the developmental cycles! But theory apart, psychologists
nowadays do not believe the maturational trend strong enough to
absorb cultural differences, nor that it is valid to generalize from an
age-sample in one community to children of the same age in other
social environments. Gesell's own samples were rather selective.
The children studied longitudinally, in many cases right up to the end
of the *Ten to Sixteen* survey (3) were in themselves a superior group
and products of the middle-class type of family and standards of child-
rearing. The socio-economic factor was uniform, which excluded an
important source of variability, and of course limited the significance
of the behavioural sequences. To take the humble example of toilet-
training, no doubt there is a maturationally 'best' time to begin it with
least emotional upset to everybody concerned and the smoothest
progress, but there are differences between home standards of cleanli-
ness and a minority of homes where there is no toilet training at
all.

This is not to say that developmental psychology has completely
shifted its ground; the idea of genetic stages is still useful in education
and so is the idea of a 'best' time to start a training campaign. There
are behavioural sequences which have been confirmed by research,
usually in respect of some specific mental task where age-related levels
of performance have been found. One example is the series of
performance-type tests called by their author *Progressive Matrices* (4).
These are designs each with a missing section to be selected by logical
inference from among possible alternatives. At the time the test was
being tried out for standardization (see Chapter 3) there was found
to be a phase of slow improvement up to age 8, followed by much
more rapid improvement between 8 and $13\frac{1}{2}$, at which point something
like adult competence appeared to have been reached. This kind of
thinking, with tangibles rather than words, is often referred to as
concrete logic, which may well have its peak maturation period in
late childhood. It is a clue to the nature of mental growth gradients
(in the first sense mentioned above) which may control the order in
which different brain functions come to their maturity.

Some of the most famous evidence on the subject comes from
Piaget's observations, which enjoy the distinction of having provoked
endless discussion and strenuous research twice in the present century.

P.E Y.—5*

A formal summary of Piaget's developmental views will come later. Meantime it may be said that the existence of a clear sequence of stages in one important aspect of behavioural growth appears to be established and that they are age-tied, though not rigidly. As in all developmental sequences the timing is individual and we are entitled to believe that a stage has no sharp beginnings but makes a few anticipatory appearances and comes into full function as a build-up of experiences. This, of course, is the educational importance of the research.

Turning now to developmental sequences which have a social rather than maturational emphasis we find that some of their psychological value rests upon the maturational principle of the 'best' time or critical period. Robert Havighurst's concept of *developmental tasks* performs the useful service of combining the maturational factors and social factors into a single developmental function. The series of cultural demands which a society makes upon a growing child are seen to coincide more or less with the phases of his behavioural growth when he is ready to fulfil them. This will not be without some effort, but it will be a more congenial one at the 'best' time than earlier, or later. Havighurst calls it the 'teachable moment' (5), and striking it exactly right for individual children requires skill. Thus, among the tasks set to middle school children are the gradual acquisition of adult thinking abilities and the basic educational skills, the social learning involved in adapting to one's prescribed role as girl or boy, the acceptance of sound ideas of right and wrong. To meet these cultural expectations more easily, children's personalities are already turning outwards to the world and away from home, towards greater bodily and mental adventurousness. The crucial consideration for Havighurst is that if developmental tasks are surmounted at the right time, future adaptation will be easier; if not—that is, if a child's environment denies him the appropriate cues to action—there will be difficulty with later tasks and the unhappiness of social disapproval.

The developmental task sequence, like Gesell's maturational one, is a device for presenting the growth of behaviour on all its fronts, with emphasis on their interdependence. Healthy growth of the whole individual in society is a principle which can stand on its own, when allowances have been made for differences between the American culture and others. But on the other hand *regional* surveys do establish real differences in personality growth patterns and can sometimes pinpoint the critical social factors responsible. This means detailed comparison and hence the behavioural sequence studied by this comparative method is usually in a singled-out aspect. Recently a favourite subject, for obvious and urgent reasons, has been the origins of the conscience, that important cluster of attitudes to self and society.

The development of conscience is an old psychological topic, but we have come a long way from any belief in a fixed maturational sequence of stages.

Havighurst was associated with Robert Peck in an intensive study of moral development in a smallish sample of young people (5a). Through case-studies and psychological tests they distinguished five levels of maturity[1] but the developmental sequence was not standard, and a key factor in any individual one was family environment.

Freud of course believed, and some of his followers still believe, that in every child's history there is the same pattern of events by which his blind, primitive wish for gratification comes under the control of other forces in his personality. But a child will not outgrow the *pleasure principle*, as Freud calls it, and come to terms with reality, without social pressure being exerted upon him. Thus Freud's view can be understood in a context of present-day social psychology, though with a little modification. We do not believe that the social pressures upon a young child must always seem harsh and punitive to him, as Freud was inclined to believe they did. A normal child will certainly fuss when he discovers that he does not always get his own way automatically, but it will be nothing like the sense of outrage he would feel later in life if he were allowed to get much older without being taught this.

The reader will see that Freud's account of how the *reality principle* must modify the *pleasure principle* is very like a developmental task with a 'best' time for it to be got over, and that there are both maturational and social factors at work when a child does achieve this. But this is a simplified summary. Many changes combine to improve a child's command over his own impulses, his willingness to wait his turn for attention, surmount frustration, and carry out his commitments. Till he has some idea of *time* he cannot do any of these things, and the concept of time is a product of intelligence and learning. A child's 'conscience' is a construct of his experience and in any community we find a great many patterns of development, as children work through to some kind of conformity with the standards of their social group. In districts where the standards of home and school reinforce each other children will have an earlier and clearer idea of what is expected of them than when home and school conflict. This

[1] Amoral, expedient, conforming, irrational-conscientious, and rational-altruistic.

comparison is a main theme in the survey by Dr Spinley of young people from two human backgrounds which could not be further asunder, London slum families on the one hand and on the other families with a tradition of sending children as a matter of course to the great public schools (6).

Ethical concepts show the interaction of different aspects of personality development, and also how the social factors influence the sequence of that development and sometimes decide it. It is important, therefore, to consider the social needs of children at successive periods of their lives.

2 Socialization

We have seen that when the first great developmental surge begins to subside children in the later primary school years can settle down to enjoy their gains in a variety of ways, Their individuality has been compared to that of young adults who are in the same happy position. The second great surge of growth is in the early teens when the common developmental changes cause thirteen- and fourteen-year-olds to resemble each other as two-year-olds going through the 'No!' stage resemble each other. But when the great changes are nearly over and have been absorbed into a new way of life adolescents can begin to create their own individuality in its adult form.

Psychologists have often written about the importance of the self-concept, the sense of personal identity, although they have used different names for it. Macdougall long ago called it a 'master' construct, meaning that it can and should subordinate minor impulses (7). Maslow likewise talks of the need for self-actualization as a stage which it is desirable to reach, because it means that simpler, more primitive needs have been dealt with and are now being satisfied in ways that let the personality grow on and beyond them. E. A. Erikson's version of the developmental significance of later adolescence is a very attractive one (8). He sees as its chief object this very one of establishing an identity of one's own. To be sure only a small minority of adolescents have the kind of mentality to think about themselves this way. But then at no time during the growing period is it necessary for children themselves to understand their developmental needs, whereas it is important that parents and teachers understand them. We must remember too, that for some adolescents the task is much easier than for others. A happy few find the educational role congenial and have no real trouble in turning into the kind of adult their social group expects. Most young people make their decisions about themselves by trial and error, sometimes clumsy, sometimes deft, depending on the help they get and on how they have managed in the past. Then there is the other minority who cannot even begin, because their personality growth was stunted when some essential condition was missing from their environment. It might have been parental firmness when it was needed to help them control their impulses or a suitable adult figure with whom to identify themselves in later childhood. Deprivation of this kind distorts the ability to adjust and in some extreme cases personality growth gets halted at the level when this took place. Such children are unconsciously searching for satisfactions which they ought to have outgrown.

For the coming to terms with an adult self in the later teens is the last chapter in a long story. It begins with the sort of episode which gives mother and child equal pleasure. She points out his reflection in the mirror and tells him 'That's you! There's Baby', and he shrieks approval or hides his face against her shoulder. Or she agrees with him: 'Yes, that's your book; you take it.' Self, for a child just beginning to speak, is built up in part by laying claim to cherished possessions and having other people support these claims. It is one of the important functions of talk and communication between the first and second birthdays. A little later it gives way to less endearing kinds of self-assertion like the 'No!' phase or the 'Me, me, me!' phase. Later still the self grows by assimilating other things than cared-for objects; personal significance comes from having one's rightful share of mother's attention, one's own peg in the nursery school cloakroom. Reassurance can come from ganging up with the rest of the play-group (play-groups of very young children are often accidental and temporary) to keep out a newcomer; which is the sort of situation where tactful stage-management is better than a scolding. There are infinite variations on these and similar episodes, but they have one thing in common. The self is realized to exist because other people do; the world of things plays its part, and a useful one it is, in giving children a sense of competence; but without a social commentary the world of things would remain inert. Human contacts, praise and encouragement, restraint by other people's wishes, bargaining, competition, and co-operative play: these are the true mediating processes which bring the idea of selfhood into existence.

It is interesting to watch them at work in any age-group, and accounts are to be found in most textbooks on behavioural development. Examples are the chapter headed 'I, Me, My, Mine' in *Children Growing up* (2) and the illustrations supplied by M. M. Lewis of how language and communication affect personal and social development in the early years (9) a topic we must return to when considering language more specifically. Meantime we must be content with these few hints about the variety of inter-personal relationships which give growing children the chance to imitate and identify with others, reject and criticize sometimes, according to age and past experience. Altogether the attitude to self faithfully reflects in the end one's experience of other people and their attitudes to onself. Jersild (10) believes that a child loved and accepted for what he is will be charitable to others; one whose confidence is damaged by rejection or by feeling rejected (not the same thing necessarily) will likewise have no confidence in anyone else.

During the last twenty years of psychology a good deal of attention has been paid to this topic and to what children need at various stages of personal-social growth. Now, a developmental need is an idea which can be misunderstood. The fact that a child happens to want something does not mean that it is a developmental right and that we are depriving him (in the developmental sense) by keeping it from him. Sometimes the developmental need is just that this particular thing *should* be kept from him so that he learns a lesson in how to postpone a pleasure or put up with frustration; the deprivation would be not to give him the chance to learn it when he is at an age to do so. On the other hand, postponement is not something that little children can easily understand; and sharing either attention or a toy is a difficult concept for them. Sometimes it is better not to let them catch a glimpse of the object they cannot have if the discipline of doing without is not a present need.

Similarly we expect a nine-year-old to have outgrown the sort of dependency which causes age seven still to want reassurance from a trusted adult when carrying out some new difficult action. Dependency should be recognized when it is the way to encourage expansion and adventure. Sometimes a little neglect of the blind eye variety is the way to let a nine-year-old squabble work itself out to a salutary end. Freedom, a good thing at any time of life undoubtedly, has different spheres of operation according to the stage. Freedom to kick and squirm is relished by a baby, but not as a general rule freedom from the security of routine. Freedom from adult poking and prying is jealously guarded at the secret society stage of middle childhood but complete freedom in the learning activities should be giving way to more

controlled educational disciplines. There is sometimes a difference
between the adolescent notion of freedom and the sort an adolescent
really needs, which is the freedom of privacy and the exercise of
preferences by which he achieves adult independence and willingness
to concede a few rights to others.

A true developmental need is for some *experience* which is essential
for further growth. We may therefore, in using the term, be referring
to a child's state of mental and emotional readiness for the experience.
Or we may be referring to the changes which should be made accordingly in his environment, new tasks that ought to be set, more suitable
kinds of treatment. We look on a developmental need in either sense,
therefore, as something bound to be outgrown because through its
very satisfaction a child is enabled to pass on to the next stage of
personality growth.

A dearly loved child who has had his baby privileges of special
attention and then been gently introduced to the beginnings of
consideration for other family members, will bring the same attitude
of happy expectancy to wider human contacts and will eventually
adjust well to school, if the teacher lets him take his time. An adult
who has had a good youth will adjust more cheerfully to later responsibilities. It is the cheated who will not accept society's expectations
of them.

How a child copes with any of his tasks will depend to some extent
on how his developmental needs have been met so far; but the most
significant index of all is his success in personal-social adaptation. We
may make use of this relationship to help us identify the real developmental needs, though in a negative sort of way, by looking back
from a youngster's present state of maladjustment to trace what was
missing from his environment at a critical stage. This method can be
justified only if we can establish a significant difference between normal
and difficult children in respect of this particular deprivation. Supposing
it is found that in a group of children who are socially retarded, poor
in communication and suspicious for their age, quite a large percentage
were separated from their mothers during later babyhood, and that
in a control group of normal children such separations were rare,
then we may assume that mother-company is a need about the time
a baby begins to distinguish his mother as a person, if trust and co-
operativeness are to be established as personality traits. (Assuming,
that is, that trust and co-operativeness are socially desirable!) Again,
out of a group of ten problem boys, six are either fatherless or have
fathers who have taken no active share in their upbringing. Evidence

from this small sample suggests that the contribution of the male parent to the family group is important if boys are to acquire mature social attitudes. In our society, at any rate!

Now not all babies whose mothers must be away from them become secretive children; not all fatherless boys show symptoms of deprivation in their personality pattern. This is because there are so many elements in a human situation. Children differ in their ability to tolerate a lack, and most developmental studies of this kind must be content with tentative conclusions. Sometimes it is possible to submit findings to the simple test of percentages. A significant need is one that is seen to affect a true *majority* of cases.

Thus John Bowlby, whose name is associated with research of this kind, established a connection between separation from the mother in the early years and inability to form mature affections later, especially when there is no prolonged fostering of the baby by any one person. Bowlby summarized the results of many surveys of maternal deprivation in a monograph for the World Health Organization in 1951 all tending to the same conclusion. Damage to the personality can be life-long. On the other hand Bowlby modified some of his own early beliefs. Although there is a need in infancy and early childhood for a lasting emotional attachment to one person it is not so critically age-tied that its effects cannot be reversed by later experience of affection, provided it does not come too late. There is a sequel to the Bowlby monograph (11) published by the World Health Organization with articles by various experts, some showing that progressive retardation caused by severe deprivation can be arrested to some extent. One very important matter is that the damage to language development and therefore of the mental growth connected with language is just as marked in deprived children as damage to their capacity for affection.

Similar well-known studies were made by Spitz and Goldfarb in America. Spitz studied the effects of being in hospital upon babies and later identified a characteristic state of listlessness and depression as the result of the loss of attention, cuddling and general mothering. Goldfarb is especially associated with a survey of typical personality differences between adolescents brought up in families (including foster families) and adolescents who had been reared in institutions under the old-fashioned conditions of impersonality. These affected not just interpersonal relations but mental adventurousness and competence, and purposeful, interested planning, in all of which he found institution children deficient.

Clearly at the beginning of life children thrive and learn through being in a state of emotional dependency upon their mothers or mother-substitutes. It is a developmental need for them. This state of emotional dependency is what we call a mediating process—that is a process which causes other processes to happen, in this case the growth of the baby's physical and mental powers and of the emotions which will bring his personality into existence. He needs continuous contact with one person before he can profit from experience. In fact without it he is hardly able to have experience at all. As we shall see, contact with other people continues to be the chief mediating process by which the self gathers shape and strength, and as the circle widens the exclusive need for one person will begin to taper off. But not for several years after birth.

Most of the ideas described in the last few paragraphs may be called psychoanalytic (although it is not a very good word) because they derive from the views of Freud, and one of the earliest workers on the effects of emotional deprivation was Anna Freud, his daughter. Some psychologists believe that the sort of developmental needs young children have are part of their maturation, that a baby arrives in the world with an instinct for dependency and that his mother has an intuitive ability to sense his needs. Other psychologists, of course, consider that dependency is *taught* to children, that they learn it as the shortest route to satisfaction and would not necessarily behave in a dependent way if their mothers did not reward that very dependency by their behaviour, such as running to the child when he cries. Now, it is not difficult to see the mechanism by which dependency behaviour *could* be learned, but it is not a proven fact any more than instinctive needs are a proven fact. All that need concern us is that a close mother-child relationship is the medium in which development progresses. A child may have an unlearned capacity to feel guilt, but it is his mother who teaches him when to feel guilty and even, in a sense, how to do it. Human children learn, of course, by direct experience but a large part of experience is interpreted by communication, which means more than simply language. Thus, deaf children are cut off not only from speech sounds but other reassurances of human presence when it is not directly visible. M. M. Lewis points out that they often develop some typical deprivation symptoms (9).

Of course sensory experience is highly important too and it will be considered along with cognitive, or mental, behaviour. Turning now to the immediately pre-school years we find that Gesell has dealt with many of the maturational personality changes. Recognition of oneself as a person is practically completed in the year between two

and three when there is characteristically headstrong behaviour and
other children are either ignored or saluted aggressively! A strong,
assertive child will snatch toys or knock another child over. A
timorous one will get behind an armchair and wait for the invader to
go away. This is the age for things, not just people; things to be
pulled, squashed, lifted and thrown, rattled and banged, climbed over
and driven. Objects are often treated as symbols and an old umbrella
that opens with a squeak can cause as much ecstasy as a formal toy,
especially if there is an adult to laugh with. But plenty of material is
one of the first requirements of the nursery, and later in the nursery
school.

Three years old, beginning to be aware of the group as such, is
content to tag along and watch, may take a tender interest in babies,
in imitation of an adult, but is not so safe from jealous feelings as the
truly protective five. But co-operative group play is not to be expected
for another year or so, as observers in nursery schools noted many
years ago, and it will of course be liable to interruption by squabbles
and blows. Four is confident and demanding and can seem ruthless
about anyone else's feelings. Adults are much needed to help a group
of four-year-olds learn the difficult task of taking turns, although
they are mature enough to do this. Tattling, tale-bearing and accusa-
tions are to be expected and vigorous competition for the grown-up
role in dressing-up games. Altogether a pre-school child is not ready
to learn from his peers without supervision. What he does achieve is
extension from trust in mother and father to trust in other adults,
which parents should encourage.

The social life of infant school children, the five to sevens, is
transitional in character. The relationship most valued is with the
teacher to whom they can be endearingly affectionate, but they are
not really aware of the individual personalities of other children, in
the way that creates choices of special friends, until near the end of
this period. Although the pair is probably the favourite play-group
it is usually formed by some accident like living in the same neighbourhood or sharing the same activity. Likewise, in the family they are
just beginning to learn the principle of *reciprocity*, that what they do
and say to others is just as important as what the others do and say to
them. Self in fact will gradually cease to contain only the idea of *me*
and will absorb other roles, like being the oldest one and a help to
mother when she is busy, or the third man in fellow-my-leader with
obligations to neighbours fore and aft. It is a time when coevals play
an important part by just being *there* with rights and demands of their

own and (sometimes) with offers of help or a share of sweet things. But group loyalty as the nines and tens—let alone the early teens—understand it is far away. One cannot easily imagine a few seven-year-olds 'covering' up for a defaulter! They still depend, though without positively knowing it, upon the adult to teach them the behaviour expected in group membership. They still find it easier to be kind to a littler one than fair to each other. Hence 'the eldest' may have quite a congenial role to learn in the transitional phase, and gets through it cheerfully, so long as not too much patience is expected towards the younger ones.

To summarize then: relationship with the mother is the medium through which experience of things and people is interpreted for a very young child and from this comes the first idea of self with rights of one's own and a few small obligations. In outgrowing this stage satisfactorily a child is able to have relationships with other adults to help him with a wider world which includes a few coevals, and so group membership is slowly learned. In the home the idea of self gradually comes to include the appropriate family role. Coevals, or peers, acquire individual significance during the same transitional phase. At the end of it children are ready to form group-relationships among themselves without adult help, which having outgrown its usefulness in this particular area, now moves elsewhere. The world has widened again to make room for different kinds of human contact.

It is a new beginning. We have already seen middle childhood as marked off by more than one psychological criterion. There is the change from the early growth pattern; there is the delay in the appearance of full sexual maturity which Freud calls the period of latency, the chance to perfect many abilities before the onset of disturbing emotions. And there is this important moment in the socialization process. It is when the children's relationship with adults, however loving and friendly, is recognized by them as a different kind of thing altogether from relations with other children in the age-group. Furthermore, it becomes increasingly important for them to keep the two kinds separate, with only the established treaty points. Adults lease out free time and space for activities; they donate means and material; in return adult regulations are honoured. It is a bargain well kept on the whole, for this is the age of fair play, but a necessary condition is that distance shall be kept as well.

Luckily for everyone concerned, adults are only too glad to comply. Although the early need for reassurance is sweet and disarming, and mothers, and teachers too, may be sorry to see it go, artless confidences can be time-consuming. When eight years old requests leave to take the last of his supper in his hand and shoots out of the back door with a wild war whoop (leaving it wide open behind him needless to say) it is something to know that blessed silence will reign until his reappearance at bedtime. For such reliefs adults are glad to approve the cult of the peer group and to have the support of the psychological manual's decision: 'Let them fight it out among themselves. It's better for them.'

The greatest socializing factor in middle childhood is the group which assembles, more or less regularly, for co-operative play, now in full swing in all its forms and ceremonies. Teams are chosen, disputes settled, personal distinctions recognized by rule and ritual. Deficiencies are allowed for (children are good about the handicapped ones, as most teachers discover) and special friendships are recognized; conversely, there are probation periods for newcomers and sometimes ruthless expulsions. But it is all in the service of the one overmastering goal; the play's the thing. If a key member is removed by adult caprice replacement is made from the ranks without unnecessary lamentation. Of course there are the ringleaders and the favourites, the inspirers of schemes, the dominant ones. But they can be done without, unlike the gang leaders of later years. The game has gathered enough momentum to go on. Rules and traditions are fixed and the whole complex of activities is cemented by the special language.

This remarkable sub-culture (as it has been called) of the human society has been studied often. There is something in it attractive to adults, caused partly by their own recollections, and partly by the interest of the lore transmitted by children to each other and the enviable success of the play arrangements. Iona and Peter Opie have done a well-known survey of the rhymes, jokes, and regional superstitions in their *Lore and Language of Schoolchildren* (12). There are many studies of children's hobbies and reading habits, preferences in television programmes and so on; which of course affect the dramatic content of imaginative play and also the developmental task of preparation for adult roles in modern society. Children of this age are more simply and straightforwardly envious of adult power and freedom, but by the same token less resentful of it than they will be in adolescence. Bouts of rebellion of course occur, but seriously to compete with adults is not their ambition. It is enough to be distinguished from the grown-ups and have their own areas.

This is the psychological function of the special group-language which these children use among each other and is different from the

THE MATURATION OF BEHAVIOUR

formal language they can switch to as required by school or parents. Talk with equals is relaxing at all times of life but for human beings just beginning to be independent personalities the reassurance of solidarity within their own group is essential. This is the function of the special language, as Lewis points out more than once in his *Language, Thought and Personality* (9). The vocabulary is different, laced with slang, 'gang' names and of course, 'forbidden' terms and references inspired by the lively inquisitiveness about all the goings-on of the adult world which adults do better to accept as matter of factly as possible. Children make guesses about sexual matters and grin at sexual jokes just as they do at bathroom jokes, and there is a minimum of sexuality in all this.

In exchange for group solidarity, children abide by the rules of fair play, which Piaget calls the principle of mutuality. It is an important factor in the maturing of conscience and social behaviour although the children themselves would hardly recognize it in this way. Being 'good' they equate, upon the whole, with accepting adult authority, although wise adults know that this alone would leave great gaps in a child's comprehension of right and wrong ways of acting towards others—and himself. The solitary child with no brothers or sisters and few playmates may be in some danger of deprivation in the developmental sense, having neither the solidarity of the peer group to give him confidence in an adult world nor the chance to learn from equals how to be socially acceptable. Harlow, in his well-known experiments with infant and young monkeys, has lately extended the idea of need-deprivation from the relationship with mother to the relationship with equals. He has found evidence that loss of contact with its brothers and sisters in babyhood helps to create social ineptness in an adult monkey, in one important respect at least, the ability to make normal overtures to one of the opposite sex. It is an interesting parallel to our observation of human children.

We should note, however, that many of the features in the juvenile sub-culture are provided and suggested by adults, by whom for example children's books are written, though the most successful often incorporate the formula of an adventurous gang with a bit of territory to explore. Significantly, it is by solitary children that they are most avidly read. Another point to be kept in mind is that the environments and personalities of middle school children vary so much that generalizing about their social relationships is useful only with modifications.

The same is true about the other aspect of their personality development which has to do with the learning of adult roles. Much of this is taken care of in the school classroom, obviously as far as the acquiring of skills and information is concerned, indirectly in the increasing segregation of boys and girls which furthers the process known as sex-typing. The expectation of womanly ways in a growing girl and manlier activities in a boy is imposed gradually and by many subtle psychological experiences, like the process of identification with the appropriate parent. It is extremely hard to disentangle the native from the cultural elements, but that the pressure is not against the grain of the children's own inclinations is fairly evident. At this stage they flatly prefer the company of their own sex; teachers, for their part, make no bones about expecting characteristically different school behaviour from boys and girls. In the Douglas survey mentioned in the last chapter (page 114) the suggestion is made that this may be because most primary school teachers are women to whose standards and preferences girls will naturally conform. The higher degree of troublesomeness in boys may mark a necessary stage in their growing away from dependence on the mother figure. Conversely, the adoration of a young woman teacher found in some prepubertal and adolescent girls is a stage in their own acquisition of her admired qualities, and will end when the femininity of their own characters is securely established.

3 The social role of adolescents

Some hostility to adults is bound to occur as a by-product of the alliance with peers. Children emerge from this middle period with greatly strengthened personalities and enough confidence to be pert and aggressive at times when they do not see eye to eye with their parents. Many of the much dreaded signs of teenage trouble make an early appearance in the pre-pubertal years between ten and thirteen. Boys become restless, noisy, and aggressively masculine in their play, which is another sign of their rejection of feminine values. Organized athletics do not fully succeed in channelling this excess of vigour, and the gang members may easily dare each other beyond co-operative mischief and into outright law breaking. Relations with a rival gang may develop from jeers and scraps into something uglier. Consequently adults find it impossible to turn upon the early teens the same benevolent eye as parents and to some extent teachers also, do in the case of primary school activities. The girls perhaps, whose cliques are smaller and made up of pairs and trios of best friends loosely united for a giggling or whispering session, may cause less uneasiness than irritation when they have bouts of being aimless or perverse. But there are many adolescent habits making their appearance about this time which are guaranteed to exasperate adults sooner or later, not least the moody hanging about with nothing apparently interesting enough to be done, although a suggestion about help with a domestic job will not be well received. Then there is the secrecy, the slovenliness, and the biting criticisms, none of them easy to shrug off. Adult resentment, though often perfectly justified, goes a little deeper than disapproval. There is a new element of antagonism between adults and pubescent or adolescent children and it can be triggered off even by a trivial occasion.

With younger children an adult feels his superiority to be secure and can make allowance. Children at the primary school stage can be fractious or rebellious but they give in, on the whole, pretty readily. Once the naivety of the early years is over, they do not seriously think of hurling their whole personalities into a struggle with an adult. But in the teens it begins to be different. Adults feel challenged on something uncomfortably close to equal terms and have to suppress twinges of real anger, along with shame that the young antagonist should be able to arouse them. Adults can hardly be expected to enjoy the consciousness of having to justify themselves to their children, or their pupils, even when their orders seem reasonable. And kindness and understanding, far from being acknowledged, seem sometimes to be positively resented.

Meantime the youngster feels uneasy too. Like the adult he no longer knows what role he is expected to play. He has outgrown a child's privilege of being readily forgiven but without the compensation of independence. In any case he is far from certain how much independence he wants and is dismayed when he has got himself into a state of opposition from which he does not know how to retreat without losing face.

So the problem is one of adjustment to changing roles which are not clear to either adults or children, because the experience of adolescence is a different one in every generation. The pattern of childhood has changed remarkably little and the provisions made for children by adults have remained fairly stable. But there is, in particular, no precedent whatever for the present explosion of the teenage culture and adult uneasiness can be readily understood. A generation ago the problem of adolescence was the adolescent's desire for adult privileges which was frustrated by lack of means and prolonged dependence. This is no longer the case, except for the young people in the middle-class tradition with their sights upon higher education and a profession. And with them there has never been an acute problem. The provision made for their adolescence has suited them and they have conformed pretty easily to social expectations.

It has always been recognized that education prolongs the period of dependency and that adolescence, even in the widest sense which includes the whole stretch of the teens, is not a true developmental stage but one culturally imposed because civilization is complex and preparation for adult life takes time. In simpler communities the adolescent problem does not exist. It is a social phenomenon.

This has been the established view of adolescence in the eyes of many psychologists since the late nineteen twenties when the field work of social anthropologists like Margaret Mead first made its impact. In the Samoan culture rebelliousness by growing-up children does not arise because positive submission to adults in our sense is not required of them. On the other hand among the Kaffirs pre-adolescent children form a sort of outlaw gang of their own with a secret language because their adults treat them with tyranny and unfairness (13). The conclusions drawn from these and other re-searches were that the adolescent age-group is an educational and cultural construct and characteristic 'adolescent' behaviour is a response to cultural demands. Problems arise because the demands are confusing and the adolescent is not sure whether he is expected to behave as a child or a responsible individual. Different groups can make conflicting demands, for instance adult society on the one hand and the teenage society on the other.

However, to explain adolescent problems on social grounds is not to explain them away! As Professor Mays remarks in his study of teenagers in modern society which he calls *The Young Pretenders* (14), the adolescent we have to deal with is not a young Samoan. For Mays, therefore, and writers like him, the most helpful psychological concept is Havighurst's developmental tasks. Exactly what these are to be for any adolescent will depend on variations in the social setting, so that there can be no one adjacent pattern for children to go through once they begin their teens. In our complex society there are important differences in the behaviour expected of children by parents in different social groups. A middle-class child, for example, will not have a great deal of difficulty in understanding his educational role since home and school will be in accord and the programme usually works out smoothly by way of grammar or public school to higher education and a responsible job. On the other hand, family relationships may be more demanding and the source of more guilt and heart burning than the more clear-cut and hard-headed demands of working-class parents.

The socio-economic factor is one source of variation in the early years of secondary school. There is also, as we have seen, a sex difference and this too is partly a function of cultural expectations and the previous sex-typing of behaviour. Girls tend of course to be better poised socially and more responsive to approval and disapproval on account of their somewhat earlier maturity. By the same token they are ready to take an interest in the other sex before the boys are at all interested in them and for a year or two girls tend to take the lead in overtures towards boy-girl relationships. Finally it is important to remember here, as always, the range of individual variations. Thirteen-year-olds, and for that matter fourteens and fifteens, have many characteristics in common and adults may be forgiven for imagining them to be the less agreeable ones. But the younger teens do not always unite for mischief or for silliness. The age marks the beginning of true affection for same-sex friends; overtures made to the other sex can be healthy and innocent; many young people are capable of friendliness to teachers and can carry out some charitable undertaking with responsibility.

By placing the adolescent process in a social framework the difficulty of establishing its maturational phases can be avoided and we can think of the first *developmental* one as being concurrent with the school years and having therefore different adjustment tasks from those of the years between school-leaving and twenty. This second phase means coming to terms with the outer world as a young adult and (usually) the first experience of financial independence. These two new conditions considerably affect the growth of the self as it was described in the opening paragraphs of the present topic. The form taken by this phase of the socialization process is one which all adults today are bound to be aware of and many view with concern. Some of the features of this cult of the older teens are a matter for the sociologist rather than the educator and therefore fall outside the scope of this book, which has for its primary subject those aspects of psychology which have to do with schooling and the human relationships within a school. As for the smaller percentage of adolescents who go on with formal education into the late teens and early twenties, the social pressures to which they must adapt their growing selves create a different set of tasks, as we have seen. Their attitudes to adult expectations are different because they themselves have chosen to postpone the time of full adult stature. Some sociologists indeed are inclined to believe that for young people reared in this tradition, the danger to their own maturation is of *too* successful an adjustment and not enough resistance or reappraisal. Thelma Veness, for example, in her well-documented study of the aspirations of school leavers (15) finds a strong tendency to social conformity in the kind of adult image these young people have created for themselves, and to a wish for ordinary security rather than adventure.

We must turn for a moment to the strange new world of the teenage sub-culture which was highlighted some years ago by Colin MacInnes in his novel *Absolute Beginners*—a title which sums up a great many new beginnings. For one thing the teenage world is an international one and its attitudes and obsessions are not so much reactionary as unrelated to adult standards in the different communities. Being a teenager is an end in itself and adult status is less envied or rebelled against than ignored. Yet within the group itself conformity is very high with crazes and ideal images which has been called a kind of mythology. The 'typical' adolescent experience does not exist as described by sensational newspaper articles and other 'mass media'; and individual adolescents may feel compelled to live up to it and to experiment with things they do not really want to do, nor enjoy very much at the time. In an investigation of the sex behaviour of young people by the Central Council of Health Education (16) this damage to the individual growth pattern by the pressure to conform was found to be a real factor.

Like the world of middle childhood and the world of school, the teenage world is furnished by adults. But with the difference that the object is not the developmental welfare of the young, nor even an educational one. Educators cannot ignore it, either, because the conditions outside the school have an impact on the younger adolescents and especially upon those who will leave school at the minimum legal age. This in effect means the population of the secondary modern schools and the non-academic streams of the comprehensives. These pupils can hardly be blamed for looking to the apparent glamour and the independence of the immediate post-school environment and for shrugging off the most sympathetic adult efforts to rouse their interest in long-term satisfactions. These adolescents have made a society to suit their present selves, and have been provided for accordingly.

This is unfortunate, particularly in view of the fact that there is plenty of adult sympathy nowadays for adolescent social impulses. It is not thought to be surprising that they want to assemble in age-groups of their own choosing and that these groups will be heterosexual. Sexually mature adolescents will seek each other's company with very little delay. First dates, and first kissings and fondlings will take place on an average about age thirteen or fourteen. Few adolescents have no experience of the kind by the time they are fifteen and adults must accept the fact that two young people who want to be alone together will manage it somehow. Severe supervision will be a temporary expedient at best and it may have a bad effect on long-term personality growth. But there is no need to take the pessimistic view of liberty. The sex impulse is innate and has a powerful motivating force, but like any other human instinct it is modifiable by social learning. It has gathered about it many related activities, the social liveliness of which girls in particular enjoy, so that postponement of specific sex experience need not seem like deprivation. Many adolescents are able to appreciate that the full adult expression of sex contains acquired as well as spontaneous satisfactions which depend on how the impulse has been directed.

In the Schofield survey mentioned above adolescents of fifteen to nineteen commonly expressed views which many theorists might imagine to have been quite old-fashioned. Most girls, while interested in sex play, do not want to go beyond a certain clearly fixed point which is well short of full experience, and adopt the traditional defensive role in the later teens. Fuller sex experience in both girls and boys tended to have been with considerably older partners, and a necessary preliminary in girls at least was a general rejection of other family values. Although there was much variation in the degree of permissiveness, and in the behaviour admitted to, most had certain standards and controls, and the evidence, though retrospective as regards the early teens, appears valid.

Obviously the sex behaviour of young people is as much in need of education as any other human activity, and the first step in its education is to acknowledge it freely, but without undue fuss. There is a real danger today that, in their anxiety to be above-board and liberal, parents may push a young and embarrassed son or daughter into the adolescent society before it is wanted. Similarly the timing of sex information is difficult. There are advantages in getting it over during the matter-of-fact days of childhood, and indeed if adults are going to anticipate the twelve-year-old jokes (which are still by far the commonest channel of information even nowadays) this is when it will have to be. But it is not at all simple to solve the problem nature sets us by its location of the procreative organs in a bodily area which is a traditional source of juvenile humour. The only way to avoid slyness and grins (or alternatively shame and distress) is by associating a very different set of emotions with the idea of sex. On this argument advice is best postponed until adolescence itself when these emotions have a chance of being understood. For example, while the satisfaction of a loving sex relationship is mutual, it is not identical for the two partners and girls and boys need time to realize the different kinds of responsibility they bring to it.

The kind of advice which adolescents might find useful, according to the evidence in Schofield's survey, would be neither sentimental nor impersonally technical and would come best from a counsellor of the same sex, preferably in the case of a girl, a young married woman teacher, unless the mother has made it unnecessary. It has been found that the better educated mothers undertake the responsibility more readily, perhaps because they have the kind of vocabulary to make it less awkward.

Altogether there is an opportunity during the school years for the pattern of developing sex behaviour to be established so that its direction is set even after fifteen which seems to be a critical point. But of course instruction is not the only medium and probably is less important than the process of identification with parents and other adults. It is true that adult attitudes to sex behaviour and to marriage are not clearly defined in modern society. There is a confusion of values and the expectations of different social groups from the individual are often in conflict. This makes it difficult for adolescents to learn their adult roles. Yet among the many surveys of adolescent habits and behaviour, one thing repeatedly appears. Adolescents are as much in need of a conscience in this generation as in any other, and as dependent upon their social experience to build one. Not all the evidence of the surveys is psychological, but this at least is of a psychological character. A growing personality needs to go through the process of identification, and especially of identifying with a stable adult figure in the early years. Lack of such stable adult figures can cause aimlessness and inability to form long-term goals; which is one of the main themes in Mary Morse's study called *The Unattached* (17). Another typical example is the second half of Geoffrey M. Stephenson's analysis of the social structure of conscience as it varied in a sample of fifteen-year-old boys (18).

These investigations belong in what we may call the Goldfarb tradition (see above page 134). There are, of course, psychologists who are in the Freudian tradition and think of adolescence itself as a state of disturbance for which there is no cure but time. One of the best known of these is Dr D. W. Winnicott whose diagnosis of adolescence is sub-titled 'struggling through the doldrums'. According to this, all adolescents are in a state of conflict which causes them to antagonize society so as to have an excuse for being difficult when reprimanded. They oscillate between defiance and dependency and nothing the adult can do is right because an adolescent does not know himself whether he wants to be an adult or a child. Extreme cases of adolescent depression, the delinquents and the drug-takers, represent the general malaise of adolescence itself. As an explanation it is rather different from the typical view of most American psychologists who believe that problem adolescents are reacting against the frustrations of trying to live up to the adolescent social role.

It would be surprising if the long process of socialization did not have setbacks and many individual casualties. Later (Appendix 2) we must take another look at the different kinds of maladjustment and their causes. But the present object has been to trace the normal course, so far as there can be such a thing in our complex society; from the stage of social dependency when a child gets the impression of himself and the world through the medium of his relationship with his mother, through the extension of self which comes from activity and things to be learned about and manipulated; then through the enclosed sub-culture of middle childhood in which preparation for adult ways and spontaneous peer-relationships complement each other; and so to the similar but larger-scaled society of adolescence, in which the needs of the strengthening self, the pressure to conformity within the vociferous peer-group and the demands of the adult world are in constant interaction.

Although it does not summarize all the diversity, it is perhaps helpful to detect in this two compulsive trends. There is the moral trend, the thrust towards regulation of the self to fit social expectations, and this is mediated in the main, though not exclusively, by relations with adults. There is the thrust towards self-expression in a chosen activity, and this is mediated by co-operation with equals. It is tempting to identify this second thrust with *play* activities, and indeed it is usually for these joyous and releasing activities we call play that the company of equals is sought. Play in this sense does not stop in adult life but it ceases to have the serious developmental function it has in the growing period. Adolescent society remains largely a play society in that it gratifies the chosen interests and so promotes the self-growth, inasmuch as adolescent interests are becoming more specialized and deeper. It has however been hinted that an adolescent may fail to outgrow this developmental stage if the thrust towards adult roles is swamped by the gratifications. Relations with adults, then, though proportionately lessening in importance, continue to fulfil their indispensable mediating function.

4 Assessing social maturity

When does the process end? In other words, what is a mature adult? We can tell, at least in retrospect, the year when a young man (or woman) becomes as tall as he will ever be. Less exactly but still with some conviction we can establish the point of maximum mental attainment. But we have no measure of adulthood of personality, particularly in view of the fact that we are less likely to agree about the components of maturity than about the components of intelligence. Psychologists have put forward their formulas just as they have their favourite version of intelligence. Some imply it indirectly by way of the failures and the misfits. A lack of self-acceptance marks the neurotic and so do inadequate solutions, which are neither satisfying nor socially approved. Emotions must often be subjugated to higher ends but mature people get satisfaction from doing this. Inability to get free of one's more primitive demands probably stems from the time when these earlier needs were not met. Winnicott, for example, believes that the last phase of the growing period will be worse disturbed if dependency was first encouraged, then thwarted some time in the early years. It will be hard for such an adolescent to struggle out of immaturity.

Other writers point out that self-acceptance means willingness to accept blame and Gabriel observes that young children look for a scapegoat somewhere in the environment—as indeed do adults when they are being less than mature themselves! Again, good solutions for personal needs means that these needs must be important enough to make sacrifice of lesser needs worthwhile, and so we have the element of *purposefulness* as a feature of mature behaviour. Impulses do not veer about with every wind that blows and mature individuals are predictable.

Most psychologists are agreed about such features as these, and feel that a child is maturing when he is able to show some of them in his behaviour—for example when he can pursue a plan without being distracted, or can smother his own preference because it will be better for the team. But these features are hard to evaluate and there is no orderly developmental scale like an intelligence scale. Personality tests of course do exist, and some are intended to measure a child's progress towards social maturity. There are straightforward pencil-and-paper questionnaires, for instance, about moral concepts like honesty. Or children can be assessed externally by being rated for a quality like hard-workingness or popularity.

A particularly well-known technique for measuring status within the peer group is called *sociometry*, or the *nominating* technique, and is associated with Moreno's work in the nineteen thirties. Children are asked to name the class-mate they would most like to sit beside or work with (and in some cases, least like as well) from which a diagrammatic sketch can be made of the relationships within a group by drawing arrows for choices. Cliques and clusters emerge clearly and special cases like the popular child (target of many converging arrows) and the isolate, chosen by none and making hardly any choices himself. For teachers planning group work in their classrooms, this black-and-white evidence might be more helpful than simple observation, since even sympathetic adults are not always in the secret of children's judgements of each other. More interesting psychologically perhaps is the hint given by some follow-up studies of further ratings by equals, that the degree of popularity may be constant since the same individual seemed to find a similar level in later groups.

On the whole however, reliability is not a feature of personality ratings—assessors at inteviews, for example, can sometimes show little correlation among their judgements. On the other hand, more formal tests, for instance of ethical attitudes, may lack validity, since what they tend to represent is intellectual not moral development.[1] Moral concepts do not guarantee appropriate behaviour! Giving the 'right' answer to a carefully structured question beginning 'What's the thing for you to do when . . .' is not spontaneous activity.

There are open-ended type tasks for the diagnosis of individual behaviour patterns. The response is only loosely structured by the test question and takes its form from the subject's own imagination.

[1] This point is noted by the author E. A. Lunzer, in his introductory description of *The Manchester Scales of Social Adaptation* (published by the National Foundation for Educational Research in 1966). These scales have been carefully standardized for ages 6–15.

He is not aware of being tested in the sense that there is no one correct reply. Of these *projective* personality tests (as they are often called) well known examples consist of reading patterns into ink blots and giving interpretations of more or less non-committal pictured episodes. As in all open-ended assessment, however, evaluating the response in projective tests is difficult and detailed, requiring prolonged training in diagnosis, which makes them uneconomic for general use. Consequently very thorough personality analysis has been biassed towards the behavioural extremes, and when attempts are made to typify the 'normal' it is often by placing them at a point along a dimension which leads for instance to outright neuroticism or depression.

· Class teachers are unlikely to want maturity ratings (in the developmental sense) beyond what their own observation of children's behaviour can supply. But should they wish to try, a useful technique is to evaluate children's responses to questions about behaviour against characteristic responses of an older age-group. This could supplement the external rating scale with five fixed points of placement for some quality like persistence on a task.

Assessment, you may remember, can be by the method of impression or by objective techniques with the behaviour itemized. Both methods have disadvantages which in personality assessment are particularly hard to avoid. General impressions are unreliable and itemization of personal qualities can be of very doubtful validity. On the whole serious evaluation requires expert psychological training. Perhaps most useful for a teacher is the knowledge that personal judgements always seem to be well-founded and are in fact seldom based on explicit variables consistently assessed. Prejudice affects the best of them—as indeed it can affect educational assessment as well.

This brings us to the end of the present topic by way of one of its many points of contact with the next to be considered. Cognitive (or mental) development may conveniently be approached through its relationship with the social environment.

A note on further reading. Several current theories on personality growth are referred to as they fit the context of this chapter. For more systematic statements see the suggested reading plan in Appendix 4.

REFERENCES

(1) Gesell, Arnold and Ilg, Frances, *The Child from Five to Ten*, London, 1946.
(2) Gabriel, John, *Children Growing Up*, U.L.P., 1964.

(3) Gesell, Arnold and others, *Youth, The Years from Ten to Sixteen*, Hamish Hamilton, 1956.

(4) Raven, J. C., *Progressive Matrices*, Lewis & Co., London, 1938.

(5) Havighurst, R. J., *Developmental Tasks and Education* and *Human Development and Education*, Longmans Green, New York, 1952 and 1953.

(5a) Peck, R. and Havighurst, R., *The Psychology of Character Development*, Wiley, New York, 1960.

(6) Spinley, B. M., *The Deprived and the Privileged*, Routledge and Kegan Paul, 1953.

(7) MacDougall, William, *An Introduction to Social Psychology*, Methuen, 1908.

(8) Erikson, E. H., *Childhood and Society*, Horton, New York, 1950.

(9) Lewis, M. M., *Language, Thought and Personality*, Harrap, 1963.

(10) Jersild, Arthur, *Child Psychology*, 5th Edn, Staples, 1960.

(11) Bowlby, J., *Maternal Care and Mental Health*, W.H.O., Geneva, 1951.

(12) Opie, I. and Opie, P., *The Lore and Language of Schoolchildren*, Oxford University Press, 1959.

(13) Mead, Margaret, *Coming of Age in Samoa*, Morrow, New York, 1928; and 'The Primitive Child', in *Handbook of Child Psychology*, 1933.

(14) Mays, John B., *The Young Pretenders*, Michael Joseph, 1965.

(15) Veness, Thelma, *School Leavers, their Aspirations and Expectations*, Methuen, 1962.

(16) Schofield, Michael, *The Sexual Behaviour of Young People*, Longmans, 1965.

(17) Morse, Mary, *The Unattached*, Penguin Books, 1965.

(18) Stephenson, Geoffrey, *The Development of Conscience*, Routledge and Kegan Paul, 1966.

6

Cognitive Development

1 The nature of mental growth

Individual personality becomes adjusted to the environment by experience of people and things, from which are crystallized meaningful ideas of how the world is arranged. In this process by far the most effective external agent is language. We have already seen something of its importance in group solidarity and how belongingness reassures each member of his own reality as a person. This feeling of the essential worthwhileness of communication is the spring of language learning, released by the earliest human contacts, with mother, co-operative adults, and other children jostling for recognition. Of course, it is the tendency of language, and particularly of read and written language, to become less *orectic*, less motivated by social emotion, and more cognitive, or intellectual in function, just as it becomes more generalized and less tied to single episodes. But even the most advanced and technical language is still communication; it is self-expressive in that it implies awareness of a listener or reader; without the motive of communication language is nonsense. The development of language is essentially making communication firstly more flexible so that it covers a wider range of communicable topics; and secondly more effective so that the words and the arrangement of words do a better job of informing a listener. Thus children gradually master speech and make it say what they want it to say. At the same time the need to tell other people sharpens the edges of what has to be told and ideas become clearer and better related. But speech is also worth listening to, and other people's words draw a child's attention to ideas he can form.

We shall have to come back to this crucial function of language and to others which go beyond the obvious one of communication though still deriving from it. Language illustrates the interdepedence of the social and intellectual factors in cognitive development. It is probably the clearest case of socially motivated learning and also, as seems very likely, of environmentally stimulated development; though it is not the only one.

152

Bodily growth can be plotted on a graph showing its progress at different points in the maturation period. We know therefore that this progress is variable. In the absence of fixed units we cannot know exactly what the variations are in cognitive increase, or whether they are maturational in the sense of being roughly age-tied, as the height-spurt is age-tied. We do not know what intellectual gain is represented by an increase in scores, although there are plenty of graphs of this kind. We do not know when a child is maturationally ready for a skill as we know that a boy of twelve is suddenly going to need a much bigger size in shoes and sweaters a year or two from now. There is a correlation between mental age and, for example, success in beginning to read—but this only means that at about the same time scores in a (verbal) reasoning test and early reading performance will have reached about the same level. This is hardly surprising. They are subject to the same powerful environmental factor, the child's experience of language.

Of course we can turn to 'performance'-type tests from which the specific verbal response has been removed—though it is not possible to remove the effect language has had so far upon the development of thinking. Performance-type tests of logic and comprehension do not measure 'pure' intellectual growth either. On the contrary, one of the most significant pointers to the importance of the cultural factor is given by the Progressive Matrices test (see above page 127). On all formal tests of ability the scores of adults sooner or later begin to show a decline and on Raven's test this appears relatively early, at about 18. But from one very large survey P. E. Vernon was led to believe that the decline began later and was not nearly so rapid among young men in superior occupations (1) demanding more mental effort. Some years later he found further evidence to support his view that intelligence itself can go on growing as long as stimulation lasts (2). Of course the achievements of an artist or scientist, of a brilliant financier, or for that matter of a grammar school boy specializing in classics, are not within the compass of a formal intelligence test; but the point is that on such formal tests an adult using his full ability will give a better account of himself, and goes on doing better for longer than someone challenged less by his way of life.

If adults are subject to environmental stimulation, then surely it must be even more effective during the maturational period, the more so the further back we go. In other words a bright child (genetically bright, that is) will get brighter if socially and environmentally stimulated and a dull child not so stimulated will get *progressively* duller. The pattern of growth in fact is not fully pre-determined.

Not so very long ago it was believed that innate capacity set limits to a child's educational intake. It was therefore educationally sound to group pupils accordingly, so that poorer pupils were not overloaded but allowed to absorb education at their own rate (see above for a statement of this view, page 111). For fast-growing pupils a richer diet was necessary. This, though perhaps never quite so baldly expressed, was the thinking behind the educational policy of *streaming* (classifying by ability in school). Doubts have been raised about the wisdom of this; and the recently published report by the Central Advisory Council for Education entitled *Children and their Primary Schools* (3) contains a statement on the subject. There has been a fair amount of research on the relationship between streaming and attainment, of which the relevant chapter in the Douglas survey (page 114) may be cited as a typical example. The sample of children whose primary school career was recorded in *The Home and the School* (4) were given a battery of tests at age eight and then again at age eleven, with their scores carefully standardized so that each child's position in the whole age-group was the point of emphasis. It was one of the major objects of the enquiry to study individual shifts of position relative to the whole sample, and there were many such. These shifts were in large measure attributable to environmental factors which operated in such a way that some children were able to hold their lead and often improve it because home conditions and the school they attended were particularly favourable. Meantime other children who showed up equally well at age eight lost their advantage because these helps were wanting. In particular nearly 500 children were identified as having been allocated to an A or B stream by ability before they were eight, and as continuing to be so taught with only a few transfers. Children in the upper stream on the whole improved their scores and this included the duller children who happened for one reason or another to have been allocated to the A class and whose scores, on the average, actually improved more than those of the brighter A children. That is, duller children who had the good fortune to be in an A stream, moved up in respect of the whole age-group. Conversely in the lower streams, it was the brighter eight-year-olds who showed subsequent deterioration, conforming, so to speak, to the general expectancy of poorer progress from B stream pupils.

Incidentally, it was believed by the investigators that the original allocation to upper and lower classes in a school year-group was made partly on social and cultural grounds. Middle-class children of even mediocre measured ability will speak more fluently and grammatically and give an overall impression of better fitness for education which is bound to have some effect, however, unintentional, upon teaching policy.[1] It is only one of many school occasions when linguistic deprivation, be it mild or gross, is only the first of a cumulative sequence of environmental disadvantages. Admittedly, children able enough to surmount early cultural handicaps and get into higher education, do eventually appear to make up the leeway in language itself. But it is surmised, and with some reason, that what they do not get over so completely is the loss of the stimulating effect of language upon their mental development in the critical early years when it seems very probable that the ability to think like a human being is beginning to take shape.

What psychologists are concerned with here are the great differences to be observed between one home and another, not so much in respect of specifically 'cultural' advantages like the presence of books, but in the quality of ordinary family talk. A flexible vocabulary, meanings conveyed by sentence structure and intonation rather than catch phrases, references to ideas and to things absent as well as to the here and now (what Bernstein means by his 'elaborated code')—all these set up a more effective complex of thought associations. Without being aware of it, children talked to and learning to talk in this way learn to think more widely and at the same time more precisely. On the other hand, the effect of what he calls a 'restricted' communication code is pointed out by Bernstein (5) in various studies of social differences in speech habits which have attracted a good deal of psychological interest in recent years. Perhaps it is not possible to agree completely with his claims that the language heard in the home exerts a fundamental influence on a child's ethical thinking and so upon his personality as a whole. Nevertheless a child is likely to *think* more carefully about what is meant when told: 'I shouldn't do that if I were you. You did promise; and if you don't keep a bargain how can you expect other people to keep their bargains with you?' than when the parent contents himself with an angry shout, or a vague general threat. According to Bernstein the more rational social attitudes of the better educated are directly due to the verbal rather than emotional expressions of feeling which children of such parents get into the habit of understanding. Because language is carefully

[1] The Plowden Report points out a tendency for girls to be favoured on much the same sort of criterion, as opposed to boys who make a less satisfactory impression upon teachers.

attended to, thought is attended to, and action in turn becomes more reasonable.

There is no doubt that in the early appearances of thinking, when a child is sorting his impressions of the world and selecting his responses to them, the environment and in particular the speech environment plays a critical role. But it need not be critical in the once and for all sense. In one very famous study A. R. Luria, in collaboration with another Russian psychologist, demonstrated how an early speech deprivation can be got over by an intensive training programme (6). A pair of twins were very retarded in behaviour and in purposeful play especially. They used, significantly, a very limited speech code to communicate with each other, with a fixed and primitive set of language references. Both improved when introduced to the company of other children but one of the twins got special language training and forged far ahead of the untrained one, not just in the use of words but in planning his activities and in general maturity of personality. Luria was associated in his early psychological work with Vygotsky whose impressive ideas on language and thinking were not generally available to British and American psychologists till their translation into English in 1962 (7). Like him and many other Russian educational psychologists since Pavlov, Luria believes that words are indispensable for the internalization of actions which make thinking possible. To this important though sometimes difficult conception we must return. It is an influential one at the present moment in the psychology of development and learning, especially in conjunction with Piaget's much discussed investigations. It has already had considerable effect upon educational practice and is likely to have more.

Besides those environmental ones there are other complicating factors in mental development. The specialization of the teens, the leaning towards the literary rather than the scientific, the technological rather than the social, may come in part from an innate mental bias, a *preponderance* of one of the special mental factors of which Thurstone once identified a modest fifty-seven and Guilford, more recently, at least 150. But Guilford, inventor of the distinction made between divergent (imaginative) and convergent (logical) thinking habits, believed this to be as much a personality as an intellectual difference; and that creative brilliance is due as much to emotional as intellectual drive is strongly argued by Liam Hudson in the lively study entitled *Contrary Imaginations* (8).

There is, in fact, no single line of mental development. At all points the environment interferes, for better or worse, with the age-tied genetic sequence. It is at least as important a determinant of when attainments will appear and the form they will take in an individual human child as his heredity is.

2 Structure and function

It would be nonsense of course to try to beat down the value of the hereditary contribution. No doubt in many individual cases, perhaps even in the majority, the full potential is never realized, but there is no reason for abandoning the common-sense view of heredity as setting an upper limit beyond which development of powers cannot in the end be environmentally boosted. The traditional evidence for the hereditary factor's influence is in such things as high correlations between members of a family for test scores and other performances. In any educational survey, too, the children of able parents make a better showing, even allowing for their educational and cultural privileges. Support may be borrowed from what is known of the structure and maturation of the nervous system. Of the many millions of neurons, its structural cells, almost all, as we have seen, are already present at birth. There is nothing fanciful in the hypothesis that the specific total count is a matter of inheritance; there is certainly room for individual variation round about the approximate average of ten thousand million!

Since the nerve cells increase so little in number after birth, the growth of the nervous system including the brain must go on through the expansion in size of the original cells and by their elaboration. Many psychologists who have studied the organization of the brain structure by various methods, believe that this is partly due to bombardment by environmental stimulation. This may well be so. Again, there is almost certainly an environmental influence at work in the increase of the connecting fibres, particularly in the so-called 'association' areas of the brain, whose function is to interpret, remember and generalize upon the evidence submitted by the sensory and motor areas which are directly linked each to a definite part of the body. For psychologists like Hebb (the same Hebb whose definition of the three distinct meanings for the term intelligence may be remembered) who try to come to grips with what actually happens in the brain tissue during activity, the period when the earliest neural connections are forming is the 'getting ready to learn'. The more intricate the linkages between cells the greater will be the future capacity to comprehend and assimilate experience. Hebb suggests that deprivation of early experience restricts the formation of interconnections in the cerebral cortex and in the association areas particularly. The nerve cells are not stimulated often enough, nor in sufficient numbers at a time, to get into the habit, so to speak, of functioning in complex groups, built out of what Hebb calls *cell assemblies*; until they do, experience cannot be organized into thought systems, enriched by comparisons between this event and past events, nor expanded imaginatively with the help of language (9).

But there is probably a wide range of individual differences in the innate *responsiveness* of the neural structure itself to the stimulation of experience and activity—for all we can tell at the moment, it may be in the very chemistry of the cell itself. Family resemblances are as obvious in gifts and abilities as in body build and colouring, and there must be some corresponding condition to explain them in the neural make-up. After all, one reason why it is difficult to fix the limits of the four *lobes* of the cerebral cortex (that characteristically 'human' part of the brain) is that the extent of these lobes differs somewhat between one individual brain and another.[1] It has been observed too that every-one has his own characteristic frequency in those famous 'brain waves' known as the *alpha rhythm* type, and Grey Walter inclines to accept this as innate and probably hereditary. He associates the respective frequencies rather with different habits of thinking than with degrees of ability; but there are other quantitative variations to be found in the EEG patterns[2] which are strongly associated with intellectual originality. This, if it exists, is a difference in the functioning rather than the structure of the neural connections, their tendency to be more or less lively, more or less on the look-out for stimu-lation (10).

There is another highly likely source of innate variability in a certain network of tiny neural fibres which interpenetrate almost every area of the brain. This is called sometimes the reticular (net-like) system, sometimes the non-specific projection system. Unlike the specific projection system (which takes messages fairly direct from a given body area into the exact brain locality which receives these

[1] The part of the brain most recently evolved is called the cortex, since it 'covers over' the older, more primitive part. It is partially divided into a left and right hemisphere, and in each hemisphere there is a frontal lobe, a parietal lobe, an occipital lobe and a temporal lobe.

[2] A graphic recording of the brain waves or fluctuations in the electric activity of the brain.

particular impulses) it sets up a sort of generalized stimulation for the entire brain and creates a state of all-over readiness to respond. Some-times, therefore, it is called the brain's *arousal* system. Psychologists associate this most interesting formation with conditions like vigilance, motivation, and responsiveness. When it is firing at high pressure, the individual is quick to perceive any one of a wide range of possible stimulations which the *specific* projection system may pick up from the eye, or the ear, the finger tips, or the taste buds. When it is relatively inactive—on a drowsy summer afternoon in school for instance!—that same individual is lethargic and inattentive. And no teacher needs to be told that there is apparently quite a difference between one pupil's arousal system and another's!

Just as there are hereditary factors in the structure and function of neural connections which regulate the intake from the environment and responsive activity, so there is a maturational factor which partially at least regulates the *timing* of mental development. Many psycho-logists are of the belief that there is a more or less uniform sequence of maturation of different brain structures and that until the appropriate one has (spontaneously) matured the behavioural function cannot appear (see above, page 108). Mental development, it follows from this belief, is not so much a product of stimulation as the simple passing of time. Now the actual changes in the cells and fibres of the nervous system and the higher brain in particular are not at all well charted beyond the very early years. In fact they have to be inferred by indirect measurements, as on the electro-encephalogram, where the 'brain wave' rhythms can be seen to change typically from infancy to about fourteen years; or else, of course, by behavioural observations. It is probable, however, that there are age-tied events which trigger off structural brain changes in the same way as the adolescent process is triggered off at the age of puberty.

One such structural change is the laying down of a substance called myelin along the nerve fibres which, being fatty, acts as a protective sheath. When a nerve fibre is unmyelinated it can carry only a rather slow electrical impulse; in a fibre that has been myelinated the nervous impulse is communicated about fifty times faster. Now in a new-born baby many nerve fibres are not myelinated or not completely. For example: the optic nerve tracts are not fully myelinated till two months after birth and there is not much myelin on the connecting fibres in the two brain areas on which are *projected* respectively the various muscular systems of the body (the motor area) and the various sense receptors (the sensory area). Myelin begins to be laid down here

P.E.Y.—6*

quite quickly, however, so that a baby becomes capable of crudely effective movement (such as the possessive clutch on his feeding bottle!) and of simple sensations from eyes and ears. What he presumably cannot do is make any sort of internal commentary, so to speak, on bodily experience. This is the early period of life which none of us can remember because although we felt stimulation and made relatively appropriate responses we were not consciously aware of doing either. What makes experience meaningful, recognizable, and so on, is the functioning of the *association* areas of the cerebral cortex to which the motor and sensory signals are referred, to be made sense of, or decoded. If a baby can do this at all it must be in a vague elementary sort of way, because the myelination of the fibres of the association areas apparently comes later in the sequence. This means there cannot be that pervasive and instantaneous communication process which makes the mature brain flicker and pulsate in a shimmer of endless activity.

Of course the increase of myelin is not the only index of development but it is a useful one because it is quantitative and because it can hardly be due to anything but spontaneous maturation. What can be observed of its progress in the early years has led some psychologists to argue that the myelination of the whole cortex goes on by genetic stages which are therefore age-tied, and that the brain is not ready to function at full adult efficiency level until early adolescence. On this view certain kinds of thinking are maturationally impossible for children. Intricate reasoning systems depend upon correspondingly intricate structures in the nerve cells, those in the association areas of the cortex being the last to be so organized. We shall return to this theory very soon in another connection, but at this point the reader must be warned how misleading it can be to talk of 'structures' in the brain. We have very little idea what the physical nature of such linkages can be; one thing at least seems certain, they are not localized here and there in the cortex, with the memory for (say) long division tucked into one corner and a taste for fifteenth-century church music in another. If the reader can imagine a functional rather than a structural unit, a flicker from one available nerve pattern to another, it might be more helpful. Brain maturity would then mean that a great many cells all over the cortex (not to mention in other brain regions as well) could get into instant communication and that every possible permutation of linkages would be available.

To sum up: even if mental maturity is brought about simply by the passing of the necessary number of years there may well be critical periods when stimulation is essential. One such, as Hebb believes, is when the association areas are first being tried out as the medium for understanding and recognizing primary experience and if this does not happen the equipment for future learning will be impaired. Another must be when language is starting to fulfil its indispensable function of replacing absent objects by symbols and bringing together for comparison events that happen apart in time. In this context too, ought to be placed the findings by ability and attainment surveys that home and school environments decisively affect mental scope.

The trend of our times is to pull the genetic factors and the learning factors closer together. One result of this is that learning has widened its psychological compass far beyond the acquisition of skills and information as we shall see in the next group of chapters. It has become a way of understanding the nature of behaviour itself. Hence the 'learning' psychologists have an interest in what may come out of the present surge of new knowledge about brain physiology. The 'maturation' psychologists have always assumed a neuro-physical basis to the development of behaviour, which implies firstly that there is an age-tied sequence of behavioural development and secondly that it takes a similar form in all children. In previous chapters we saw how by using large samples and shrinking the results by statistical methods, meaningful mental age-norms can be arrived at with the variance defined. But now we come to what is probably, at the present moment, the most famous attempt at a genetic explanation of mental development from birth to adolescence, and certainly the most talked about.

3 Piaget's theory of mental development

The feature of Piaget's developmental psychology which has provoked as much discussion as any is that he makes little use of the two normative methods just referred to. He does not consider large samples necessary to validate his conclusions about the general pattern of mental development; nor does he summarize them in the form of mathematical statistics.

In the first place he uses clinical methods. The children are observed in limited groups, sometimes in pairs and often singly. Their behaviour is often spontaneous and the records of it descriptive, not quantitative. Normative surveys are based on fixed test questions so that the scope of responses is restricted to a range that can be measured; but Piaget and his collaborators apparently present their problems in no set form of words, which some critics declare makes standard assessments impossible of one child's performance against another's. To counter this, however, it must be appreciated that Piaget is concerned not so much with assessing a performance and giving it a value (such as a percentile rank or a mental age equivalent) as in identifying the thinking process by which the child arrives at his answer. His tests are most ingeniously contrived to do exactly this. Using concrete material (lumps of plasticine, bottles of beads, mechanical dolls running a race) he asks for a comment on what has actually happened (has the plasticine increased in amount by being rolled out thin? has the doll which started further back taken longer to reach the goal?) and so fixes the links in the thought process between the child's observations and his conclusions about them.

He does, of course, believe that certain thinking forms, or rather certain thinking deficiencies are characteristic of certain ages. But this is not an *assessment* of the child's answer; it merely is his way of declaring that it takes a given number of years for adult-thinking abilities to be perfected and that at so many years after birth a child's thinking is likely to be thus far on its way to maturity. Naturally, brighter children may well reach the successive stages earlier in time; naturally, experience must make a difference so that a child may well be able to think out the logical answer with familiar material though he fails in an artificial experimental situation. But for Piaget's theory these variations are incidental and he is willing to concede them. His point is that all children, bright or average, do in fact go through these necessary stages in the evolution of the thinking ability and that it takes a number of years for this to happen. What takes place during these years is of course something else again. Does the thinking spontaneously mature or does it grow by exercize? Piaget has his ideas about this, as we shall presently see. So far, we have been concerned to see why his theory can be called genetic: it contains the idea of a developmental sequence that is age-tied, in the sense that one thinking stage grows out of the preceding one and that each stage takes its own time to be outgrown. It is the pattern of this process which Piaget is trying to trace out, the growth of thinking in the abstract, so to speak. A physical parallel would be the increase of myelin which can be studied also as an independent maturity index. Of course both myelination and the developing thinking ability can only occur in individual examples. But that does not prevent them being thought about and described in the abstract.

For the recording of scientific observations in any field, whether of

physical or behavioural phenomana, technical language is a helpful
shorthand. We are quite used to this in the traditional sciences and no
one is perplexed by chemistry's $CaCO_3$ or algebra's x's and y's and
minus signs. But it is a relatively new technique in psychology and
many students are put off by statistics, let alone by still more austere
ways of expressing behavioural observations like C. L. Hull's theorems
about the laws of behaviour and Kurt Lewin's topological diagrams
representing motivational forces (11). Now, just as the results of the
normative surveys need statistical treatment to bring out the pattern,
so in Piaget's belief the study of thought structures, and of the successive stages they go through in the years of maturation, needs an
abstract language to state its conclusions. This is his second point of
difference from the methods of other developmental investigators. He
uses, not statistical conclusions, which are based on mathematics and
quite often upon straightforward arithmetic, but symbols and signs
borrowed from something less familiar.

To give an approximate explanation: this means using letters to
symbolize not numbers as they do in mathematical algebra, but such
ideas as a *class* or category (for example, sea captains) and its *sub-classes*
(sea captains with beards and clean-shaven sea captains). Meantime
the signs in logical algebra symbolize the relationship between the
things the letters represent. By adding together all the sub-classes we
arrive at the total class itself, so we may use the plus and the equal-to
sign for this relationship. Then again *sub-classes* are mutually exclusive.
A bearded sea captain cannot be (for the period of the beard's duration)
a clean-shaven one and for this relationship of mutual exclusiveness we
can use an oblique stroke. So what we know so far about our class and
its sub-classes enables us to say: 'The population of sea-captains is made
up of sea-captains with beards and sea-captains who are clean-shaven,
which we may render as:

$$B \text{ (the class)} = A \text{ (sub-class)} + A' \text{ (sub-class)}'.[1]$$

On the other hand, the class of sea-captains can be composed of sub-
classes distinguished by a different criterion altogether, for example
by whether their command is in coastal waters or upon the high seas,
and to this arrangement our formula may also apply, since the two
sub-classes are again mutually exclusive: $B_2 = A_2 + A'_2$. But captains'
beards abound both in coastal waters and upon the high seas and
neither sea area has the monopoly of clean-shaven captains. So we

[1] Formal logic strictly speaking would prefer the capital letter for the class
and the same small letter for the two sub-classes but the present system is used
for clarity.

have four possible variants of sea-captain which we may show as a little grid or matrix.[1]

Such a matrix is a logical structure which Piaget believes not only represents the information we possess in a systematic way but also *represents* the structure of our thinking on the subject. (Needless to say we can think out the relationship without knowing anything about the matrix ourselves just as a child can know what his score is without knowing that it is on the 75th percentile!) To understand how many *possible* types of sea-captains there are we must balance in our heads two distinct pairs of alternatives. Otherwise we might see having a beard as a necessary *condition* of having a command on the high seas, or as a necessary *result* of having a command on the high seas, instead of as being quite unrelated to it.

In the same way an object which is *broad* cannot at the same time be *narrow* and if it is *heavy* it cannot be *light*. It can be both narrow and light, or both broad and heavy; but two other possibilities are perfectly consistent with the logical structure of the information. It can be narrow *and* heavy or broad *and* light. To perceive this requires the ability to think of weight and width as independent and distinct. Frequently of course an increase in one does happen to be accompanied by an increase in the other, but one does not logically *cause* the other.

Now, according to Piaget it is inability to balance the claims of two independent variables that characterizes the thinking of young children. They form connections which are inconsistent with the logical structure of the information presented to them. Thus a *tall* thin jar must *contain* more, they argue, although it has just been demonstrated by their very own actions that it gets filled to the top by exactly the same number of beads as a short, squat container. Their thought structure in fact is not tight-knit and consistent with due reference to all possibilities. When this in the course of time and experience does come about Piaget says that their thinking has reached stability of equilibrium. It has a system of explanations for events such that no explanation will contradict the one offered for something else.

[1] Bearded sea-captains in coastal commands. Bearded sea-captains on the high seas. Clean-shaven, etc.
or

	A_2	A'_2
A_1	$A_1 A_2$	A_1 A_2
A'_1	$A'_1 A_2$	A'_1 A'_2

For instance, children admit quite early in their mental growth that the amount of plasticine in a ball does not increase when it is rolled out thin but longer, and they give reasons consistent with the fact that long-short and more-less are two *distinct* modes of distinguishing one blob of plasticine from another blob of plasticine (or two distinct modes of composing the whole class 'blobs of plasticine' from two sub-classes). But they do not extend this logically to the dimension of *weight* as well as quantity and they are still later in sorting out *volume* (the object's displacement of water) as being something not necessarily altered by other changes in that object. The total logical structure with every possibility allowed for that can be made up from shape, weight, and bulk, takes time to build up.

Probably the best known example Piaget offers of a young child's inability to understand that a class is composed of all its sub-classes and therefore must be bigger than any one of them, is how they answer the question about the brown and white beads. All the beads are wooden but more of them are coloured brown than white. Asked if there are more *brown* beads or more *wooden* beads in the box, children under seven will answer 'More brown beads because there are hardly any white', even though a moment ago they have agreed firstly that all the beads are wooden and secondly that not all of them are brown! Piaget argues that children cannot hold in their heads simultaneously the two ideas of decomposing B (wooden beads) into its two elements A (brown) and A' (white) and of seeing that B *continues* to exceed either brown or white, each by the amount of the other one (A is B less A' and A' is B less A).[1] Decomposing B for a young child makes it disappear from the structure as a whole because he cannot *think back* to its wholeness and simultaneously think of it in two parts (12).

The reader may have found these examples complicated enough, but they are among the simplest of the ways in which Piaget uses logical structures to describe how thinking works when it is systematized and consistent, and exactly what is missing when this is not the case. The problems so far referred to (changes in the plasticine, composition of an assembly of beads) are concrete problems where there is a physical demonstration and where the reasoning, though logical, is restricted to this particular case. (We have seen how children able to argue out that change of shape need not affect quantity are often unable to transfer this conclusion to weight as well, although

[1] Readers may prefer the alternative notation to help them clarify this example. $B = b + b$.

the argument is identical). But reasoning in the *abstract* works from possibilities, or hypotheses, not actual occurrences, and furthermore draws on an understanding of logical relationships in general. This kind of thinking does not, according to Piaget, appear before adolescence.

To take again as simple an example as possible. From our knowledge of magnetism we might logically deduce that an iron filing placed between two magnets at the point where they are exerting equal force would be bound to stay there, although it would be hard to demonstrate. If on the other hand an iron filing accidentally deposited between two magnets did behave in this manner, one might reasonably assume that they were exerting equal force upon it. Besides accounting for the present observations it would not contradict the system of information which includes an understanding of magnetic fields and the nature of metals, nor the wider system which contains the concept of equality.

One might then logically deduce that this relationship between, first, the pressure of two equal magnetic forces, and, second, the motionlessness of the iron, would permit *three* possible arrangements of those two states of affairs. First, that they are both the case. In the presence of two equal magnetic forces the iron is in fact motionless. Secondly, that neither is the case. In the absence of equal magnetic forces the iron moves. Thirdly, that the first is not the case, the second is. In the absence of equal magnetic forces the iron (can) remain motionless. But the *fourth* possible arrangement would invalidate our hypothesis; that is, if the first were ever found to be the case and not the second, so that in the presence of equal magnetic forces the iron does not remain motionless.

Since there are no other possible arrangements, if we could demonstrate that the first three do happen but the fourth does not, our hypothetical proposition could (logically) still stand.

There is an algebraic formula for the foregoing taking p for our first item (presence of equal magnetic forces) and $\bar{p}$ for its negation (absence of equal magnetic forces), q for the motionlessness of the iron and $\bar{q}$ for its negation. It would run like this:

That p implies $q = pq$ or $\bar{p}\bar{q}$ but not $p\bar{q}$.

Supposing now you are observing another pair of conditions and wish to test the truth of a different sort of proposition about the connection between them, such as that the two are incompatible, then you could logically work out what arrangements of p and q could be found to happen without disproving your theory of incompatability. (By this we mean that if one is there, the other cannot be.) There are in fact only two arrangements of p and q which allow this hypothesis to stand: p present q absent or p absent q present. The other two occurrences are logically impossible and if they are found the hypothesis must be abandoned and a new relationship proposed between p and q. For instance one might set out to prove the incompatability of 'It is raining' and 'The pavement is dry' but have to abandon it in favour of the complete *independence* of the two states of affairs. Pavement under an awning can be dry during a shower and it can be wet (not dry) for reasons other than rainfall.

To test a hypothesis, then, a thinker must reason out what possibilities *may* be found to occur and what *must not* be found to occur, and then proceed to demonstrate that the first do and the second do not, in fact, happen. This propositional thinking is necessary when one is confronted by an event which may be caused by any one of a large number of variables that happen to be present, or by any combination of them. Piaget observed adolescents who had reached this level tackling problems of explanation by systematically working through the possibilities and their implications. He believes that by using algebraic calculations of the kind referred to in the last paragraph it is possible to unravel the shuttling to and fro of abstract reasoning within a frame of organized knowledge.

The technique is complicated and further explanation would take up too much space in the present context, the aim of which is to indicate what it is that Piaget is trying to do. He himself attaches a good deal of importance to his methods and believes that they do in fact create a *model* of the thinking activity itself as well as demonstrating how it evolves to its final form. Examples of the more intricate logical structures are to be found in his own book *Logic and Psychology* (12) which has a useful introductory note by Professor Mays, and is the most convenient original reference available to English readers. There are relevant chapters in Robert Thomson's *Psychology of Thinking* (13) and E. A. Peel's *The Pupil's Thinking* (14), both of which emphasize the developmental aspects of Piaget's psychology.

Undoubtedly the difficulty of Piaget's technique is one reason why educators have some trouble in sorting out the significance of his work. It is also puzzling that its impact should be felt so late, as he has been a prolific writer and worker for the last forty years. But for English readers of course, his books had to wait for translation; some were not available until he himself had gone into new lines of enquiry, in the course of which he had abandoned some of his own earlier speculations, so that we may well be selecting for special appraisal something which he himself no longer regards as central to his views. For example the Russian psychologist Vygotsky (see above, page 156) disagreed with Piaget's early idea of the egocentric talk of young children—the sort of running monologue without reference to any particular listener with which they so often accompany what they are doing. In *Language and Thought of the Child* (15), one of the best known of the early studies, Piaget identified egocentric talk with inadequate ability to communicate and its gradual decrease with improvement. Vygotsky, however, was convinced that monologue is a necessary step in the process by which speech becomes internalized and so helps thinking to develop out of concrete activity (7). This was exactly in accordance with Piaget's own later observations. In the same way he accepts the point made long ago by Susan Isaacs, that logical insight is fully as dependent on adequate experience, the chance to study and manipulate the concrete environment, as it is upon spontaneous maturation. Hence children with opportunities of this kind may well acquire it earlier, especially with familiar material.

The reader may perceive that this is in full accordance with modern educational practice with its stress upon activity rather than instruction as the medium for learning and for the formation of those thinking abilities which guarantee further learning. This is yet another reason why Piaget's work is now having (to date) its greatest impact. In any case it is now apparent that his plan of attack on the development of thinking is not finished, although it was always present in intention. The 'early books' as they are known in psychological circles, were on various general aspects of children's thought and surveyed the field. Later books have filled in different sections like pieces of a puzzle, very much as Piaget sees the thinking structure itself to be gradually put together by growing experience. It becomes at last the tool, the machine by which human beings can tackle the environment; but the devices we take for granted in an adult's approach are simply not there for a child to use even on simple everyday problems; the instant grasp of relationships (this is bigger than that, this caused that, this belongs to that) the 'obvious' deduction (he started earlier but arrived at the same time so he must have taken longer) and the interlocked system of knowledge.

When Piaget was still in Paris at the beginning of his career, Simon, Binet's collaborator, asked him to standardize the reasoning tests invented by the English psychologist Cyril Burt upon French children, and characteristically he was far more interested by the errors the children made than in evaluating their successes. It was shortly after this that he recorded his conclusions about the thinking abilities in the first years of life, such as he observed them to be in his own children, and as Director of Studies at the Institut Jean-Jacques Rousseau in Geneva did his investigations on samples of children of various ages, the results of which were published in the famous five volumes of the years between 1926 and 1932 (15). His name has always been associated with Geneva where he became professor of psychology at the university and latterly director of the International Bureau of Education affiliated with Unesco. He and his collaborators (notably Dr Barbel Inhelder) constitute what has become known as the Geneva school of developmental psychology whose influence on recent educational research has been very great in Britain and America. Piaget himself has been associated with many discussions and conferences on education and psychology; some of these have been on an international scale, such as the study group inaugurated by the World Health Organization on the psychological development of children. Reports have been published as live discussions (16). Of more localized interest was the series of lectures to teachers given at the University of London Institute of Education, and published in a useful little volume subtitled *First Years in School*, where readers will find some first-hand information about Piaget's own work and the kind of follow-up research it has inspired (17).

In the first five books (which were quickly translated and started a great deal of controversy which is still going on even though Piaget's own theories have expanded beyond them in several ways) he stated his belief that children's thinking is *different* from adult thinking and in order to describe and explain these differences used a vocabulary of special terms. The belief he has not abandoned but he has largely given up the rather generalized terminology in favour of more detailed explanatory systems. We have seen how he once used the term *egocentrism* to define the deficiency in a child's power of communication. Another such term was *syncretism* by which he meant that children will arbitrarily explain one phenomenon by another which merely happens to be there at the same time and has nothing logically to do with it (e.g. 'The sun does not fall out of the sky because it is hot'). Again he took *animism* as the identifying feature of the pre-scientific stage through which, in accordance with his theory, he believed that children's thinking about natural phenomena must pass. (The wind, for example, they say deliberately 'pushes' the boats, and this they mean in an explanatory not a fanciful sense).

As has been indicated, some of the early speculations he has given up, having found in logical algebra a better medium for systematizing his theories. What he did carry over into later work was his concept of certain fixed growth-stages in thinking, with age seven or eight as the dividing line between typically childish thought devices and something which has the adult characteristics of consistency and insight, though of course in a strictly limited way.

4 Piaget's account of the stages of mental development

These stages Piaget now sees as four[1] with two before the seven-eight period and two after, though with many possible sub-stages composing the total succession. Obviously it is going to take a minimum number of years to get through the whole sequence, and in this sense they are age-tied, which does not preclude the individual maturational factor. Bright children are bright inasmuch as they are getting through the stages faster, which is why some psychologists have tried to locate Piaget's stages at *mental* rather than at chronological age-points (although this in a sense is merely saying the same thing in two ways).

Each stage is developmental in the fullest sense. It has a task to be achieved on which the successive phase is based. Thus between birth and two years old children are acquiring the notion of permanent objects which go on existing when they cannot be seen, or have shifted their setting. For instance by eighteen months a child can go to look for a lost shoe if it is not in its usual place beside the other one. It is still a shoe though it is elsewhere; it can be got and brought back. Furthermore it can be brought from various places—under the sofa, behind the curtain. These displacements (as Piaget calls them) and the variety of actions involved in them, are collected in a simple system of information about the shoe and its existence in a collection of localities. My shoe=my shoe beside the other, on my foot, hidden behind the sofa. This *group* (a mathematical term) of displacements of the shoe entails various activities by the child, all leading by devious routes to the restoration of the shoe to whatever purpose it is wanted for.

This example has been given in a little detail to illustrate an important point. It is movement and other activity which creates the shoe's significance as an object, because having to do something about it is its significance for the child as an individual. Learning, for Piaget, depends on this impulse to make the objects of the world serve one's

[1] Or five, by some arrangements. See footnote on next page.

needs and this means having to adjust one's ideas about the real nature of objects and what can be done with them. 'It is my shoe (that is the function of its existence) but it will not come to me if it is on the other side of the room and I want it. I must recognize that it is my-shoe-over-there and to make it my-shoe-in-my-hand I must crawl towards it.'

These two aspects of learning about the world Piaget calls *assimilation* (the my-ness of things, things exist for my purposes) and *accommodation* (things have an existence of their own with rules which one has to come to terms with if they are to serve one's purpose). Between them learning is motivated and action is the medium by which the learning happens. When *assimilation* and *accommodation* are balanced (that is the use to me and the actual nature of the interesting object complement each other and do not clash) then the child's idea of reality (in this particular case only, of course) has reached what Piaget calls *equilibrium*. One other of his key ideas is also illustrated though in a crude sort of way by the child's action in retrieving his shoe. This is the beginning of *reversibility* in thinking, the power to see what has happened and if necessary undo it, by going back to the beginning again, to the *status quo*.

At about eighteen months or two years old, a child's repertory of objects and actions is tidied up by his being able to label them in words, which ends the naiveties of the foregoing *sensori-motor stage*. Between two and four the ability to symbolize absent things by sounds and also by imitative actions indicates that the child is internalizing the world by building up a set of images of it in his mind. But at first the collection lacks system and order. Words will be used in an undiscriminated way to refer to any one of a loose collection of objects. For instance having learned the amusing new word 'pom-pom' he will call everything a pom-pom and will be puzzled by adult corrections. This is a part of our old friend egocentrism. So, too, is the obvious inability to dis-tinguish between the image of an object and its own reality. Words gradually come to be used in accordance with adult guidance, the right word with the right object, but not Piaget believes, spontaneously out of the child's own understanding of things and the arrangement of things.

However, between four and seven, the processes which are the developmental task of this *pre-operational stage* are making great strides.[1]

[1] Commentators on Piaget sometimes distinguish 2–4 as the stage of intuitive thought and 4–7 as the *pre-operational*. Others see 2–7 as one continuous stage. But one need not worry too much about labelling details. The principle of Piaget's theory remains the same.

As the child performs more activities in a widening world, he begins to classify these events into permanent objects with permanent features (objects, classes, and sub-classes) and into various relationships that link up one state of affairs with another state of affairs (cause and effect, comparisons, duration, and so on). 'If you suck a piece of toffee hard and it gets smaller and then is gone—like pudding when you take big spoonfuls—but I am going to suck slow and keep it longer than you can!'

Piaget believes that to understand such a relationship a child must be able to participate in it himself, if not actually then by identifying himself with what is being done. Secondly it is a piecemeal process with equilibrium achieved in one specific set of events at a time but not by analogy in any other. This is because at this time and for many years to come, children live at the level of the concrete and not by abstract principles.

Furthermore, as we have seen, children in the pre-operational period up to about seven find it hard to balance two modes of thinking about the same thing, like the end-state and the starting-state. Hence in concentrating upon the length of the rolled-out plasticine, or the height of water or beads in the thin jar, or the tips of two sticks brought level, they cannot argue from the fact that the plasticine was shorter and thicker a moment ago, or the beads were counted out equal to the beads in the dumpy container, or that the other ends of the sticks are now not level. When they can do this they are no longer tied to the visible results of an action but have formed in their thought structure what Piaget calls an *operation*. This is the mental equivalent of a generalized action; unlike any single action, this generalized idea of it is *reversible*, the thought of the starting-state being contained in the end-state and vice versa. Similarly, as egocentrism diminishes, a child perceives that something is hit by the ball he throws. He sees it, so to speak, at the receiving end of the missile, as well as from the throwing end. By the same token he will now admit that 'Jacky is my brother, so I must be Jacky's brother', thus incorporating two points of view in his idea of brothers.

Now that he can move to and fro in the world of things and events (or the relations between things) he is on the way to having an orderly thought system, by which everything that happens here and now can be fitted into a structural framework without dislocating any other part of it. This state of equilibrium is extended from one area of experience to another, during the stage of *concrete operations* which, as we have seen, begins to function about age seven and goes on roughly throughout the primary school years. For Piaget's account of the development gains of this phase, which are exceedingly important, the source is the so-called 'later' books, each one describing the investigation of one specific item of mental equipment. They are thought of as the later work because their impact on recent education has been delayed by the varying gaps between their original appearance in French and their English versions, which makes them hard to place in any meaningful chronological order. In fact *La Genèse du Nombre chez l'Enfant* appeared in 1941 which was actually nearer in time to the last of the 'early' books, *The Moral Judgement of the Child*, than to its own translation into *The Child's Conception of Number* in 1952. *Le Développement des Quantités chez l'Enfant* also belongs to 1941, but it was late in the fifties before all the research programmes got under way which were inspired by Piaget's downright statements about the respective concepts of material substance, weight, and volume. Piaget went on to other specific topics, such as the child's notions about visual *space* and related concepts like area and geometrical measurement, and *time* in the sense of the duration of actions and the related concepts like velocity, or movement speed (18).

Besides these there are several books with more comprehensive subjects (19). *The Child's Construction of Reality* is of interest in showing how young children build up their working ideas of the world around them. In *The Psychology of Intelligence* Piaget describes the internalization of actions to form the concrete operations of middle childhood and subsequently the abstract structures of adolescent thinking. The famous and influential *Growth of Logical Thinking* traces the development of reasoning past the stage of the concrete problems which are within the scope of primary school children to the thinking techniques which adolescents are able to use. (See the 'iron filings' problem on page 166 for the kind of hypothetical reasoning Piaget means.)

It has been hinted that Piaget has no qualms about making downright statements on the basis of the test situations he has invented. The following are among his conclusions.

Firstly, a child's understanding of one area of experience is independent of his understanding of another. Hence his working model of the world, and by inference his thought structure, will be incomplete until each component has appeared.

Secondly, the components appear in fixed succession and are consequently age-tied. *Number* and *quantity* as stable properties of material which do not change simply because of other changes in it (e.g. butter does not increase by being melted nor do five beads become more numerous when spread out) are understood at age seven. *Weight* follows at between eight and nine. The ideas of 'time taken' and 'distance covered' are not distinguished from each other till age eight likewise, therefore *velocity* cannot be understood as the relationship between these two measures until after this age.

Thirdly, each separate concept develops in its own fixed sequence of stages. The properties of measurable space (size, distance from other objects, shape, etc.) are understood bit by bit. At the beginning for a child spaces are 'topological', objects are seen together as a loose group or a general mass, not exactly placed or outlined. Then relative position is understood and objects are seen as left/right, before/behind. Perspective, or allowance for distance, appears in drawings at age nine; and finally between ten and twelve, proportional differences are made in reduced-scale pictures of scenes.

Now it is the exact age-placement of these steps which has drawn the most criticism, especially since Piaget's samples were often, though not always, small. It is not surprising that extensive research like Lovell's (20) have often shown when the tests were tried on other and larger samples of children, that failure at certain years was not nearly so widespread as Piaget claimed in accordance with the sequence. Also, by Piaget's own argument that thought-structure grows from experience, cultural background must make a difference as indeed it has been found to do by many experimenters. Children could be at the concrete operational stage with some material and not able to use the same concept in other, less familiar situations. These empiric variations are hard to reconcile with the idea of a genetic sequence, although Piaget and his collaborators answer this criticism by saying that being able to generalize from one discovery to similar discoveries is itself a stage in the emergence of the idea.

What is of great value about Piaget's evidence in general is that it draws attention to the kind of thinking of which primary school children are capable and, more important, to the uselessness of abstract verbalization as a teaching method. Just as infant school children depend upon active experience to develop the first ideas of number, for instance, so children between eight and eleven depend upon it to evolve the later forms of mathematical and scientific concepts appropriate to their thinking level. Furthermore if regard is paid to their natural mode of learning, they may turn out to be more capable of thinking clearly than used to be believed and will pass on readily to the next stage where abstract ideas do have meaning for them.

This final stage begins to function at about eleven. Piaget calls it the stage of propositional thinking or *formal operations*. The difference between these and concrete operations is that they are forms of thought, not solutions to particular problems. All logical solutions are consistent with other knowledge the thinker has, hence all *operations* fit into a system. That is why, for example, to understand numbers a child must allow for the several aspects of number, such as classification and seriation by equal differences, and an answer he gets to a concrete number problem must be consistent with this system. But a *formal* operation manipulates not facts as perceived but the possibilities of various relationships between these observed facts, and rejects all solutions except what fits the structure of logic itself.

In examining possibilities therefore, adolescents must also become capable of combining every possibility with every other possibility and deducing the hypothetical results (this kind of systematic attack Piaget calls a *schema*) and also of envisaging proportional variation, such as is involved in understanding the differential calculus. The best known illustration of a feat that needs a combinatorial schema as the strategy of attack is the 'five liquids' problem, in which adolescents are to work out which three out of five colourless liquids will blend to form a colour, the fourth (unknown) being a neutralizer and the fifth (unknown) having no effect. The general upshot of all this is that an adolescent can do formal mathematics and think logically. It does not, of course, mean that he can think about logical thought structures; that is something else again, as the student struggling through the present topic must have decided some time ago!

One reason why Piaget is so prominent a figure is that few psychologists have attempted a thoroughgoing attack on the nature of human thought processes, let alone launched a theory about their developmental history from birth to adolescence. But we must not identify the sheer bulk of his output with its scope. In fact the aspect of mental development Piaget analyses is quite limited; the development of certain kinds of concept, mathematical, scientific, and technological. This may well be a good *index* of general intelligence but it leaves out large areas of cognitive experience, some very important. Language itself Piaget studied largely as a means of getting at how and what children were thinking and less as an important developmental field in its own right. Others have perhaps less general significance than language, but matter for creative and productive thinking, since they contain emotional and temperamental factors, which brings us back to individual differences and a final comment on Piaget's educational ideas.

Logical reasoning is a specialized activity and rather rare. Its social and psychological importance is less, upon the whole, than its intellectual importance. Many human beings have no occasion to engage in advanced mathematical and scientific hypotheses. Many quite satisfactory pupils do not reach this level. Whether more of them will do so because of better adapted educational methods remains to be seen. Primary school mathematics and science are growing subjects at the present moment; it is not psychologically impossible, as we have seen, that mental development itself will be stimulated and that more efficient thinking strategies can be induced in children of all levels of ability. There is nothing in Piaget's developmental theory inconsistent with this possibility.

5 A summing up

In this respect Piaget's work fits in very well with present-day views about mental growth and the educational practice which would follow. With no fixed unit of measurement we are not in a position to plot the age-trend of mental development, but do not in any case regard this as genetically pre-determined. There are many media, language and communication being perhaps the most obvious, through which the environment must affect it. Attempts to assess these social and environmental factors are generally in the form of home and school surveys, though other evidence can be found. For instance adults whose education continues, or who are in more stimulating occupations can increase their scores on formal tests beyond the age, when, on an average, scores reach their maximum and begin to decline.

Hereditary factors of course must play their part, particularly in the maturation of nerve tissue, and there is probably an age-tied genetic sequence of maturation which regulates the acquisition of neural functions. Innate individual differences of brain structure and development and therefore of brain function may well exist. On the other hand observations like those of D. O. Hebb support the kind of evidence that is referred to in the last paragraph, and suggest that efficiency in brain functioning is partly the result of environmental stimulation, particularly as it affects the so-called association areas in the cerebral cortex. Obviously there must be some kind of physiological basis for the gradual evolution of adult thinking abilities and in this process there may well be critical growth periods when stimulation is important for laying down the capacity for future learning.

Language appears to play a crucial role in the development of these thinking structures by facilitating the internalization of experience and activity. This has been emphasized by two well-known Russian psychologists, A. R. Luria and L. S. Vygotsky, whose work usefully supplements the conclusions of Jean Piaget. Piaget's theory of development can be called a genetic one in having for its central idea an age-tied sequence of stages in the evolution of thinking ability, with a point for transition from one kind of thinking to another. This has been upon the whole confirmed by further research with Piaget's test material upon larger samples of children than he usually observed. But much variability has been found, which is not surprising since by his own argument thinking mechanisms are created by inter-actions with the world of objects and their inter-relationships, whose mental counterparts are called operations which form an internally consistent system of explanations for events. Two, alternatively three, stages of thinking are pre-operational in the sense of lacking this consistency and equilibrium; at about the age of seven children become capable of logical understanding though not simultaneously in all areas of experience and it is during the stage of concrete operations that each area in turn comes under the control of operational thinking; from this emerges the stage of *formal operations* or hypothetical thinking consistent with abstract logic. It is through active experience that the interlocked scheme of thinking operations comes into exist-ence. This is the most important educational corollary of Piaget's theory.

Unlike Vygotsky, whose psychological views are similar but who sees social instruction and guidance as essential to the formation of a child's thinking mechanisms, Piaget has chosen to concentrate on the time-sequence in which they appear rather than on the role played by learning. Thus his theory of cognitive development cannot be called comprehensive, especially since he limits his survey to the kind of reasoning for which logical calculations offer, as he believes, an explanatory model. Some important aspects of cognitive experience are omitted, including language growth and other mental activities which have motivational elements in them. One of these is the impulse to learn which Piaget does not directly consider, but takes for granted as a part of the *assimilation-accommodation* process. Another is the effect of present (or past) learning upon future activity. Both are subject to great individual variation. The impulse to learn is selective not indiscriminate; a child may be intelligent or slow but will absorb into his personality only what seems worth his individual while.

Individuality itself grows out of learned experience and so creates an even greater degree of selectivity.

It has been hinted in this chapter that learning has greatly widened its psychological meaning. We do not now think of it as the process by which an individual acquires certain adjuncts to his personality like a vocabulary or table-manners, the knack of driving a moped or working a computer. These are special forms of learning which are included in the idea of it as the whole history of an individual's interaction with his environment, in the course of which he interprets and manipulates it and is at the same time changed himself by adjusting his strategies of attack and in a sense his own wishes. The individual human being and his environment will be the topic for the next section of this book.

REFERENCES

(1) Vernon, P. E. and Parry, J. B., *Personnel Selection in the British Forces*, U.L.P., 1949.
(2) Vernon, P. E., 'Recent Investigations of Intelligence and its Measurement', *Eugenics Review*, 43, 1951.
(3) Central Advisory Council for Education, *Children and their Primary Schools*, Vol. 1, H.M.S.O., 1967.
(4) Douglas, J. W. B., *The Home and the School*, McGibbon & Kee, 1964.
(5) Bernstein, B., *British Journal of Sociology*, 9, 1958 and 11, 1960.
(6) Luria, A. R. and Yudovich, F. G., *Speech and the Development of Mental Processes in the Child*, Staples, 1959.
(7) Vygotsky, L. S., *Thought and Language*, M.I.T. Press and Wiley, London, 1962.
(8) Hudson, Liam, *Contrary Imaginations*, Methuen, 1966.
(9) Hebb, D. O., *The Organization of Behaviour*, Chapman and Hall, 1949.
(10) Grey Walter, W., *The Living Brain*, Duckworth, 1953.
(11) Hill, Winfred, *Learning, a Survey of Psychological Interpretations*, Chandler, San Francisco, 1963.
(12) Piaget, Jean, *Logic and Psychology*, Manchester University Press, 1953.
(13) Thomson, Robert, *The Psychology of Thinking*, Pelican Books, 1959.
(14) Peel, E. A., *The Pupil's Thinking*, Oldbourne, 1960.
(15) Piaget, Jean, *The Language and Thought of the Child*, 1926; *Judgement and Reasoning in the Child*, 1928; *The Child's Conception of the World*, 1929; *The Child's Conception of Physical Causality*, 1930; *The Moral Judgement of the Child*, 1932. Kegan Paul, London.
(16) *Discussions on Child Development*, Vols. 1–4, ed. Tanner & Inhelder, Tavistock, 1956–1960.

(17) *First Years in School*, Univ. London Inst. of Education, Evans Bros., 1960.

(18) Piaget, Jean, *Le Développement des Quantités chez l'Enfant*, Paris, 1941; *Le Développement de la Notion du Temps chez l'Enfant*, Paris, 1946; *La Geométrie Spontanée chez l'Enfant*, Paris, 1948; *The Child's Conception of Number*, London, Routledge & Kegan Paul, 1952; *The Child's Conception of Space*, London, Routledge & Kegan Paul, 1956.

(19) Piaget, Jean, (a) *The Psychology of Intelligence*, 1950; (b) *The Child's Con-Construction of Reality*, 1955; (c) *The Growth of Logical Thinking*, 1958. Routledge & Kegan Paul.

(20) Lovell, K., *The Growth of Basic Mathematical and Scientific Concepts in Children*, U.L.P., 1961.

PART THREE

Individual and Environment

I

Living Behaviour

1 *The problem of individuality*

When psychological methods are applied to the behaviour of individual human beings, the problem is usually how to explain it and not simply to record and describe. For example, at any moment, what accounts for the selectivity of an individual's sensory intake? Not only will his version of the present environment be remarkably unlike the sum-total of the physical features presented to his eyes and ears but it will be different from the version of someone else who happens to be in the same room at the same moment. His *life-space* (to use Kurt Lewin's term for an individual environment) and the reactions he makes to it will be the unique result of his particular equipment, mental and bodily, and his history so far.

A teacher, even a hardened campaigner, might be taken aback by the present composition of a pupil's life-space. Elizabeth, a model pupil, has narrowed her visual and auditory field down to the diagram on the blackboard and the words of explanation; and her motivational one to understanding it just ahead of everyone else, and so earning that little conspiratorial half-smile from the teacher which has so much positive *valence* for her. (Valence is Lewin's word for motivating attractiveness). Meantime the largest object in Christopher's life-space is his memory image of the vintage Rolls-Royce they were dismantling in the garage he passed this morning. We might say that the classroom has nothing for him but negative or avoidance valences, which make him shift his sitting position and draw an audible sigh of frustration. This brings direct awareness of Christopher into the teacher's life-space. There is a sharp auditory stimulus as the pointer raps the desk top on which he has been unawares leaning his elbow, and the composition of Christopher's life-space shifts like a kaleidoscope.

Now the interesting thing about the episode is Christopher's success in switching off the teacher's by no means unobtrusive presence and hearing instead the remembered clink of the mechanic's spanner. Similarly, by what mechanism will he hear his own name called after him in a busy street, louder than at conversation pitch perhaps, but not louder than the clatter of buses and the gabble of other pedestrians? Readers will note that the 'why' of this problem is not nearly so puzzling as the 'how'. Everyone knows that a mother can sleep through a thunderstorm and yet alert at the first whimper from the cot. If we were asked to predict her behaviour, or Christopher's, we could make a good guess. But the filtering or screening of intake which an individual operates is very hard to explain. At what point does it happen, and how?

Another problem is how to explain the varying amount of control an individual has over what he learns and how he subsequently responds to a situation. Someone half-way across an intersection gives a sudden start when the traffic light flashes red. Yet at no time did he set out to make this response a part of his repertory. Nor does it, on this occasion, function usefully, since it momentarily inhibits the useful response of nipping smartly to the other side.

Then, the wish or intention to learn does not always have the effect the learner would like. Although he is in no doubt about the desirability of the goal (promotion, maybe, or just freedom from anxiety) and makes corresponding efforts, his inner self refuses to be won over. The learning remains work in the most dispiriting sense and refuses to stick.

Yet there are times when goal-directed, or extrinsic, motivation leavens the lump, the goal itself ceases to be the direct object and the work becomes its own *raison d'être*. This is the best of all bonuses for effort. Unfortunately we do not know how to make it happen except by practising the starting effort till it becomes a habit-response to sitting down and opening the book. The firing point itself must be the result of a complex of variables such as mood and expectancy—for which psychologists have been obliged to invent the descriptive title of *set* without being able to explain it very well.

How to make learning successful is very nearly the same problem as how to motivate learning, although not quite, since there are kinds of learning in which conscious involvement does not appear to be the important thing. Some psychologists, like Piaget, take motivation for granted as an ordinary condition of behaviour, which of course implies that motivation is not something that can be manipulated to the best advantage. Other psychologists, especially those interested in animal learning, have regarded it as a sort of mechanism for getting behaviour started and have established a state of need or discomfort in their subjects. Relief of discomfort is the complementary mechanism for clinching the new response. This use had the effect of concentrating psychological attention on external rewards and goals. For present-day educational procedures, a more helpful concept of motivation, upon the whole, than either of those is that it is something which grows with the activity and is therefore capable of being modified and adapted to new purposes.

This view.

Arthur Koestler points out (1) that a living creature *attacks* its environment to find out what it is made of and how it can be exploited. Learning is one of the strategies which make this attack more successful. By learning a living creature files away information about its environment in a systematic manner (Pavlov's dogs, as we shall see in due course, rapidly sorted out the signal that mattered from those which meant nothing), selects effective actions from its available repertory, and apparently finds certain experiences worth while and adopts a life-style accordingly. Since no two individuals can have an identical history of interaction with the environment, it follows that behaviour will be organized to an individual pattern in each of its three aspects. These are: the organization of the sensory input and understanding of how the world is ordered; the organization of available responses for dealing with it; and the organization of interests and purposes. There is no agreement about the last, since it can only be inferred from what is observed to happen in perceptual learning and the acquisition of new responses, which will be the topics of the next group of chapters. Naturally something will have to be said about the motivational factors without which these two processes cannot possibly be understood

Flow chart.

We must begin however with something which can be directly observed and goes part of the way towards explaining the nature of behaviour itself, its physiological mechanisms.

2 *Behavioural equipment*

A living creature can employ simple or very complex strategies for dealing with its environment. But even an unenterprising specimen like the sponge can be just as competent at 'answering the end of its being created' as the human subject of Prior's poem from which this quotation is taken. Unlike Jinny the Just it neither loves nor hates; but within the limits of its behavioural equipment it is functioning very well. Human behaviour likewise takes place within set physiological boundaries.

Living activity can be distinguished from non-living activity such as the movement of winds and tides, cosmic radiation, or the electric currents that go through the lattice structure of transistors in a computer. But it does not contradict the ordinary scientific laws of the physical universe and a living creature has many points of contact with the physical continuum in which it is set, and which may be described, depending upon the context, as consisting of matter or energy. Living organisms use this, sometimes by absorbing it, as a plant does light or a human child a lump of sugar, thus altering it to its own particular form of matter or energy. The other kind of use is modification of some structure in the physical context; straw and mud can be worked into bricks for a pyramid, or by a thrush into a nest that fits the niche between two branches.

To turn the energy of the world to its own purposes (like keeping warm enough or moving to somewhere more comfortable or interesting) a living creature must be aware of it and in particular of any changes in its direction or amount. Human beings have several channels by which energy changes can be communicated; many of these we share with other mammals. These are the sense *modalities* and it is convenient to distinguish the different sorts of energy to which they are tuned in. The electro-magnetic radiation which pulsates at certain speeds we perceive through our eyes and call light; other vibration rates too low for us to 'see' we sense through our skin surfaces as warmth. Likewise we can be alerted to the mechanical energy of movements and collisions in two distinct modalities. We can feel it, for instance as a knock on the skin, and an impact further away will jostle the air-molecules between its locality and our eardrums, and we call it such things as a bang or a squeak.

The eye mechanisms may be referred to as *photoreceptors* and the ears as *mechanoreceptors*. For completeness we may call the taste buds on the tongue surface and the odour-sensitive cells on a square centimetre or so of the nose lining, the *chemoreceptors*, since they register the energy of chemical alterations like melting and evaporation. Altogether our receptors or sensory mechanisms are tuned in to changes which demand a corresponding shift in our behavioural energy. To a *continuous* stimulus like a ticking clock we become rapidly adapted so that we can push it to the background and get on to whatever needs our immediate attention now. We shall see later on that quite complex responses can be relegated to this automatic functioning zone, provided they need no further adjustments.

Besides the familiar sense organs for vision, hearing, taste, touch, and smell, there are several other receptors of which ordinary experience does not make us aware. You will find in a textbook of experimental psychology reference to the tiny organ in the inner ear upon which our equilibrium adjustment depends, and to the muscle spindles which are embedded in the muscular tissue and which when compressed give us our sensations of movement as joints are flexed or extended. A modern textbook naturally includes some of the discoveries of chemistry, physics, and the related medical sciences, and the structure and function of our sense organs can be much more minutely analysed than when the first psychological accounts of sensation and perception were written many years ago. But the main puzzle remains much the same as it was. There is no exact correspondence between the physical events on the one hand and our sensory experiences on the other.

For example, each of the tiny taste-buds is particularly responsive to one only of the four elementary tastes. But the 'sweet' buds near the front can be stimulated to much the same sensation by either sugar or saccharin and yet the molecular change is quite different in the two cases. Conversely our colour discriminations cannot be explained away as the result of quantitative averages of the different light-wave frequencies. Yellow is not a primary colour to a physicist but belongs to the same secondary order as lilac, in which we can see the blue and the light red without difficulty, whereas yellow simply does not look like reddish green. It looks like a unique colour sensation in its own right. There is no completely acceptable theory about how we see colours.

Sometimes, then, we distinguish fewer, sometimes more sensations than the physical stimuli would predict and, altogether, far more than the structure of the sense organs can account for, intricate though they are. This is asking readers to take a great deal for granted and they will find better substantiated explanations of the psychological difficulty in textbooks like *Scientific Principles of Psychology*, a useful general account, and *The Human Senses and Perception*, which assumes a fair amount of scientific information (2). A little, however, must be said here about the eye and ear to show how far their structure explains our range of visual and auditory discrimination and what other kinds of explanation are needed.

Neither eye nor ear should be called a single receptor, in the way that a nerve-ending just below the skin surface is a single receptor for pressure, warmth, coolness, or pain. They are aggregates of receptors, some of which appear to be differentially tuned in to a particular frequency of the incoming sound or light waves. They have, besides, an array of accessories for conducting the stimuli and focussing them upon the small sensitive zone where the critical function of any receptor is carried on. This consists of translating the energy of the stimulus into the energy of the impulses which travel along the nerves, and happens in the retina, as most people know, which is part of the lining at the back of the eyeball, and in the third or inmost division of the ear at the tiny so-called organ of Corti, which looks a little like a microscopic set of pipes arranged in a spiral. Being in contact with the sound receptor cells, it sets up in them (although this is a very much simplified description) a series of resonances to the incoming vibrations. Up to this physical point what we are going to 'hear' as 'sound' is a sequence of bumps and jostlings. When some physical body (like a metal rod) is struck, it vibrates like a pendulum but faster, crowding the air molecules immediately around it, which crowd the next concentric ring, and so on. Behind each crowding is a vacuum, and these alternate compressions and rarefactions of air form the crests and troughs of the sound wave. The bigger the vibrating disturbance the loftier the crests and the noisier the sound. But the quicker they succeed each other (the *frequency*) the more high-pitched it is.

The different frequencies appear to affect particular receptor zones and are transmitted to different nerve paths, so the incoming bursts and volleys of the neural impulses are partly sorted out before reaching their destination in the auditory cortex—that area of the brain which deals with signals from the ears. But final identification of noise and tone differences must be a function of the cortex itself.

The first specialization in the *photosensitive* cells of the retina is into the rods and cones (so-called from their shape). The rods need less radiant energy to stimulate them and pick up what light there is. They are the agents for night vision when the cones switch off, and the colours with them. Among the cones there must be some further specialization for differential responsiveness to the colour frequencies.[1] Its nature, however, is not understood either from the retinal structure itself or from psychological evidence like the phenomena of colour—blending, after-images of colours complementary to the original stimulus colour, colour-blindness, and so on.

We can tell apart hundreds and hundreds of colour shades, far more than we have names for. To provide an individual receptor for each

[1] Electromagnetic radiation is measured by the distance between two wave-crests which varies from miles down to trillionths of an inch. We can see about one-seventieth of this total range of frequencies. Within this visible spectrum the shortest waves give rise to sensations of violet-colour and the longest to red.

would make the eye enormous. Similarly, the evidence is against there
being a special *neuron* to flash or fire for every one of the endless fine
discriminations we can make not just in the highly informative
modalities of sight and hearing but in smell, for example, or fingertip
pressure. Many incoming signals from the receptors must use the same
nerve fibre, or channel, as the communication engineers would call it.
It is apparently an identical impulse, yet it signals a different starting
event or stimulus from the last time it was used, and we can identify
it unhesitatingly—greenish-yellow, not golden yellow, the sourness
of lime juice, not vinegar, the initial phoneme of *mine*, not *nine*. How
are we able to read our incoming neural impulses so precisely?

A term that is sometimes used to describe what probably happens
is *coding* (again borrowed from the technology of communication, the
transmission of messages by all sorts of media, including human
languages as well as hardware like a morse transmitter). It means
turning a piece of information into signs or symbols selected in a
certain grouping or order which means just that and nothing else.

Supposing in a mechanism there are three wires carrying a current
which can be on or off in any one independently, then there are no
fewer than seven possibilities and therefore you can 'say' seven distinct
things, one by each arrangement (eight, if *all three off* also means something). For instance, first position *on*, second *off*, third *on* could signify
five, as indeed it does in the binary system of numbering.

Readers will have perhaps recognized an elementary account of how
a computer works. Every age has had its favourite model, or counterpart, of the functioning of the nervous system and the brain in particular; and each has added to our overall understanding on at least one
aspect of its complex behaviour. Not unnaturally ours is the computer;
the 'on-or-off' mechanism fits in very well with present-day neurology
since a neuron is known to fire, or be activated, on the all-or-nothing
principle and so, like our electric wire, can only be either 'switched'
on or 'switched' off.

By the computer principle, then, one exact signal may be said to
be distinguished from all other possible signals (e.g. this is red, not
yellow and it is crimson, not scarlet). It seems likely, too, that the
intensity of a stimulus is also computed, not by the strength of the
nervous impulse, which does not vary in any one nerve fibre, but by
the number of times it occurs per second, strong stimulation—bright
as against dim or louder still from loud—causing the frequency to rise.

For an earlier generation of psychologists the model was a telephone
exchange, the brain's function being thought of as linking up each

incoming message from a sense organ with an outgoing message of instruction to an appropriate muscle or gland which was to effect a response. The functioning unit of this system was seen as consisting of three essential neurons, sensory or ingoing, motor or outgoing, and central or connecting, and was called the sensori-motor arc. Its other name, the reflex arc, indicates the rather limited, push-button concept of behaviour that could be represented by such a model. It fits best one of our repertoire of automatic unlearned responses. In the heyday of *behaviourism* some psychologists would have said that it summarized the only aspects of behaviour which are proper for scientific study, the stimuli that can be experimentally manipulated and the observed responses.

Unfortunately much that is significant in behaviour, and especially in human behaviour, cannot be directly observed at all. The stimuli to a mathematician may be no more than a few scribbles that express an unsolved equation; the 'response' may be no more than writing a single cipher. In between there is a long interval when his overt behaviour consists of staring motionlessly at the paper. Our computer model at least has the advantage of emphasizing the neural activity that is going on, and is useful in another way as well.

It is perhaps natural to think of the brain as 'mirroring' present impressions and 'storing' past impressions like little images of the outside world. But this is only a manner of talking. If one is looking at a kitten playing with a ball of red wool there is no corresponding *picture* in the visual centre of the brain; there is an interplay of neural currents or impulses. If the brain can be said to store anything it is clusters or networks of neurons which have got into the habit of functioning together. This subject was referred to in the chapter on mental development and the points made there need not be repeated.

In connection with sensory signals, however, we must ask ourselves whether we are born with the neural patterns for discrimination already wired up, or whether they are formed by early experience. The *gestalt* psychologists believed that we are able to distinguish broadly between things from the moment we open our eyes upon the world. But needless to say finer trained discriminations like the wine-taster's or the phonetician's are the result of learning, and there can be little doubt of our ability to form new neural assemblies for understanding impressions and organizing complex responses.

It could be the case that as this happens the brain becomes specialized and committed to certain ways of functioning and that as time goes on it becomes more difficult for 'replacements' to be made or brain

damage to be made good by new formations. It may be that certain
higher mental functions have more circumscribed neural pathways
and are more localized than psychologists have believed so far. The
orthodox view was that of Karl Lashley who thought that the cortex,
or 'higher' brain operated as a whole, and that it was the amount of
damage, not its locality that mattered. However, from the evidence
of brain surgeons like Penfield and Roberts there appears to be some
localization of the higher functions. There are definite areas associated
with the production and perception of language symbols and they
are almost always in the dominant one of the two hemispheres.[1] In
most respects the hemispheres are duplicates, but not for speech, and
Eric Lenneberg, a Harvard psychiatrist interested particularly in language development, believes that the speech areas are gradually 'laid
down', so to speak, during the period that hand preference is being
established and one of the two hemispheres is becoming the dominant
one.

This is a difficult subject and if specialization does take place on the
lines suggested by Lenneberg, we are nowhere near understanding
how it happens. It has long been known, however, that certain parts
of the cortex do receive the signals from the specific receptors. There
is a visual area and an auditory area. Touch signals are projected on to
the *sensory* area and messages from the finger-tips get a bigger share
of it than those from, say, the outer surface of the calf. There is also
a *motor* area whose existence has been known for a long time, since
electrical stimulation at a given point of it can produce an involuntary
movement in the part of the muscular system that is projected there.
The distribution again is according to importance, not size. The nimble
tongue, for example, gets as big a spread as the whole of the foot and
lower leg.

Even a sketch description of the central nervous system, as the brain
and spinal cord are usually called, takes up a good deal of space and
only such comments have been made as are relevant to the account of
perception and learning which follows this chapter. A little must be
added about the autonomic system, since it regulates most of the reflex-
type responses which were utilized by Pavlov in his learning experiments.

These are muscular and glandular responses which have to do with
the smooth working of our biological machinery. If there is an increase

---

[1] As many students will know, the cerebrum, or higher brain, is partially
divided into two hemispheres, the left and the right, and one of these is the
leading one.

in the temperature, we perspire; if soluble material gets into our mouths, we salivate. Tiny muscles in the iris of the eye make the pupil expand and contract at changes in light brightness, We do not consciously instigate these, and are unaware of most of them, but it is of course important that they should go on without our conscious supervision, and the special nerve centres or ganglions which regulate them lie outside the spinal cord. Fibres from these ganglions go to the glands and certain other, mostly internal, organs, and these fibres can either activate or inhibit. Organs involved in the peaceful routines of ordinary health, such as digestion, are kept ticking along by fibres of the autonomic system's *parasympathetic* division, while those of the *sympathetic* activate organs concerned with sudden emergency, like the adrenal glands, and at the same time switch off the routine work while the emergency lasts. That is why appetite deserts you if you get upsetting news in the middle of a meal.

Now the reflex responses themselves are not consciously manipulated, but the ganglions of the autonomic system have fibres connecting them with the spinal cord which receives the sensory stimuli that trigger off the responses. Many of these stimuli are not consciously perceived (you need not be aware that the room is getting warm in order to perspire) and the whole behaviour takes place at the automatic level on the reflex-arc pattern. But they *can* be relayed to the conscious centres and they can in the course of experience become associated with situations where intelligent appraisal is fully operative. Before the sympathetic responses go into frantic activity (drying up the mouth, accelerating the heart-beat) danger must first be recognized. The reflex responses, as we shall see, are often an index that learning has taken place.

Our behavioural equipment consists of a system of receptors, a nervous system, and a system of muscles and glands sometimes called *effectors* since they are the means by which our overt or observable responses to the environment are carried out. The function of any receptor is to transform the particular energy of the environmental change to which it is sensitive into the energy of neural impulses. Thus neural activity in the form of these electrochemical impulses appears to be the means by which the nervous system, particularly the cerebrum, carries out its function, which we may identify as the organization of incoming sensory impulses into meaningful signals and the organization of outgoing impulses into effective responses. These responses may be immediate or delayed. The timing and choice of the response are the product of the neural activity that goes on between it and the stimulus. Some of the functioning groups or assemblies of neurons are probably innately determined, but in the course of experience and learning new assemblies must be formed. It is possible that the higher brain becomes to some extent specialized and committed to certain modes of functioning. Some of these may be localized though with a complex of inter-relationships. There is some support for this view from the location of the speech and language centres in the dominant hemisphere.

There is a fixed and presumably innate connection between stimulus and response in the case of the reflex actions regulated by the autonomic nerve centres. Conscious manipulation and timing of these organic responses is not possible. However through learning the stimuli concerned may become associated with situations intelligently perceived. This is an important form of the perceptual and cognitive learning processes which will be the topic of the next two chapters.

REFERENCES

(1) Koestler, Arthur, *The Act of Creation*, Hutchinson, 1964.
(2) Lewis, Donald J., *Scientific Principles of Psychology*, Prentice-Hall, New Jersey, 1963.
(3) Wyburn, G. M., Pickford, R. W. and Hirst, R. J., *The Human Senses and Perception*, Oliver & Boyd, 1964.

Learning: Perceiving and Attending

1 The nature of perceptual learning

In its early days when psychology would have been called the mental science, rather than the behavioural science, psychologists were interested in the general process of *perception* by which we are conscious of, identify, and make sense of incoming signals from eye, ear, and finger-tips. The shortest access to this process was by introspection and personal report. But of course such evidence cannot be checked by a second observer. Some experimental psychologists believe that only overt behaviour can be scientifically studied and that the only data for psychological inferences are the stimuli applied to the organism (these are the independent variables in the experiment) and the responses observed to follow (the dependent variables). Processes which happen in between, like the hard thinking of the mathematician in the last chapter, can be inferred but not quantified. They might be listed as intervening variables, just to complete the account of behaviour which would be given by an extreme *behaviourist* as psychologists concerned only with stimulus-response connections used to be called.

Not many, however, adopt this position. There is some important psychological information which could not possibly be obtained without subjective reports, for example the experience of colour. The electromagnetic radiation is not *coloured* but differentiated by energy quantities and wave lengths. The disturbance in the retina of the eye is of a chemical and electro-chemical nature. The neural impulses are not *coloured*. And so on. One cannot guarantee what experience is going to result from the physical properties of the stimulus energy, and the physiological events in the receptors and nervous system.

Even though the study of perception, and the related process of attention, went out of favour for a time, it has always been accepted that what we observe, or take in, especially at the conscious level, is not identical with the physical events. There has been a recent revival of interest in perception and attention in connection with this same old problem. What filters through to us is only part of the possible stimulation and it gets altered in transit. It is quite a distorted version of the *proximal* stimuli (that get into the receptor itself) but the strange thing is that it is usually much nearer to the real nature of the *distal* objects, the things out there in the environment, which we can locate and identify.

Common observation would see a difference between attention and perception—for example between deliberate eavesdropping and accidental overhearing—but it is difficult to arrive at a useful psychological one, since both terms refer to the same phenomenon, the selective nature of our sensory intake. In experimental practice, when the aim is to identify the conditions which make one sensory event stand out from its background in the first place, and secondly take a certain form or pattern for the individual (like the group of vocal sounds overheard in a crowded room as an articulate remark) this would probably be called a study of perception, for which visual stimuli like pictures or diagrams can conveniently be used, since they are static and give us time for analysing the intake pattern. Since an act of attention implies directing observation towards a result, and therefore has a more obvious beginning and end in time, an attention study might consist in asking someone to listen to a message, or to 'shadow' it as some experimenters call repeating it aloud as it went along. But this is not to say that attention is active whereas perception just happens to us because the stimuli are present. When we perceive we are hard at work, omitting this and including that to suit our present state of expectancy or *set*. Of course we are not directly conscious of all of this activity. Some of it is the now automatic result of a learning or adjustment process we have forgotten all about. Some of it never gets into consciousness at all but must happen at preconscious levels. As in many another case of efficient habit, we may be jolted into noticing it only when it has gone wrong.

Sometimes we make an allowance for distance where it is not justified, like the writer who woke from a nap and thought he saw crawling down a ridge on the other side of the valley, a monstrous white creature which turned out to be a moth on the window pane. But usually it works with perfect reliability. We can cover a tall tree on the other side of the park by holding up one hand—but we do not assume that it has shrunk to fit. On the contrary when our eyes rove over a landscape or an interior we do a good job of seeing things the right size and shape, wherever they are. We usually have to make a special effort even to see that a receding object *looks* smaller and smaller, or else have it presented to us in special experimental conditions which cut out, among other things, the clues offered by the visual context.

This is called the phenomenon of size constancy and was one of the first things that directed attention to the difference between the visual input and our perception of what it implies. It is related to the artist's dodges for representing depth on the flat surface of a picture, because our retinal surface is likewise two-dimensional, with images of objects in vertical and horizontal relationships only. Yet we perceive the distance dimension with just as great a feeling of certainty.

How we do it all is quite puzzling. We may get clues from sensations in the tiny muscles which alter the curvature of the lens to suit near and far objects, so that we associate such and such a sensation with such and such a distance. And the difference in angle of vision between the two eye-images probably indicates depth on the principle of the old-fashioned stereoscope. An infant or young child gradually may learn how far he has to extend his arm to reach something when it *looks* a certain size and so, by active involvement, builds up a notion of an object's constancy. Thus he learns to *see* it, at any distance or angle, as the size and shape he knows it to be. (Readers will remember how Piaget insists on experience as the builder-up of steady concepts in the sensori-motor stage.)

Children who are furnishing their world in this way with reliable properties seem to learn their lesson thoroughly. We are all familiar with the records they keep in the form of *drawings*, not of what things happen to look like from an accidental viewpoint but of what they know them to be. A table has four legs thrusting out one at each corner and is rectangular as one would only see it by looking down from the ceiling! They draw a face in profile with the whole eye it has, not the half-eye that is visible. A house has transparent walls to show all the furniture, since you must not be fooled by its temporary non-appearance. Children tend to abandon the pictorial notebook as they get better at verbal stocktaking but in the pre-school years their drawings are an index of what they have found out. It is significant that the artist's tricks of perspective, which go all the way back again from the known reality to the appearances, have to be specially taught to almost all children.

For obvious reasons not much is known about this long learning, nor about its extent. There is one very striking experiment in which human babies are set to crawl on a glass-topped table with a simulated drop beneath the surface towards one end of it (1). Their avoidance seems to indicate that perception of depth either has an innate factor or is learned very early. Likewise when young primates have been rewarded for selecting the only one of two or three drawings which has three-dimensional effects, they subsequently choose a real solid object rather than a flat two-dimensional one, and readers will often have noticed a baby trying to pick up the picture of something off the page.

Of course we can all find our way about the real world without consciously sizing it up; but this does not mean we could always do this, since things thoroughly learned do become automatic. We cannot, for example, look at a printed word and not read it. But learning to read was once a conscious effort which the early perceptual learning can never have been. For one thing, remembering all the clues and making all the allowances for size and distance would have been quite a feat of logic! There have been several ingenious experiments which try to duplicate early sensory adjustment. For example, as many people know, it is an inverted image of an object that is projected through the pupil on to the retina of the eye, but somehow or other a baby becomes able to see the world right way up. Experimenters have worn inverting lenses and have been able to set objects on their feet again after only a few days' fumbling. But the experimenter knows what he is trying to do, in the same way as any beginner knows what he is trying to do when he first attempts the fine discriminations that will make him a specialist one day. The baby's early perceptual learning cannot be quite the same.

We may call it intuitive learning because of its absence of plan and because of its speed and spontaneity. Children usually find their own way about the chairs and tables, plates, and spoons, and adults seldom draw attention to the shapes and contours. It can be left to the children's own apparently built-in tendency to sort and identify. It is perhaps the case that simple forms and relationships are innately understood, but the educationally important thing is that given ordinary experience a child is certain to learn to organize sensory information, just as later on he can be shown how to perceive differences in letter shapes and weights and measures.

Now, how is the visual intake, for example, organized? Well, instead of coping with the whole medley of coloured surfaces that is the visual array, we collect certain ones into prominences and get rid of the rest as indeterminate background. Something causes a selection of our sensory impressions to gather into a coherent whole that fairly jumps out of the context. It becomes the *figure* of the *gestalt* psychologists (whom we shall come to in a moment) and the rest becomes the *ground*. Why? Why, if we are shown an empty room with one chair in it standing against a wall do we see a chair rather than a wall, although there is far more wall than chair, let alone a whole empty room? The easy answer is that the chair is a familiar and useful object; but readers are assured that the same thing happens with an impersonal array of dots on a page. Even when they cover the surface they seem to form themselves spontaneously into groups.

Sometimes we see things that *are not so*, because to see them this way is easier, neater, makes better sense. It is less clumsy to see a three-dimensional figure in an arrangement of lines because 'seen flat' it has no intelligible pattern and is hard to hold. The cube shape keeps jumping back. In other cases we cannot accept the true sensory information at all. The illusion persists even when actual measurements are taken and the trick is pointed out. Suppose you see a drawing of a receding street with everything in it scaled for perspective except the second lamp-post which had been drawn exactly the same size as the one 'nearest' to you. It will, of course, appear to be much taller but that is not all. Measure the two with a ruler, and *still* you will see it disproportionately tall. More recent curiosities than these traditional illusions are the so-called impossible figures which can be drawn but could not exist! They give an uncomfortable, astigmatic sort of sensation because they are completely upsetting to our perceptual plan of attack (2).

We 'prefer' our illusions because they make better sense, just as some things in the visual array make sense and others recede. The *gestalt* psychologists (so called because they used this German word as a label for the 'figure' object) concluded from numerous experiments in human perception that we tend to the simplest possible answer, the most economical arrangement. Sometimes if a new feature is inserted, it will be economical to change the whole structure or *gestalt* completely. Three dots make a triangle. Add another and you have a diamond shape, not a triangle with an extra dot tacked on. It is not the dot total that matters. It is their relationship, just as a melody in another key is still the same melody though every single note in it has changed.

According to the *gestalt* psychologists we see one pattern rather than another in accordance with certain principles. Some of them are obvious enough, like the the principle of *size* or *area*. The chair is taken in as a figure more readily than the wall because it is smaller and more compassable. Associated with this is the *proximity* principle. If two lines are close together they are more likely to pair off than when they are far asunder. Similarly, something *closed off* from its surroundings has a better chance of being seen as a whole and even of having any missing bits of the outline filled in. Afterwards, it would be quite hard to remember just how much of the outline had been there and how much inferred.

Some of the other principles of configuration are not so obvious. One, for example, proposes a perceptual tendency to see symmetrical rather than irregular arrangement, and to continue a pattern in the direction of its apparent flow. But in any case all these principles are perfectly consistent with learning from experience. It does not take so long to run an eye or our finger tips over a smaller objects as over its larger background. A child is quite likely to encounter the appearance of the chair's blue cushion and the smoothness of its wood all in the same few seconds of exploration and therefore will remember it as a connected whole. But he may have lost the sensations he got at the start of crawling across a big floor by the time he reaches the end and is therefore less likely to remember it as all one floor. But the important thing is that within the limits of experience, he does in fact 'structure' his impressions of the chair into a whole and is quite well able to complete a drawing of it if you show him one with an essential part missing. (This is a well known Binet-type test, by the way.)

The original *gestalt* psychologists were the German philosopher Max Wertheimer and his followers Kohler (whom we shall meet in another context), Koffka, who was mainly responsible for publicizing the principles of organization, and Lewin who developed from *gestalt* psychology his well-known ideas about individual life-spaces. They all eventually lived in the United States where about thirty years ago a great controversy raged between the *gestalt* views about perception, thinking, and learning on the one hand, and on the other the views of the stimulus-response psychologists who took their lead from Pavlov and Thorndike. Nowadays, for practical educational purposes at least, one can work out a version of cognition and learning that makes use both of the *gestalt* ideas of *structuring* and of the Pavlovian ideas of *conditioned responses*. We shall come to Pavlov, Thorndike, and other stimulus-response (or *connectionist*) psychologists presently. Meantime we need only note that gestaltists believed in an innate tendency to impose pattern upon incoming sensory information—which of course implied that it must have a physiological basis—and that the various laws of organization described how the brain mechanisms actually functioned.

Perhaps they were right and some of our understanding of our environment does not need to be learned, but it is more important educationally that we can see new relationships and so make our thought schemas more complete. Piaget was content to take this innate capability for granted. Some of our new *gestalts* we seem to arrive at by the spontaneous learning typical of the pre-school years and of free-chosen activities at any age. But this does not mean we must always acquire our *gestalts* in this way; there are many which we can be taught. A letter-shape for example, is a *gestalt* and readers will be familiar with the devices a teacher uses to help beginners to see the internal structure of these new forms. You will also remember, that having 'seen' it a learner usually finds it impossible *not* to see it and respond appropriately. It has become his *cue* for making the sound sub-vocally, for example, or at a later date in his education for spotting the accusative form of the Latin noun.

We have to set our minds to some *gestalts*. The structure of the Latin declension does not 'come' spontaneously, and we may have to puzzle quite a while before we see which is the missing section of a matrix diagram. Obviously percepts like these contain, besides the immediate sensory input, elements from past knowledge and also present purpose or interest. This brings us to the selectivity of individual attention which was mentioned in the last chapter.

2 Learning and the control of attention

We all know that individuals perceive the same occasion differently, according to personal interest, amount of expertise, and, for children especially, age and experience. There are some things which cannot be missed by any observer. They jump out of their background by their loudness, or brightness, or extreme coldness. But even a moderately strong stimulus can be adapted to if it goes on long enough in the same way, and we are quite good at damping down even a varying background stimulation, although we appear to be better practised in this for auditory changes than for visual ones. Somehow or other we filter out unwanted stimulation, although we cannot tell how. We do not manipulate this peripheral activity directly, but by directing attention to something else. Even the voice pitch changes if unwanted.

Educationally it comes back to the figure-ground process. We channel a child's attention by outlining, emphasizing, and clarifying the *gestalt* and we will succeed best if we keep in mind the size of his intake capacity. This means, of course, not the sum-total of the items but the complexity of the total design. Quite a long sentence can be held in attention if it is a sense unit to which every word is necessary. On the other hand quite a short one may have to be re-structured before it can be grasped. For instance you would have to insert extra words to explain a proverb of the *Penny wise, pound foolish* pattern; and re-group with mental parentheses for place-keepers an ambiguous phrase like *The friend of my cousin's wife.* Several examples of this re-structuring are to be found in the appropriate chapter of James M. Thyne's book on the application of learning principles to classroom practice (3).

The so-called *span of apprehension* (a psychological concept that goes back to the days of Galton) is a simple item-count and has a certain limited usefulness as a measure of attention capacity, since it increases steadily with physical growth. It fitted in well with Binet's maturational approach to assessing intelligence and he usually includes a digit-repetition test in the questions for an age-level. But its correlation with general ability falls off after about age ten. This is near the time when, by Piaget's calculations, there begins a new appreciation of logical relationships. In any case, at any age, the items taken in vary with the kind of activity and the amount of patterning that is possible. So while it is important to remember that for most school material a young child's stretch of intake will be shorter than an older child's (the length of sentence he can get through without forgetting the opening words, for example) and very much less than the teacher's, it is not a fixed measure that cannot be extended by intelligent presentation on the teacher's part. The word *aeroplane* for instance can be read as a pattern though it has far more letters in it than other words in the primer. There are plenty of other examples that could be cited from constructive number play, or indeed from almost any activity except the routine drills like spelling, where the number of letters that can be memorized per word has some relevance.

An important experiment carried out in 1960 demonstrated that the *potential* span of intake is actually greater than the number of items actually quoted from immediate memory. For a tiny fraction of time we appear to 'hold' all the sensory information in suspension, so to speak, but the instant we quote or use some of it, all the rest decays. This is how our selective attention process acts in order to protect our functioning apparatus from overloading so that it can work effectively (4).

But how much can be effectively handled? We have seen that it is the *pattern* of items that matters, not their total. But can we attend to more than one pattern without relegating most of their contents to the background? Can we really attend to two parallel goings-on, or only to either alternately? Much research has been done on this question.

It is not true, of course, that we can attend only to one thing at a time. Everyone knows that a routine skill like the mechanics of driving a car, can be managed on the periphery of attention, while a series of decisions is taken at the focal point, in this example concerning shifts in the structure of the traffic pattern. But this is not the only way in which two behavioural sequences can be carried along together. Control can be effective so long as there is some *predictability* about the phases of at least one of them. For example the ending of the query *Can you tell me the* ——? is much more predictable than the ending of *Where is the* ——? Even an absent-minded person might find himself answering the first mechanically—and indeed we are all quite good at carrying on commonplace conversations and quietly pursuing our own thoughts at the same time!

But predictability in what comes next obviously depends upon previous experience. Compared with the glib adult a young child is apt to be tongue-tied when meeting a stranger, not from shyness but because taking in the new voice and features is all he can manage. We (and his coaxing mother) will have to wait until the precept fully develops before he can cope with the speech formula. Similarly we get a more coherent impression of a narrative when it has a point that seems to us to follow, logically or psychologically, our expectancy (the point of a joke makes use of the same expectancy but overturns it instead) and we are likely to tidy it up in the re-telling.

Teachers are well aware that time and experience are needed before an activity becomes manageable enough to be carried on along with a parallel intake process. Making allowances for age, knowledge, and individual ability is ordinary good classroom procedure, and is the way we hope to create in children the *habit* of giving attention at choice instead of having the content of the input largely thrust upon them by environmental shifts, as happened when they were younger. Like other habits it is adopted by the learner because the behaviour it consists of has been *reinforced*. He has, that is, discovered its worthwhileness.

It is not nearly so helpful to educators as it sounds to say that attention is regulated by 'interest'. We are off on a false track if we hope to sort topics and activities into the interesting and the not interesting. For children, as for adults, prolonged interest is not something tacked on by an external inducement, nor by novelty. It is activated by a goal or purpose. The interest value of the most spectacular toy wears off very rapidly unless it can become a medium for discovery, or a property in dramatic play, to mention only two kinds of involvement that can be quite strenuous. But strenuous effort can get all the motivation it needs by its relationship with a goal—provided the worker can see this relationship—and quite young children can sustain effort towards some end; the age-difference is in their time-span, not motivation. A young child needs shorter-term objectives to keep him happy and attentive. At first he is dependent upon the teacher's prompt if he *Worksheets?* is to practise the behaviour of directing his attention, instead of letting it be accidentally caught; but when he experiences the goal-motivated interest that results from making this response, then he will adopt it as a habit. This habit will generalize at first to other forms of activity, and then from situations structured by the teacher to situations and projects structured by himself.

Part of a teacher's skill is to make sure that the experience of planned attention does turn out to be satisfying, as it will if the goal and the length of effort are chosen with regard to age, ability, and temperament differences between children. Slow-learning children are going to be slower to pick up the habit and the readiness to transfer it to other kinds of work. They have not found the experience of voluntary involvement particularly rewarding. Therefore they need shorter-term projects, like younger children, and the point and purpose of any effort must be kept well to the fore.

Perception, with the related process of attention, is that function of our cognitive activity which regulates our intake from the sensory environment. First, the sensory intake is *selected* from the whole array of available stimuli and second the impressions received are *adjusted* and do not correspond exactly to the physical and physiological occurrences. They are often nearer to the 'true nature' of the object or event than to the so-called proximal stimulus in the sense organ. The commonest case is that of size-constancy. Illusions, which misrepresent the sensory facts may actually fit in better with our tendency to structure the world in an orderly and economical way.

Perception is regulated by an individual's present expectancy, purpose, or *set* and by his past history of learning and conditioning. But much of our selectivity is not consciously willed and most of the adjustments we make for immediate appearance are automatic. This makes it difficult to establish how perceptual learning has taken place and how much of it was actually necessary in a period of life we have all forgotten.

In any case the speed and apparent spontaneousness of a young child's perceptual learning are strong evidence for an innate *predisposition* to structure experiences. The *gestalt* psychologists believed that they had experimental evidence of natural principles of organization. However although perceptual learning in the pre-school years is spontaneous, later *gestalts* often require a deliberate effort of attention by the learner and of explanation by the teacher. To make new patterns stand out it is often necessary to re-structure the material. The *span* of a child's intake is not an aggregate of items but the complexity of design he can perceive. It is possible to carry on more than one complex activity at a time when the relationships between the items of at least one series are highly predictable. Learning and individual ability are significant factors in this.

Children who are developing their scope of attention are at the same time acquiring habits of volitional attention to goal-directed activities. It has been suggested that these habits are acquired by the normal learning condition of reinforcement and that the *satisfier* in this case is the interest which is activated by goal-direction.

Perception and attention are called the *cognitive* processes but they are an *active* coming to grips with the environment in themselves and lead to the further activity of selecting responses to the situation as perceived. Not every response is a conscious strategy, in the sense that an artist gauges the pressure and direction of his brush-stroke by the image of the tree he means to paint, or a chemistry student decides the moment for altering the conditions in an experiment. When a hungry boy's mouth waters at the smell of cooking it is not a conscious strategy. But the *timing* of this reaction is significant, as we shall see in a moment.

REFERENCES

(1) Gibson, E. J. and Walk, R. D., 'The visual cliff', *Scientific American*, April 1960.
(2) Penrose, L. S. and Penrose, R., 'Impossible Objects', *British Journal of Psychology*, Vol. 49, 31.
(3) Thyne, James M., *The Psychology of Learning and Techniques of Teaching*, University of London Press, 1966.
(4) Sperling, George, 'Information available in brief visual presentations', *Psychological Monographs*, 74, no. 11.

3

Learning: The Perceptual Organization of Responses

1 Pavlovian conditioning

It was once said that a living organism can do only two kinds of thing. Responses to the environment may either be mechanical (for instance when the speech muscles move) or they may be chemical or electro-chemical (for instance when digestive juices are secreted or the photosensitive substances inside the eye are altered by radiation from a light source). Overt behaviour consists of a limited number of physiological occurrences; some can be observed and others can be measured and quantified by instruments like the misnamed lie-detector. In any two healthy individuals the inventory of possible responses would come out much the same. The *variability* of behaviour, what makes it plastic and adaptable, is how and when these responses occur. Firstly, they can be grouped into endless combinations. A pianist runs through an air on the keyboard for the very first time and every single finger flexion has been made before but never in this identical order. Secondly, they are not made at random. They are *timed* to signals from the environment and though the scope of the response is limited, there appears to be no limit to the addition of new signals for making it. No two individuals will respond to exactly the same array of signals. All Pavlov's dogs could salivate. Because of different training experience some did so to the sound of a tuning fork and others to an electric bell; because of differences in perceptual discrimination not all learned to distinguish the circle as a 'mouth-watering' shape from the ellipse which was not.

Before we come to these famous experiments, a comment must be made on the difference between conscious and automatic responses. It is quite obvious in ordinary experience but hard to define psychologically. A learned response readily becomes automatic so the difference is not between innate and acquired behaviour. Moreover a judicious behaviour pattern can be no more than a chain of many unconscious sub-units. Our pianist does not consciously dictate the separate flexion of each finger muscle although he does intend the striking of each note in its proper place. Then later, after practice, he ceases to identify the separate note-strikings but still intends the playing of the whole phrase when he lays his hand on the keys. The same response can be conscious in one context or on an earlier occasion, that is unconscious or automatic later. Many psychologists have found it useful to think of a behavioural unit when it is conscious or purposive as *molar* or *whole* behaviour because it cannot be adequately represented by totalling up the (unconscious) sub-units of which it is composed.

The easiest kind of response to classify categorically as automatic is one regulated by the ganglions of the autonomic nervous system. Nearly all our familiar reflexes belong here. A reflex-type response is well suited for scientific observation because it is fixed and occurs with monotonous regularity as often as the stimulus. This means that the experimenter can vary the stimulus and trace its precise effects, which he could not do if the response could vary in itself.

The dependent variable in Pavlov's experiments was, then, one of the autonomic reflexes—secretion from the salivary gland which can be regularly activated by the injection of nutritious material into the mouth. He set out to discover whether any stimulus of quite different quality from this natural, unconditional stimulus can produce mouth-watering in a living and relatively intelligent organism, and if so, in what circumstances. On this one response he carried out investigations extending over many years in the last quarter of the nineteenth century and the first quarter of the present one. He invented the world-famous principle of the *conditioned reflex* and became one of the founders of a whole school of psychology.

Pavlov was a physiologist and his choice of the salivary response was in part accidental. He was in process of investigating digestion in dogs and noticed, as many people had done before him, that a dog's saliva would flow during the familiar preliminaries to the feeding ritual. But unlike other people the scientist was not content to accept it without trying to find out why and how. By arranging suitable apparatus and optimum laboratory conditions he was able to demonstrate certain behavioural changes and the exact conditions for their occurrence.

An animal which responds automatically or unconditionally to a normal or natural stimulus will produce the response to a different sort of stimulus altogether, provided this other neutral stimulus occurs often enough in conjunction with the first. Thus Pavlov's dogs, as many students know, produced the mouth-watering response to the sound of a buzzer which had regularly preceded the food-stimulus. In time the response to the buzzer became so firmly established that it would persist even after a number of occasions when the buzzer did not turn out to be followed by food after all. And even when the dog had, so to speak, given it up as a bad job the response to the buzzer might suddenly appear again on a much later occasion. (We should compare the common human experience of going absent-mindedly to a shelf for something which has not been kept there for months.)

Now the point is that any neutral stimulus would have done. There is absolutely nothing mouth-watering about the sound of a buzzer or the click of a metronome. It becomes a stimulus to mouth-watering only on certain conditions and is therefore called a conditioned or (better) a *conditional stimulus*, conditional upon repeated association with the natural trigger. Conditional too, upon something else. To become effective it should not just be close in time, but should *precede* it. In fact it must fulfil the requirements of a *signal*.

Now the dog obviously did not instruct itself to salivate—any more than a human learner could instruct himself 'Now turn pale' at the sight of familiar handwriting on an envelope. But that is not to say that the signal itself is not consciously perceived. Pavlov's experiments could not prove that it was—nor, of course, disprove it. On the contrary he did find some dogs quicker in the uptake than others, more sensitive to conditioning and able to discriminate between the signal followed by food and other signals which were not. It was *perceptual* problems he set his dog subjects.

This is the aspect of his work which has been followed up by other Russian psychologists interested in learning, notably Vygotsky up to the time of his early death and A. R. Luria, who have both used Pavlovian principles to analyse human performances like language and inner or *covert* behaviour like concept-forming and thinking (which see below). In this field, of special importance are Pavlov's two further discoveries: stimulus generalization and higher-order conditioning.

Subjects trained to respond to one conditional stimulus will show a strong tendency to respond to another stimulus similar in kind— a musical tone higher in pitch than the one used in the experiments— and to respond to it in other related ways as well. Thus a human child will react to the same words of encouragement although spoken by a new person and in quite a different voice. Conditioning is not limited to just one specific bit of training.

To account for our responsiveness to all sorts of objects and events, higher-order conditioning is even more important. A conditioned dog could be conditioned to a *second* stimulus which preceded the buzzer (say a visual one like a coloured card). Some dogs went as far as third-order conditioning, that is at one more remove still from the final outcome of the food powder, but Pavlov did not succeed in taking it any further at the level of dog-intelligence. But it is a very neat account of how human learners, capable of grasping more intricate sets of associations, could acquire sensitiveness to a very large array of response-getting stimuli or signals to action.

Some part of language-acquisition can be explained in this way. Everyone knows that a child will respond to a parent saying 'No, no!' with expressions of anxiety and even crying. The vocal sound itself is not at all damaging or frustrating—but it happened to be the sound he heard just before his mother stopped him from taking something, or perhaps allowed herself some relief for a long morning's exasperation by administering a quick smack! Now, the response to a conditional stimulus need not always be an overt one like crying, or more than just a little fragment of the total response. After all, when we read in a book the words *a savage tiger* we do not leap up and bolt for cover. But there may well be a minute physiological tension of the same kind as we have experienced when menaced in the past by something powerful and hostile; and if hardly even that, then almost certainly reactivation of some of the links in the neural networks in the brain which would be activated by the original experiences.

The above is a much simplified reference to how the effect of language can be partly explained by some type of *sign-theory* like that of Professor Osgood of Illinois University (1). Naturally the associative networks triggered off by a single word-signal would be a great deal too complex to describe, let alone by words strung into abstract statements. Naturally it is a speculative account. Both Vygotsky and Luria are convinced, through research into children's thinking and performances, that words are capable of triggering off a complex of inner reactions because the same word has been associated with many concrete occurrences, and, through higher-order conditioning, with other word-signals to other reactions. Unfortunately, direct access to these crucial inner processes is not experimentally possible, though Osgood, in his chapter on 'Language Behaviour' (2) quotes several Pavlovian-type experiments which show how a response to a concrete stimulus readily becomes conditioned to the word or name for that stimulus.[1]

Pavlov's discoveries greatly influenced American as well as Russian learning psychologists. The most famous of these in the early days was J. B. Watson, a behaviourist. Watson is remembered particularly for an experiment in conditioning an emotional, as opposed to a simple response, in his famous young subject Albert. The appearance of a small animal, formerly rather a favourite of Albert's, was regularly followed by a sudden loud clatter till soon the animal aroused in Albert a general fear reaction of starting and whimpering and a disposition to crawl rapidly away.

Now we have seen that there is a connection between, for example, fright or anger and activity in the 'emergency' division of the autonomic nervous system which accelerates the heart-beat, switches off appetite, brings us out in a chilly perspiration, and so on. Watson satisfied himself that a complex 'experience' like emotion can be interpreted, if necessary, as a network of physiological responses, not psychologically different from the overt responses like running away. One need not, however, accept this *mechanistic* theory in order to understand that a neutral stimulus can indeed become the signal for emotional excitement, if it regularly has occurred before something painful, or alarming, or highly agreeable for that matter.

A strictly Pavlovian experiment uses one of the unlearned automatic responses which are completely under stimulus control. These may be in the autonomic range, or, like the knee-jerk, dealt with at spinal level by the central nervous system. In either case there is no decision to make the response, no consciousness of choosing it from among other possible ways of responding. However, a selected or intentional way of responding can, as was noted in the opening paragraphs of this chapter, start as conscious effort and then, as the invariable way of responding to the stimulus, gradually become fixed to it and virtually reflex in character. Such an acquired response to a stimulus can then be extended to a second stimulus according to the association pattern of Pavlovian conditioning. For example, a child trained to repeat words after a teacher is shown a printed word, hears the teacher saying it aloud, repeats her spoken signal and after repetitions is conditioned

---

[1] Suppose the appearance of a yellow card was followed by a puff of air which caused an eye-blink in the subject of the experiment, while a red-coloured card was not, then subsequently the eye-blink could be elicited by merely reading or hearing the word yellow.

to say the word aloud to the visual stimulus of the print-sign that has preceded the spoken cue.

This is demonstrably a two-stage learning sequence. Before the Pavlovian linkage of print-sign with spoken stimulus, the pupil must formerly have acquired the inclination to respond to the teacher's speech by imitating. Inducing such a voluntary response as this (in a situation where other responses are available, such as pointing to the object whose name has been spoken) is a different form of behavioural control. The response desired by teacher in classroom or experimenter in a psychological laboratory, cannot be summoned by the simple application of a stimulus. Often its spontaneous occurrence must be waited for in the first place, and to control its reappearance means abandoning the Pavlovian experiment in favour of some other method. This is, in fact, what most American learning psychologists have done, as we shall see in the next chapter.

One may, of course, shorten the waiting time before the response turns up by emphasizing features in the situation which might suggest the behaviour in question to your learner. What are being utilized in this case are such things as his perceptual ability, his readiness to try things out for a purpose, his recollection of past successes. These *mediating processes* (as we call the inner activities between presentation of situation and effective action) are not accessible to us in an animal learner, and it is very hard to frame the sort of experiment which will give a clue to what they are like at any level below the primates. To get at the more efficient cognitive processes of thinking and solving problems we need the short-cut of language. Language can be used for two purposes in the investigation of learning processes, firstly for manipulating behaviour much more quickly than by situational control, and secondly for getting more evidence about the inner activity than from the overt, problem-solving response itself, which is often a very meagre index of all that has led up to it.

On the other hand, the true nature of thinking cannot be understood without taking the response into account, as we shall presently see.

2 *Thinking and action*

More is known about conditioned reflexes through psychological experiments than through common observation. We can have quite an assembly of conditioned reactions to our credit in ordinary life, without being able to list them. Although special circumstances might draw our attention to one, we could give only a sketchy account of how it was acquired—nothing like the precise demonstrations in laboratory conditions. But it is the other way round when we come to the sort of behaviour commonly (and psychologically) identified as thinking. Its existence is hard to prove experimentally and only a start has been made in analysing it; but there is plenty of common-sense evidence to satisfy any human observer, and he would rightly resent any attempt to remove his own belief that he makes conscious, planned responses to the demands of the environment as he perceives them to be.

The psychological definition of behaviour must be one that can include human thinking. On the other hand, there is nothing mystical about thinking. It, too, is a form of behaviour with properties in common with other forms. This need not do away with its importance as a behaviour form that is particularly human, above all when it is abstract thinking carried out through language and other symbols for concrete experience. But like other behaviour it must develop and be subject to improvement and change of use through learning.

In conversation, 'thinking' is a word-token that can stand for almost any kind of mental activity. *What are you thinking about?* means remembering. *No, I don't think so* means believing. But asked to define 'real' thinking most people old enough to understand the question would offer much the same kind of instances as a psychologist would. 'Say something in Latin? You can't just *say* something in Latin,' replies thirteen years old witheringly to inquisitive eight. 'You've got to stop and think.' 'Wait a minute till I think this one out. I haven't come across it before.' And so on.

Thinking happens in many situations and thinkers work with different materials; but there is a common pattern in the behaviour. It arises, characteristically, when the situation and response are not obviously linked, as they are, for example, in smoothly polished habit behaviour. Thinking contains the element of novelty or even unique-ness of action. You do not have to understand something more than once. After that first struggle, when you deal with it successfully again, you are not thinking out, you are remembering. This sense of struggle is another marked feature of thinking, quite different from the effortless way stray ideas wander into consciousness.

The amount and duration of effort varies. Sometimes, though the situation is quite novel, the effective response is picked out from the array of possible responses quite unhesitatingly. Conversation qualifies as thinking behaviour in this sense, but the effort to choose the right

So q. A type with one word answers is not thinking it's conditioned reflex.

words is hardly noticeable in comparison with other forms of language behaviour like giving a lecture, writing an essay, or even making a diplomatic reply when someone asks you to admire the new dress which you do not like at all. At the other end of the scale of effort, the effective solution is hammered out only after much searching and discarding.

This brings us to the third main feature of thinking. It is directed or controlled. The search or struggle is for a response to bring about a certain end-state, not just for any sort of reaction that would be appropriate. After all when you are asked for your opinion of the dress you could make a dozen possible replies, none of them positively nonsensical. But your objective is to make one that combines sincerity with kindliness. This tiny example is like all thinking. It is highly motivated.

Does this mean that we think because we must and only when we must? If the obvious, or mechanical response were always effective would we not think at all? In a well-known book called *How we Think* which has had a good deal of influence upon educators ever since its first appearance, Dewey indicates something very like this (3). Thinking arises, he says, because there is something we want to do or to have and the situation frustrates us. Our immediate (perhaps habitual) response comes to grief, so the whole context must be re-appraised and a new way of dealing with it discovered. This new response in turn we will go on being content with until it too breaks down and forces on us the exertion of thinking again. Or, of course, of giving up and running away from the problem—perhaps into fantasy and make-believe.

Now Dewey's pragmatism, as it has been called, was an educational antidote to the old idea of thinking as something that went on and ended 'in the head'. It is an active business, not a passive listening to explanations. Children will get into a habit of thinking if they are given practical things to be done, in the course of which they will meet and overcome problems for themselves. The project method which was popular in schools just before and after the war owed much to the influence of Dewey's theory of active thought. Unfortunately, like many good things it could be misapplied, especially since about this period there was a strong movement in psychology towards explaining all learning, or at least all the exertion that leads to new responses, in terms of discomfort reduction. From this viewpoint activity is the outcome of some form of discomfort or deprivation and when means are found to satisfy it, either the animal sinks back into apathy or mechanically repeats the successful response, without any apparent impulse to vary its behaviour. However, no one observing human children would ever be satisfied with this narrow concept of motivation; their delight in exploring and manipulating is far too useful to be ignored. The whole trend of recent educational policy is to exploit it.

Many experimenters have now satisfied themselves that animals, too, have impulses to explore and be active. It is not surprising that such near-relatives as the monkeys will learn how to open a hatch which gives them a wider view of the world. But even a white rat appears to seek stimulation for its own sake. Readers who want to go more deeply into the experimental evidence will find some references in the second last chapter of Winfred Hill's book on learning (4) and in what Robert Borger and A. E. M. Seaborne have to say about reinforcement and motivation (5).

Provided we do not take *problem* in too narrow a sense and remember that human thinkers will readily involve themselves in problems offering no reward but the satisfaction of solving them, then problem-solving behaviour is a good working definition of thinking, as stated by George Humphrey: 'What happens when an organism, human or animal, meets, recognizes and solves a problem' (6). This implies that a thinker must be intelligent enough to see that something is 'wrong' with what he is doing if he is to go on to pin down the difficulty and find a response to fit.

It was chiefly the *gestalt* psychologists who studied problem-solving behaviour at the animal and human level. They explained solutions as an act of *re-structuring* the situation, seeing it in a fresh light, perhaps with a shift of emphasis on to some small feature that had been overlooked (this was how the Curies finally identified radium). Among the earliest subjects of problem-solving experiments were Wolfgang Kohler's chimpanzees. For experimental economy, the behaviour has to be got going by a specific material reward, and Sultan, his most intelligent subject, was willing to undertake remarkable feats of mental exertion for one inaccessible banana. Kohler set box problems and stick problems, none of which could be solved by direct action. Some intervening action was always necessary—the boxes must be carried from elsewhere to be climbed on, or even stacked one on top of another A short stick must be used to fish a longer stick into the cage which could then be used to reach the banana. The ape must turn his back temporarily on the goal and invent a devious route instead of persisting with ineffectual grabs. He must, that is, *see* a relationship between the final response of getting the banana and intervening responses of getting stick or box; he must also re-think his previous experience of boxes and sticks from *things to throw about and play with* to *tools* for effecting a new purpose.

Kohler believed such *insightful* solutions were new behaviour. Furthermore, the new behaviour structure or pattern could be transplanted to another situation with different materials, since it was a *pattern* that had been seen, not just an accidental arrangement of objects and responses that turned out lucky. Insightful solutions are not the result of blind groping. They are once and for all solutions that burst ready-made upon the scene.

The *gestalt* psychologists were content to take 'insight' as part of the inborn trend towards re-structuring for one's purposes. Productive thinking, according to Wertheimer, did not build up gradually out of past learning but was a new event. His best known example is of how quite young children who knew how to get the area of a rectangle, suddenly saw how to get the area of a parallelogram by re-shaping it into a rectangle.

Norman Maier listed three kinds of 'new' response. The first arose from the sheer variability of behaviour, out of which some responses would be accidentally successful and be adopted as habits. This is 'trial and error' learning. Secondly, the connection between a situation and a response could be seen and made use of in an equivalent situation. This is a form of learning *transfer*. But a really new problem could not be solved by pattern. It was thinking, not learning. Details of his famous experiments with human subjects, the pendulum problem and the hat-rack problem, are to be found in Hilgard's book on learning theories (7) and Robert Thomson's *Psychology of Thinking* (8).

Meantime to summarize: problem-solving behaviour is still a useful definition of thinking, with modifications. Thinking is searching for an effective response that is not automatic nor obvious. It is highly motivated, since thinking is goal-directed and strenuous, but the goal need not be an external reward. Any intelligent response can be called thinking but the degree of effort and the delay in finding it will vary. Finding the response was called by the *gestalt* psychologists an act of insight and they thought of it as new behaviour not to be explained as a build-up of previous learning, as the stimulus-response psychologist wished to explain it. There has been a recent trend towards reconciling these two extreme viewpoints, which has very interesting educational implications. Some of the investigations are now to be considered.

3 Acquiring thinking strategies

Thinking should not be over-simplified but it must conform to the ordinary behavioural rules of learning and development. Competent thinking strategies must have a life-history. We are indebted to J. S. Bruner and his collaborators for this idea of *strategies* which performs much the same service as Havighurst's *developmental tasks*. That is, it summarizes in one phrase a whole approach to the explanation of behaviour. Thinking strategies, or learning strategies (they mean very much the same thing here) refer to the planned attacks upon puzzling new experience which are adopted by a learner out of his own past successes in understanding and organizing his impressions of the environment. He expects to find rule and order and therefore does so more quickly.

It is still a remarkable achievement and in one important form it is peculiar to human beings. Harlow, whose experiments on the problem-solving behaviour of Rhesus monkeys have had a great deal of influence, believes that man possesses no *fundamental* intellectual process that is biologically different, and therefore that animal learning can be taken as a simplified version of human learning. But he makes an exception of language, which is a pretty considerable exception! He admits that words are far more effective stimuli than objects and events for learning experiments because they elicit more competent and far-reaching responses (9).

But this does not mean that human beings need not learn how to manipulate words and other symbols. Sir Frederick Bartlett is very emphatic about this. Thinking he calls a high-level *skill* which like any other skill has its trained experts (10). The bodily skills—crafts and games—consist of practised movements timed to a plan. Thinking manipulates symbols, especially words, instead of concrete things, but it too is timed and directed by a plan. It is acquired and improves through practice. A teenage pupil looks for a systematic attack when asked to learn something. When told that there is none and that the thing must be memorized, item by item, just as it comes, like the genders of nouns in a foreign language, then he feels affronted. But he did not always have the habit of looking for economical rules and generalizations, this mental set or expectancy.

This is in keeping with Piaget's theory. He has occupied himself mostly with the developmental account of the growth of the thinking strategies as activity organizes experience. Other psychologists have been more concerned with the learning side of the story and therefore with the individual differences in the ability to think which result from different opportunities for learning how to set about it. Thinking, like general ability, as we saw in an earlier chapter, is partly a product of environmental stimulation.

The effect of past learning *experience* upon present *competence* to learn is part of the old-established psychological concept of *transfer*, which is a very wide one. In its narrowest sense, that is between related types of tasks or skills, it is sometimes called transfer of training, and readers can no doubt think of many obvious illustrations—between tennis and badminton, between the use of the subjunctive in French and in Latin. Much of this specific transfer can be conveniently accounted for by common elements in the two performances, not in absolute improvement in the learner's own competence. It should be noted, too, that the transfer effect can be a negative or adverse one. If much the same sort of stimulus in the new task calls for a different response, then there will be interference from the impulse to go on making the old response, and this is the more likely if the two tasks are attempted close together. We shall come back to this point in connection with forgetting (see below, page 243).

Specific transfer is very like Pavlovian generalization. Once made responsive to a stimulus a learner becomes alert to the same sort of cues elsewhere. Another kind of transfer that we have come across is recognizing a new situation as equivalent in structure to one we have dealt with successfully before, even though many individual features have been altered (see the reference to Meier on page 214). This is transfer of *rule*, such as we find in applying a mathematical principle to fresh examples. When this happens, we can complete our thinking out of the present problem with far fewer clues, as Bartlett points out in discussing the problem experiments at the beginning of his book (10). On the other hand, equivalence or rule transfer is not an automatic thing. Learners often need guidance if they are going to profit from similarities of this kind, as every teacher knows.

Experiments for measuring the amount of transfer effect between specific task learnings are not really difficult to design. The *control group* is the traditional way and there are plenty of detailed accounts in experimental psychology textbooks. But it is a different matter when we come to the kind of transfer that is implied by an alteration in the learning competence itself, which is why Harlow aroused so much interest by his successful demonstration (11). A typical experiment of his would be to conceal a prize consistently under the odd one out of three objects. This odd one might be a different colour from the other two on one series of trials. Having learned by experience to choose the odd-coloured one, the monkey would be presented with another series where the oddness of the third member took a different form, say of size or shape. In the end it would always choose the odd item right away, even in a form of oddness never before encountered. In its monkey way it was saying to itself something close in *concept* to the child's solving of the verbal problem: 'Which is the different one in this list: apple, potato, pear, plum.'

The monkey was being given a chance to learn that rules do exist that make discovery easier. After training, a monkey could only be wrong once, on his first choice of all. If this happened he would unfailingly choose another, get it right, *and then go on choosing the corresponding item throughout*. Harlow called this expectancy of rule and order a *learning set* although it has passed into psychological lore as 'learning how to learn'. It is regarded as one of doubtless many intermediate changes by which a learner ceases to be at the mercy of chance trial and error and perfects an organized attack upon his environment to achieve his objectives. We are to assume that Kohler's maturer apesubjects already had a learning history of this kind, and that learning experiments in a laboratory show how favourable conditions may hurry up a process which would happen in the ordinary life-situations of the learner, but with longer delays. It is a more promising approach to human education than the idea of insight as something which simply comes about.

In learning to systematize experience we group together things and events which appear to be related. This is another way in which our particular experiences affect our present thinking.

4 Concepts and social transmission

As was pointed out, we do not have to create a child's ability to make his way among the objects and occurrences of his world, let alone his wish to do so. But adults do direct it to the particular features that matter in the society to which they and their children belong. This effect of social transmission, as the Russian psychologists are fond of observing, is most obvious in formal education, but is to be seen in human communication of all kinds, both in and out of school. The *concepts* a growing child collects in his card-index of the world will be those that are thought to be useful in the culture, and for that matter that the culture makes possible at all. In his book *Language, Thought and Reality* Benjamin Lee Whorf (12) goes so far as to suggest that the words available to the speakers of a language regulate the scope of their thinking. The Hopi Indians, who do not have a word meaning time, nor use present, past, or future forms of the verb, may not by this argument understand the passing of time as we do, nor have any concept of time as it applies, for example, to history or geology. Whorf's ideas are speculative, although they have stimulated much research by linguists and psychologists upon the performance of children from different races and linguistic cultures. Yet it is plausible to imagine a very great difference between the intricate number relationships that can be understood through our decimal system of representing numbers and the limited concepts of someone who had to 'think with' Roman numerals. Harder to imagine is how one would in practice think numerically in this way. Once you have 'seen' a visual pattern, you may remember, you cannot *not* see it, and once a concept is in use as a regular thinking token you find it very hard to go back to the clumsy stage of working with concrete examples and roundabout description. Everyone finds this when trying to talk to a young child about an abstract idea like *coincidence* or *sincerity*.

Concept is an old psychological term but often rather vague. It has been thrust to the fore again by the recent surge of interest in Piaget, and teachers and students are only too ready to agree that children's 'time concepts', for example, are not quite like their own. But Piaget's studies of the fundamental thinking process itself do need supplementation to be practically useful. He does not choose to stress the individual case and those special variations that are brought about, for example, by the cultural and family background of a particular pupil and even by the kind of material used. Concepts are built up by specific learning occasions. Naturally some of these happen long before school and out of school without the benefit of adult interference. Most of a pupil's language competence, for example, is not the product of the formal English lesson, and Vygotsky is saying the same thing when he distinguishes between 'spontaneous' and 'scientific' concepts. The first are the result of learning from experience without setting oneself to do so. 'Scientific' concepts mean the formal explanations which tend, upon the whole, to be imposed by adults and which hang together in a system. They are the subject-matter of formal education.

A concept of anything is our past experience of it summed up for future use. We approach no current experience as if we had never come across it before. We either note automatically the 'kind of thing' it is and act accordingly, or we try to place it in *some* category. That's a queer-looking flower.' 'Is it a flower?' Or, perhaps, about a strange character in a traveller's tale: 'Wait! I think he is trying to warn us about something.'

We are often told that the core of a concept is the response implied —what the learner feels the situation calls for. A young child's spontaneous concepts make this clear enough. Ask him what a chair is and ten to one he replies, 'You *sit* on it!' Logical, dictionary definitions come later than psychological ones. They are not how we learn our living concepts but the label we stick on them later. Meaning for children, and adults, too, for that matter, is how they have been actively involved in something.

The easiest kind of concept to trace the history of is the class or category concept—our general idea of the thing in question. This not only makes us able to recognize an example when we next meet it (even an unusual one) but also to think about it in an unspecified general way. Any and every sort of house and no one in particular comes into our idea of 'houseness'. This is house reduced to its absolute essentials, which are sometimes called its *critical attributes*. In the case of a house this need not be the doors, windows, or even walls. Children are quite capable of agreeing that a shell is the snail's little house, although it has none of these.

Going one further we may abstract the critical attribute. In lipstick, ripe tomatoes, and old-style pillar boxes the common attribute is redness, and this justifies lumping them into one class or mathematical set. If we spot the correct critical feature then we will get the thing properly classified as a whatever-it-is. If we do not, then we get it wrong.

This is the kind of concept-attainment which Vygotsky describes at length in his influential study (13). Using an assembly of blocks of different size, shape, height and colour, he would pick out one of them, tell the child that it was a *lag* (or other nonsense name which was printed on the under side) and ask him to pick out the other lags. The child was to work out what the critical attributes of a lag must be by eliminating the irrelevant features as the examiner indicated which of the chosen blocks were 'wrong'. Such a striking attribute as colour, for example, was to be ignored, as the child gradually discovered. Height, on the other hand, counted. Young children based their groups on the irrelevant attributes, even when repeatedly told that a block was 'wrong' that had been chosen for its colour, say. Furthermore, they kept switching the criterion, now going after shape similarities, now distracted by colour, so that their groups were complex in their arrangements and obeyed no tight-knit rule (13).

Vygotsky found age-stages as Piaget did, but unlike Piaget emphasized the part that adult inducement could play in hastening the
attainment of rules and concepts. He was interested in the dynamic
effect of language. If you know there is a word for a 'something' then
you set about finding out what that something is and what the attributes are by which you will be able to spot the examples and discard
others that do not belong. Most of the time, especially after we can
read, we do not make up our own concepts from the foundations.
We do not, that is, collect impressions which appear to belong together
and then look around for a suitable general label. Mostly, our concepts
are conventionalized for us. We are trained to look for certain things
and understand certain relationships by our social environment and
above all by our common language. Thus *sincerity* is a concept which
someone in our religious and moral culture would be expected to
have at least an intellectual idea of, and an older primary school child
would be expected to offer one or two concrete definitions, such as:
'Well, it means when you don't cheat people—pretend about something wrong—say one thing and think another.'

This example reminds us that concepts also have an emotional or
motivational factor, a feeling element as well as a thinking one, as
religious and political names make very clear. The literal meaning of
Shakespeare's *multitudinous seas* is less important than the emotional
and pictorial effect. There is no one *correct* explanation and therefore
this kind of meaning is hard to measure, although C. E. Osgood, who
has already been mentioned in connection with the psychology of
language, has systematized a technique using word-associations.
Obviously it is important for the creative thinking that is to be
discussed in the last section of this chapter. But even our ordinary real-
life decisions are only partly logical. In their *Study of Thinking*, J. S.
Bruner and his collaborators were able to externalize the steps by
which a competent thinker attains a new concept by arguing out what
the 'critical attributes' must be (14). One of the things they found was
that quite different strategies or *learning sets* were used when the
material was thematic and not impersonal. (Thematic is a term for
problems which bring emotional pressures to bear and which generally
concern social relationships.)

Naturally many of our concepts will have special individual properties, the result of our peculiar experiences, and will go on being
modified in the same way. Children who get the benefit of fluent and
informed conversation with parents will develop wider, more flexible
concepts to 'think with'. But there are some concepts which have

fixed meanings and everyone who understands them does so in very much the same way. They are not *special* to a small social group or an individual and understanding them is a once-and-for-all process. So we may call them the *closed* concepts. The *vocabulary* of a language consists largely of open concepts, since the meaning of a word will often be slightly different to different people and can be given a new shade of difference by the context. The word *transport*, for example, has quite a lot of meanings in the modern world which it did not use to have. But the *grammar* of a language, which has to do with the correct word order and parts of the verb, consists of closed concepts.

5 Teaching the mathematical concepts

Probably the largest system of closed concepts which is taught to children consists of the kind Piaget was concerned with—concepts of number and quantity and logical cause and effect relationships. These concepts are the kind we use for problems where we must narrow down the possibilities to the one and only 'correct' solution. Brain-teasers come into this category as well as the mathematical activities of the classroom and it is rather surprising how many human beings like to become involved in them, considering how impersonal they are, and that all the agreeable distractions must be excluded. If your object, for example, is to count up a total of items then you must ignore all their individual properties except the one which admits them to membership of a *set*. Suppose you want to allocate one book, or one piece of chocolate to each child, then you need only consider the correspondence between the number of children and the number of objects. It does not count that one child is hungrier, more intelligent, or more deserving and better-mannered. The logic of sets means excluding other properties and we have seen from the Vygotsky experiments that young children have trouble with this exclusion.

   Modern primary school mathematics teaching is an attempt to meet the double problem of motivation and understanding. Piaget's view is that the need to assimilate experience for one's purposes and to accommodate one's purposes to the facts of reality is a basic human motive. Following this, the way to fulfil both the motivational and intellectual requirement is to get the pupils involved in concrete activity and manipulation. Out of this will grow the mental strategies which make the manipulation of written symbols in formal computations both meaningful and enjoyable. This is the learning theory which supplements Piaget's developmental theory. It admits firstly, that the ability to think out a problem rationally has to be acquired, and secondly, that the enjoyment of problem-solving is partly a learned attitude.

Naturally, it is not all guaranteed by learning. There are individual differences! Many teachers suspect that the old-fashioned notion of a sex difference in mathematical performance and preference may have something in it. In mentioning the social and motivational factors in his book on the growth of mathematical concepts, K. Lovell quotes some research that indicates both personality and sex factors in ability (15). At the secondary school level this may well be due to social-role typing. As for the general intelligence factor, it would be nonsense to deny its importance. But the traditional view that success in arithmetic and mathematics depends on ability may be putting it the wrong way round. Present ability may rather reflect past opportunity to learn how to handle mathematical concepts.

This casts a different light on backwardness in arithmetic and its causes. Educationists do not now so readily accept dullness as a prime cause of backwardness and environmental conditions, like absence and poor home backgrounds as having only secondary effects. Rather, the dullness and the backwardness are thought of as two ways of describing the same cumulative handicap. This means that poor performance in mathematics is a complex of even more factors than was recognized in the past and that it is extremely difficult to measure the degree of backwardness as though it were a single variable. Besides, the mathematical work of the primary school is nowadays a more comprehensive activity than when it contained a large load of memorized number facts and it was comparatively easy to measure performance and diagnose one specific recurrent error.

The present techniques are the result of extending the concrete number work of the infant department into the junior school, and secondly of new learning theories about the most efficient forms of concrete experience. When *gestalt* psychology was at its height *visual patterns* like domino cards were thought to be the way to clarify the number structures. Today, we have manipulation of one kind and another, to get the pupil to think what he is doing, and to think back to how it was before he altered the material. Opinion is divided, however, between the Piaget view that realization comes about in its own good time through ordinary events, and the belief that the natural process can be hastened by designed experience with special material like Dienes's (of which an account is given in Lovell's text) or the now well-established Cuisenaire rods.

We ought to keep in mind Vygotsky's interesting definition of ability as potential rather than an absolute stage reached so far. It is not just what a pupil can do for himself but what he can be induced to do with adult guidance. This is a possibility which Piaget, in accordance with his fixed-stage theory, naturally pays little attention to. At present we are still living in the educational reaction against verbalism, rule-of-thumb methods for getting children to work mechanically with symbols and calculations they cannot possibly understand. Vygotsky himself calls these old tricks of the trade the *pseudo-concepts*, meaning that children can be drilled in getting the right answers without at all knowing why. But this does not mean that real experience of just any kind is effective and that the structure of a lesson can take care of itself.

In this and the preceding section we have been considering a learning process of great social and educational importance. By getting involved in activity a child naturally will condense its many impressions of the world into a limited number of classes of 'things' and 'happenings' which have the same pattern and can be dealt with by the same generalized response. Some of these concepts are formed spontaneously; others a pupil attains to through adult direction.

A class concept groups things together which have the same common property, or critical attributes. The ability to classify is a logical one and children appear to go through certain stages in acquiring it. However, educational opportunities may hasten this natural process. A child exposed to linguistic stimulation will attain the concepts available in his culture far more rapidly than by personal exploration.

Members of the same community will have many concepts in common, but because of individual experience everyone's concepts will have individual elements and will change with further experience. We may call them flexible or open concepts.

Other concepts have fixed meanings and uses and are sometimes called the closed or logical concepts. The largest system of closed concepts taught to children are the mathematical ones. They present a double problem, how to motivate the learning of them and how to make them understood. It is believed at present that out of concrete activities pupils develop both understanding and enjoyment of abstract problem-solving at a later stage. Backwardness in mathematics may result from deprivation of this active experience when it was a developmental need. Conversely well-designed classroom activities almost certainly hasten the development of useful mathematical concepts.

Altogether, thinking can be described as a high-level skill which uses abstract symbols, the meaning of which has been learned through experience, along with the habit of using them in certain ways which Bruner and others call the thinking strategies. There remains to be mentioned a particular kind of active thinking, which does not consist of narrowing down the logical possibilities to the one correct answer. Because there is a movement away from a fixed definition of human ability, this kind of thinking is the subject of much psychological interest and investigation at the present moment.

6 Original thinking

Everyone who writes about it distinguishes logical thinking and creative thinking: on the one hand, things like problem-solving and concept-attainment, and on the other, works of art and scientific inventions. But what is the difference between the two performances? Is a pupil gifted in one unlikely to be gifted in the other? Or are the real stars the lucky ones who are both critical and clear-sighted and copiously productive? Is the difference one of temperament as Liam Hudson (16) believes upon the whole, the logical thinkers being phlegmatic and the creatives being energetic, lively, and aggressive? How do we educate pupils to be inventive and constructive? What motivates the urge to create: to write, to paint, to make a melody, even to do something out of the ordinary and entertaining?

Perhaps education in the past has been directed too much by the need for logical and realistic thinking. If so, we must ask what sort of changes in the home and school environment would encourage an exploring and productive turn of mind in pupils. Liam Hudson, a lively and speculative writer on the question, thinks that family atmosphere is responsible for a child's mental as well as emotional bias; and there may well be a connection between repressive school discipline and unadventurous thinking habits. But these are only general hints. Analysing logical thought is far from easy, but what we do know about it seems to be on the right lines and suggests definite educational techniques. What happens in creative thinking is hardly understood at all; and we do not know what kind of education helps it to develop.

Readers might find useful some of the distinctions made by recent writers. Peter McKellar in his *Imagination and Thinking* (17) compares the associative links in fantasy and day-dreaming (which he calls A-thinking) and the logical links of R-thinking. In the second there is strict conformity to the observed facts or reality; in the former flexibility and freedom from restraint. It ought to be emphasized that neither activity is *wrong*, but a thinker would be well-advised to decide which one is in order for his present purpose. Darting off at a tangent would destroy a reasoned argument, but it could lead to the very flash of intuition that solves an inventor's problem. Indeed, good thinking probably veers between the two extremes of disciplined or reality thinking, which keeps the thought processes in order, and inspirational thinking which ranges about in search of hints and sudden illuminations.

Bartlett distinguishes thinking in closed systems from adventurous thinking (10). The first consists in filling a gap by selecting the missing piece and is controlled by logic. This is the kind of hard mental effort required by the standard intelligence-test questions, like completing a number series. In adventurous thinking there is no 'correct' answer. The thinker is creating a whole new plan or system and the connections are not there waiting for him to understand them. Only when it is all complete can he look back and see them. When a scientist has made his discovery he sees why certain processes have had this result, and when a writer finishes a novel he sees the actions of the characters as inevitable in the unfolding of the story. But as he goes along an adventurous thinker has to choose what to do next out of an array of suggestions provided by himself, with only a general idea of the finished product to guide him. In a more modest way, the struggles of a student to work out what it is he wants to say in an essay are the same sort of thinking behaviour.

Original thinking needs plenty of suggestions and also readiness to take surprising excursions away from the direct line. Teachers have been known to find this turn of mind exasperating in a pupil. Asked to carry out some routine project he will reduce the rest of the group to giggles by his tongue-in-cheek interpretation. A zebra crossing, for example, he will draw as a little zebra holding up the traffic as it minces from kerb to kerb. His initiative may be the delight of the speech and drama mistress and infuriating to the housemaster on speech day who wants nothing from the rank and file but decent and unobtrusive conformity. He can make a shocking job when he is not interested and work night and day when he is. Bone-laziness and prodigiousness of output are both characteristics of the divergent thinker.

Divergent and *convergent* in relation to thinking were popularized, as you may remember from the chapter on intelligence, by J. P.

Guilford, whose address in 1950 to the American Psychological Society is sometimes taken as the starting-point of the present interest in creative as opposed to logical ability. You may also remember from the discussion of Thurstone's work on mental measurement (page 86) that American psychologists have never been happy with the idea of one general mental factor and one single measure of its performance. It was in this tradition that Guilford was working. His model of the structure of intellect is a complicated one and need not be described here. What he meant by divergent thinking is perhaps clear already but it may do no harm to summarize it as copiousness and variety of response whereas convergent is an economical narrowing down. Like other writers Guilford implies that good thinking consists of both.

Measuring ability of the divergent type is a problem since it cannot be done by 'correct-answer' test questions. Open-ended tests (see the chapter on assessment) give the necessary scope but when performances are too varied they cannot be assessed one against the other. There has to be some kind of common basis. In a well-known survey by Getzels and Jackson (18) the creativity tests used the sort of structuring devices which allowed the thinking to stretch. For instance subjects were asked for as many uses for certain commonplace objects as they cared, or were able, to think of, for verbal associations for different meanings of the same word (this was to get at the tendency to playfulness and joking which characterizes the high creative) and for a sad, a moral, and an entertaining finish to the same fable. Getzels and Jackson wished to show that creativity and traditional intelligence were partially independent and therefore made a point of distinguishing the group of high creativity rating and lower I.Q., from the control group where the reverse was the case. On the other hand, the minimum intelligence score in both groups was a high one by ordinary standards; the inference was that beyond a certain level of measured ability other factors must decide the kind and quality of achievement.

This point is a favourite of Liam Hudson's. Using some of the same tests as Getzels and Jackson he finds that while creative achievement needs an obvious minimum of conventionally measured intelligence, scores that go higher do not guarantee any greater degree of creativeness in themselves. A brilliant artist might be expected (for what it is worth) to have an I.Q. of at least 120—but would not necessarily be any the better for being nearer the 150 mark. Hudson, on the whole, prefers the other possible approach to creativity, which is by temperamental not mental factors. Creativity is an individual quality, better understood by the clinical study than by surveys.

This brings us back to education. Obviously information and training do not create genius in children, or even talent. This does not mean that they will destroy it, but the way they are introduced will probably have some effect upon their mental attitudes. A child who expects pleasure from exerting himself will go on doing it. Motive is essential to creativity from the simplest kind upwards. The spirit of the education matters more than the content.

Children do have one special talent which better informed older people may readily lose, just because they are better informed. Once something has been well understood it can be dealt with habit-fashion. But originality really means a re-thinking, taking a new look at a familiar thing and noticing something special about it which we have been ignoring because it does not 'count' as a critical attribute of the concept. This is what an artist does, or a poet when he puts aside the idea of (say) a cabbage-leaf as an edible vegetable and sees instead that it has beautiful and exotic colouring. It is what we were all able to do as children. Children really look at the environment. They have to, since they do not know enough to take its features for granted.

They often make better audiences for experimental music, just because they have no preconceived standards. They often surprise us by making a vivid comparison which our better knowledge of the real facts prevents us from even seeing. A four-year-old of the writer's acquaintance, watching dark-brown flakes of muddy snow being squirted up by car-wheels, announced that it looked like mince. Which indeed it did, although the adults had pigeon-holed snow and mince so far apart that they needed the child to point out their resemblance. Bringing together widely unlike things is the essence of inventive imagining, both scientific and artistic, and over-systematic educational methods may discourage it.

On the other hand, undisciplined fantasy is not productive. Original thinking is hard thinking with a goal in view. No artist can do without his tool-set of skills and mental habits. Because habit-behaviour can be left to function by itself the thinker is free to tackle artistic decisions and special problems as they occur. Thus a trained ballerina does not worry where her foot should go next but can give her whole attention to the meaning of the dance. A skilled debater could not make the lightning ripostes for which he is famous if he had to stop and think about the grammatical forms of the words. For this reason alone, habit-acquisition should be understood by teachers; but it so happens that it casts some light on the nature of learning itself, as we shall see in the next chapter.

REFERENCES

(1) Dalrymple-Alford, E., 'Psycholinguistics' in *New Horizons in Psychology* (ed. Foss), Penguin Books, 1966.

(2) Osgood, Charles E., *Method and Theory in Experimental Psychology*, Oxford University Press, New York, 1953.

(3) Dewey, John, *How we Think*, Heath and Co., Boston, 1933.

(4) Hill, Winfred F., *Learning*, Chandler Publishing Co., San Francisco, 1963.

(5) Borger, Robert and Seaborne, A. E. M., *The Psychology of Learning*, Penguin Books, 1966.

(6) Humphrey, George, *Thinking*, Methuen, 1951.

(7) Hilgard, Ernest R., *Theories of Learning*, Appleton-Century-Crofts, Inc., New York, 1956.

(8) Thomson, Robert, *The Psychology of Thinking*, Penguin Books, 1959.

(9) Harlow, Harry F., 'Learning to Think' in *Scientific American*, August 1949.

(10) Bartlett, Frederick C., *Thinking*, Allen and Unwin, 1958.

(11) Harlow, Harry F., 'The Formation of Learning Sets', *The Psychological Review*, 1949.

(12) Whorf, B. L., *Language, Thought and Reality*, Cambridge, Mass., Technology Press, 1956.

(13) Vygotsky, L. S., *Thought and Language*, M.I.T. Press, Massachusetts, and John Wiley, New York, 1962.

(14) Bruner, J. S., Goodnow, J., Austin, G. A., *A Study of Thinking*, Wiley, New York, 1956.

(15) Lovell, K., *The Growth of Basic Mathematical and Scientific Concepts in Children*, University of London Press, 1961.

(16) Hudson, Liam, *Contrary Imaginations*, Methuen, 1966.

(17) McKellar, Peter, *Imagination and Thinking*, Cohen and West, 1957.

(18) Getzels, Jacob W. and Jackson, Philip W., *Creativity and Intelligence*, John Wiley and Sons, Inc., New York, 1962.

4

Learning:
The Organization of
Responses by Reinforcement

1 The connectionist explanation of learning

We must begin with a short account of an experimental tradition which has greatly influenced psychology, particularly in the United States, throughout the whole of the present century. Stimulus-response, or connectionist psychology is the most consistent attempt at a true science of behaviour. From a survey of the atmospheric conditions meteorologists aim at predicting weather effects. Similarly from an analysis of the variables in a situation in which a living creature finds itself, including the internal stimulation from its own organic state, a psychologist aims at predicting its behavioural responses and at expressing them quantitatively. A systematic connectionist psychology will derive formulas, equations, and mathematical theorems from the experimental results, and use very abstract hypotheses about the aspects of behaviour not directly observable. Any explanation worth giving of a system like C. L. Hull's or K. W. Spence's could only be done at considerable length and would take up more space in this textbook than is really justified by its present educational importance.

For scientific exactness, the behaviour units studied by such methods must be exceedingly small and restricted by special conditions which allow the experimenter to identify all the variables and note the effects of changing any one of them. In technical terms we may call the behaviour *molecular* rather than *molar* which means that the results of experiments cannot be immediately used in a practical, real-life situation like a school lesson, into which a great many other variables must enter that have not been reckoned in the experimenter's conclusions. Perhaps general hints and comparisons might be drawn, but that removes all the scientific accuracy of the behavioural laws that have been based on the experiment itself. At the moment, a learning theory like Spence's is pure psychology, not applied psychology. Spence himself believes that by his methods it will be a long time before there is a complete scientific account of learning and that meantime little direct guidance can come from the psychological laboratory to the classroom. A comment on his viewpoint will be found in Morris L. Bigge's book which relates the various learning theories to the teacher's requirements (1).

Other learning psychologists have, however, extended their theories to cover learning in all sorts of ordinary educational and social situations. E. L. Thorndike, who may be called the founding father of connectionism, was an enthusiastic educationist and applied his *drill and habit* theories to educational subject-matter of all kinds, from vocabulary to arithmetical tables. E. R. Guthrie would have liked to see all learning explained in terms of one simple principle—that the response you make to a situation is the one you are likeliest to make when that situation crops up again. But the best-known practical successes of his methods are in the comparatively limited zone of habit-breaking. Psychologists, even in the connectionist tradition, are beginning to give up the search for a single, all-embracing explanatory formula and to look instead for specific educational methods which can be experimentally shown to work. This has been, with certain exceptions, the position adopted by B. F. Skinner, who is famous for the techniques of programmed instruction which he derived straight from his experimental methods for controlling the responses of pigeons. Programming comes nearest to being an educational application of a learning theory, but its success depends on other considerations as well. Meantime, we should have simply no idea where to start in breaking down a complex activity like a school lesson into minute stimulus-response variables; until this can be done we do not know how far human learning follows the patterns shown in the experimental laboratory.

We call this kind of psychology connectionist because it studies how connections are forged between stimuli—the environmental features and events—and responses by the organism. Learning is the establishing of this connection so that in due course when the stimulus is applied this is how the organism will respond to it. Learning is a behavioural change, because to start with the organism did not respond in this way. The response has become connected to the stimulus or situation by some factor or condition in the learner's experience. But what the factor is, what establishes the connection, is not easily settled,

There is disagreement about it even among the connectionist theorists themselves.

Pavlov, you remember, wanted to show how perceptual responsiveness to a new *stimulus* could be built up, and used the reflex reaction simply as an indicator that this had, in fact, happened. In the Thorndike type of experiment the object was to induce the animal to pitch upon one particular *response* out of a large array of possible responses which it could make to the situation, and, in so inducing it, to discover what the crucial conditions of inducement were.

Thorndike's belief was that the response was eventually selected, or adopted, by the animal because of its discovery of its worthwhileness. Not that Thorndike himself would have allowed the notion of selection, or discovery, in any literal sense in relation to an animal's 'learning'. For him, it was all blind and random activity in the course of which, sooner or later, an effective response was bound to occur. A cat in a cage with a spring-catch will, provided it is active and hungry, be bound to hit the spring eventually by accident, get out and eat the fish that was just beyond its reach. The effective action comes sooner and sooner on subsequent experiments and at last the cat reacts at once to being in the cage by releasing the catch. The connection between response and situation has been forged. It has been *reinforced* whereas connections between the situation and all the other movements made by the cat have not been reinforced. The reinforcing agent, or condition, is the reward of getting out and/or eating.

Thorndike called this reinforcer a *satisfier* and this idea (along with his famous Law of Effect which explicitly states how the satisfier functions by stamping in the effective response) is itself his most satisfactory contribution to our understanding of learning and the motivation of learning in particular. One may find objections to some of his other ideas, especially that all animal learning is blind and at the mercy of chance. But although his early work was done at the very beginning of this century, the psychological idea of reinforcement has steadily gained ground. Thorndike himself gave up the corresponding idea of an annoyer or punisher as an effective teaching device and to this day the psychology of avoidance learning, the learning *not* to do something, is not well understood. The usual conclusion is that when punishment seems to work it is because some alternative behaviour pattern has been found more rewarding. Punishment may stop a response once, but if a substitute response is to be adopted by the child (which after all is what the parent or teacher wants to happen) the same learning principle holds as for the adoption of any habit—

its worthwhileness or effectiveness. In other words, do not punish a child—give him (literally) something better to do.

Later learning theorists like Clark L. Hull and Neal Miller, tried to identify the nature of Thorndike's 'satisfiers'. In Hull's system (which is a highly scientific one) reinforcement is synonymous with the relief of a state of need, discomfort or arousal, such as thirst or fear. This sally into the motivational aspect of learning implies that new activities are only tried out under stress and a learner would rest content with his old habits so long as they remained effective. This leaves the problem of the *variety* of human behaviour still to be accounted for. Miller, in his *Social Learning and Imitation*, explains it as a collection of acquired or secondary appetites or drives. They are drives towards goal-objects which have become accidentally desirable because of their association with the satisfaction of primitive organic needs in the first instance. For him, as for Hull, learning is largely unintentional; behaviour is either random activity under pressure, or rigid habit patterns, the shortest routes to satisfaction. Variations on the basic pattern are caused by the accidents of individual experience and by generalization to similar habits.

Other learning theorists took a broader view even of animal performance. Some, influenced by *gestalt* psychology, believed that an animal has some comprehension of the relationships between the goal and the actions which will lead to it. The connections between the situation and its responses would then be more complex than a habit-chain of single moves which gets to the goal eventually without organized planning. The animal, as well as adopting responses, also learns to recognize *signs* and *signals* pointing to success. This is close to the perceptual associations learned by Pavlov's dogs between buzzer and the approach of food. Recently O. H. Mowrer has emphasized the difference between this *sign-learning*, which is a cognitive or mental event with outward responses only of an involuntary type; and *solution* learning, which consists in narrowing down all possible voluntary movements to the one which turns out effective. Mowrer's point is that one kind of learning is not going to be enough to explain how all new behaviour patterns are acquired.[1]

Turning now to the less theoretical and more practical demonstrations of B. F. Skinner, we find that he is not at all concerned with speculating about what happens 'inside' the organism, but only with

[1] The arguments of the learning theories are complicated, but readers may like to consult an account like Winfred Hill's or the later edition of Hilgard's book, see reference (2) at the end of chapter.

noting the changes in rate of occurrence of what he calls its *operant* responses. By an operant response he means one which makes a change in an organism's environment. The change may be one that reinforces the response, and for Skinner such a reinforcer is simply anything as a consequence of which the rate of occurrence of the response increases. Thus if a pigeon pecks a key and then gets a food pellet, it pecks oftener and faster at this key and less often anywhere else in the experimental box. A reinforcer is a practical method of getting a response to happen.

The next practical question is how to make the reinforcer more 'reinforcing' and Skinner has demonstrated that the pigeon pecks most assiduously if it gets rewarded intermittently and with an irregular number of unproductive pecks between the lucky ones. Also, the pecking goes on longer after rewards have ceased altogether, than it does if *every* peck has been rewarded and then rewards suddenly cease. This carries the educational implication that a behaviour pattern will be most persistent if haphazardly successful than when consistently successful right up to the first failure. If a child gets away with a forbidden gratification just now and then, we ought not to be surprised that our intervening attempts at discouragement have little effect. Skinner, of course, like Thorndike is no believer in punishment as a formative device. Its popularity among teachers is its temporary immediate effectiveness—which he says reinforces the habit of applying it!

The core of Skinner's technique is controlling the behaviour by adjusting the reinforcements. In its most precise form it is known as *shaping*. Suppose you have in mind a complete behaviour pattern you want to induce in your learner, say turning a full circle clock-wise. Then you wait for the first hint of a pivoting to the right and reinforce it. When it has become a regular response, you withhold reinforcement until there is a more decided right-hand movement. As each successive approximation is established, get to work on the reinforcement of the next. By such degrees, pigeons have been brought unawares to turning figure-of-eights, playing ping-pong and other complex behaviours which would have been beyond all likelihood as single acquisitions. This is the model for an instruction programme of the Skinner type. By proceeding from one reinforced step to the next human learners can be brought without any sense of strain to a level of task difficulty that would have been unthinkable as a whole requirement. This, of course, is what good teachers have always done, perhaps intuitively. Skinner has made the process explicit. (It is also a well-tried propaganda technique. People seldom surrender their freedom whole—but may be induced to do so imperceptibly.)

Before we leave this topic it should be pointed out that reinforcement of the connection may take the simpler form of repetition. A
response which has occurred once or twice is more likely to recur,
with or without the learner's intention. This was E. R. Guthrie's
straightforward explanation. Goodness knows, you can find yourself
'practising' the same maddening mistake and teachers who find their
pupils doing this and cannot immediately work in a substitute response,
might be advised to bring the lesson to a halt and give the unwanted
response time to extinguish itself. On the other hand simple repetition
can often work behind our backs, so to speak, and present us with a
useful routine we hardly noticed ourselves acquiring. It is doubtful
if one experience of reward is enough in itself to ensure the retention
of a response without the repetition of it that reward usually ensures.
Skilful teachers try to induce the response several times over and there
are plenty of things to be learned for which this works much better
than entering into long explanations of what is wanted.

We cannot tell whether an animal learner is co-operating in any
way in the process of operant or instrumental conditioning just described (so-called to distinguish it from the Pavlovian type). It looks
as though it were a non-purposeful experience, at least in the rather
artificial laboratory conditions; possibly it may solve its ordinary life-
problems more purposefully. But this we do not know.

2 Human habit-learning

We cannot tell either what proportion of human learning is made
up of this unconscious, unintentional adaptation. Common sense
suggests that there must be a good deal and that, like other learning
forms, it has its own kind of usefulness. There are skills and attitudes
which are better acquired without too much conscious worry by the
learner and in which explanations would defeat their own purpose.
Analysing a complex movement for a beginner will often confuse
him and make him tense; explaining your preferences about how he
should come into the classroom, or where he should throw his muddy
boots, may easily put his back up. In the first case a good teacher will
try to arrange the physical conditions so that some at least of the many
false moves are made unlikely and will reduce tension by providing
expendable practice material so that mistakes are less threatening. In
the second, you might do better by making the unwelcome habit
physically impossible—just long enough for the other way round to

become a matter of course. All mothers, and most teachers of young children, do a little brainwashing of this kind in the interests of sparing nervous wear and tear.

The sensori-motor skills and social adaptation are the two educational areas in which unconscious learning appears most useful. Effective responses are picked out for repetition and others equally possible are discarded as, for example, the French rolled r and the German guttural vanish from an English baby's vocal repertoire, though he can make them very well in the early days of babbling. A child from a demonstrative extraverted family circle will usually adopt overt expressions of affection. The universal human habit of imitating may perhaps have an innate kernel but it need not. It would be almost impossible for it not to become a reinforced and generalized response in any human community, as Neal Miller and his co-author J. C. Dollard have pointed out in a famous book (3). For the very few occasions when doing the same thing as someone else leads to trouble, there are hundreds when it turns out rewarding. Conformity, in fact, is very likely to be reinforced and deviation, upon the whole, tends not to be. Community living depends to a considerable degree upon this tendency; and also upon the tendency for habit-behaviour to go on under its own momentum without conscious supervision.

The amount of conscious guidance which a teacher can give to a beginner in a sensori-motor skill like handwriting or driving a car is of course limited. There is no way of indicating directly what neural mechanisms will produce the wanted effect—the letter shape or the gear-shift—and the learner cannot himself deliberately activate them. He can only let them 'find themselves' by experiment. For very good reason the coach tells the newcomer to keep his eye on the ball. If he keeps his eye on his own wrist or tries to keep a mental eye on his own kinesthetic (muscular) sensations, he will almost certainly miss.

The real teaching agent is the *reinforcer* of success which gradually narrows down or shapes the behaviour until the precise pattern emerges out of the trial-and-error approximations. Such a skilled response is not exactly identical on every repetition. (Neither is a physiological reflex; we do not yawn or sneeze with the same force or the same grimace each time.) But the differences are so small that they can be ignored; there is no need to choose between one version and another. Practically speaking they are all equally effective and hence can be delegated rapidly to the zone of automatic control.

There is only one way in which this invaluable asset can be destroyed. If a skill when it is still at the stage of deliberate effort is practised in two different patterns, then there will always be a conflict between the two impulses and a hesitation, however momentary, while one or the other is chosen. This will mean that the response pattern can never become smooth and automatic, because the essential condition for this is absence of decision and judgement. As was indicated in the early chapters we have only to think of the trouble we would be in if we had to take conscious charge of all our biological reflex mechanisms. It follows that the more of our acquired or learned mechanisms which can be made at least partially automatic, the more of our conscious energy will be released for intelligent activity like problem-solving and inventiveness. A teacher who insists on the routine practising of the drills and skills is not being tyrannical; her aim is to release the pupils from the nuisance of having to think about something which does not deserve judicious attention.

Exactly the same thing applies to the routines of social conformity. Most children will fall into them with a minimum of resentment; indeed the resentment is directed against noncomformists in their own ranks. Luckily for parents and teachers, children like to know exactly where they are and on the whole prefer routine.

A comment should be made about the habit element in hand preference. As most people are aware there was a strong reforming move between the wars against clumsy, old-fashioned methods of dealing with left handers. This reforming zeal was justified to a considerable extent but it has now been somewhat modified in its turn. It was true that many left-handers did suffer in their personalities by a forced change-over; and a relationship could sometimes be traced between such a history and certain speech disturbancies. But it is by no means a simple relationship; and it is now believed that the harm was done not by the special difficulty for the left-hander of acquiring the writing habit. After all, most of us have quite an assembly of 'other hand' habits, like the use of the fork at table. There is no reason why any given habit should be a specific right- or left-hand prerogative, provided it is learned so from the beginning If it can be induced, then, as a new and specific skill, an effort might be made to teach the sinistral right-handed writing.

But it must be done with caution. When a child is required to give up a behaviour pattern that fits naturally into his style of life, and which nobody in his social environment has objected to up till now, then he may very easily get the impression that there is something wrong about him, and become anxious or insecure. Or, if he has a sturdier temperament, he will become hostile and unco-operative in other school activities. In other words, the harm done by the change-over was in *how* it was done. The slightest hint of tyranny and unfairness is damaging to a child's personality growth, and teachers must be on the watch for unhappiness in the left-handers and decide each case individually.

A stammer in a left-hander can be a symptom of emotional reaction to coercion. But there may also be a physiological cause. The development of cerebral dominance (the emergence of a leading hemisphere) is partly maturational and partly brought about by sensori-motor practice. The preferred hand is controlled by the dominant hemisphere and probably in turn affects it reciprocally. Thus interference with the developing pattern of the motor habits may well be interference with the cerebral patterning as well, and it is in the dominant hemisphere that the speech centres are located. But the history of all this is far from clearly understood and particularly it is not known whether the innate or environmental factor is the determining one. A child may be a left-hander because his mother was and he has either inherited the maturational pattern or imitated her habits spontaneously. Or, more simply, she may have carried him in such a way that his left hand was more available for grasping and manipulating. As in most other cases of individual development and learning, there is no single explanation of sinistrality.

In this chapter we have considered the connectionist explanation of how responses are learned and related it to human habit learning. There must be a certain amount of unintentional adaptation in human learning through the same reinforcement mechanisms which control the patterning of animal responses. Reinforcement means the strengthening of the link between a given situation and certain behaviour reactions. It may be in the nature of a satisfier, as demonstrated by Thorndike, Hull, Neal Miller, and Skinner, or simple repetition and practice as emphasized by Guthrie. The areas of human learning to which connectionist theory can be most practically applied are the sensori-motor skills and the social habits, but it is not, of course, a comprehensive explanation of how all learned behaviour comes about. In its present form, its educational usefulness is a limited one.

REFERENCES

(1) Bigge, Morris L., *Learning Theories for Teachers*, Harper & Row, New York and John Weatherhill, Inc., Tokyo, 1964.

(2) Hill, Winfred F., *Learning*, Chandler Publishing Co., San Francisco, 1963; and
   Hilgard, Ernest R., *Theories of Learning*, Appleton-Century-Crofts, Inc., New York, 1956.
(3) Miller, N. E. and Dollard, J. C., *Social Learning and Imitation*, Yale University Press, 1941.

5

Formal Learning

1 Memorizing

Learning, outside a psychological textbook where it has many meanings, for most people means sitting down to memorize a task. This is a peculiarly human activity and usually carried out on verbal material; it is difficult to arrive at hard-and-fast conclusions about it because even more than most human learning it is affected by many variables from past experience. There has always been disagreement about how much should be memorized, how it should be done, and even about whether formal learning is valuable at all.

Undoubtedly most of our remembering and forgetting is spontaneous and motivated by factors beyond our control. Formal learning, the conscious deliberate effort that is, usually implies that this spontaneous motivation cannot be relied upon and artificial devices must be substituted. There have been educators who believed that this is always unfortunate and that all learning should be of the spontaneous, free-activity kind. But our society needs people with special training and information which they would be unlikely to pick up without giving their minds to it; it is more realistic to accept this need for formal instruction and aim at making it as expeditious as possible. This is the objective which modern programming techniques have in common with Ebbinghaus's principles of memorizing which belonged to the very earliest days of experimental psychology.

Ebbinghaus tried to get rid of the special variables which affect human learning on different occasions and for different kinds of subject-matter by using impersonal material. In this way he restricted the factors in a memorizing experiment and was able to isolate the effects upon retention and recall of altering one of them. His methods, therefore, were truly scientific and an account of them from this point of view is given by I. M. Hunter in his book on memory (1). Many of the old-established principles of formal learning go back to Ebbinghaus and to later research done on the same lines.

Naturally they have to be modified for meaningful learning, which is affected by all the other factors like understanding, interest and work-habits. Furthermore, meaningful material is not usually learnt word for word but by rules and patterns (*gestalts* in fact) which can be transferred to other contexts. This means that the memorizing, the retention, and the recall takes a different behavioural form as we shall see.

Remembering always contains these three processes. There is the original experiencing and recording of the item, either spontaneously or deliberately. There is recall either in the form of recognition or reproduction. Between the two there must be a state of retention which holds the material available somehow or other for re-activation by an appropriate stimulus. Obviously retention is unconscious. It is only when we *recall* that we are aware of remembering.

But though unconscious it is not inert. There is activity of a kind between the learning point and the recall point. The material is worked on, often for the better. An overnight problem can be ready-solved when we open our eyes in the morning, as we know. We may re-member better a few days after, than immediately after, learning. This has been called, rather inaccurately, the *reminiscence* effect. The *gestalt* psychologists believed that during the time of unconscious retention the material becomes better organized and more insightful, partly through selective forgetting.

This means that to some extent recollections are always distorted. They are not a photographic record, nor would they be much use to us if they were. It is true that we can easily convince ourselves of some-thing that did not happen. For example, people who have vivid sensory images will often insist in all sincerity that a narrator actually described something which they themselves pictured as they listened to the episode. But it is because we do fit our recollections into the framework of our own experience and understanding of the world that they form useful *concepts*. When we cannot do this, when the material is too unconventional and strange to be assimilated, we are apt to carry away only useless fragments. This was demonstrated by F. C. Bartlett's famous experiments on remembering an anecdote, for an account of which and of the reminiscence effect in general, readers should refer to the appropriate chapters in Hunter's book.

The story which Bartlett's subjects had such trouble in recalling comes from the folk-lore of a very different culture from our own, North American Indian, and embodies a different 'world-picture' with features we do not observe at all or do not emphasize. We therefore tend to have no immediate words for them and to have to describe them in a roundabout way. A familiar idea, on the other hand, can be referred to quickly by its word-label without any clumsy thinking out and choosing of terms. Readers may care to look back to page 218 and the mention of Whorf's theory that we think with the ideas our language has words for, and not very easily otherwise. Certainly, we seem to remember things better when we can name them, or (to use the term of the psycholinguists who study the effects of language upon behaviour) 'code' them in with some established labelling system. We can find a useful model once again in our old friend the computer which you may remember codes its stored facts by means of different combinations of electric pathways and can easily accept more on the same principle.

The storage-potential of new items that we see, listen to, or read about, is increased if we can 'place' or code them. It is only at the time of the overt behaviour, the memorizing and recalling, that the retention process itself can be helped to be actively useful, since it is unconscious. For instance, spacing out the learning time seems to give better long-term results than cramming it all into one or two days. This is almost certainly because the unconscious selection and sorting out gets a chance to operate progressively. *Recalling* between the actual learning sessions accentuates this effect. It has been shown experimentally that when children are regularly tested they remember better at the final grand testing than a group who learned the material with them in the first place but have not been asked to recall it in the interval.

The advantage of distributed over massed practice sessions is one principle that goes back to Ebbinghaus. Of rather more doubtful value is the theory that it is better to learn the material itself as a meaningful whole (a poem or a chapter entire, for example) by reading it through over and over again, than to take it in small snippets. But very little experimental differences in recall has been found between 'part' and 'whole' methods; young pupils especially prefer the sense of getting on which comes with mastering a bit at a time. If teachers are afraid that this will cause a stuck-gramophone-record effect they should use their own discretion about compromise procedures.

But the object of learning anything is not retention; it is appropriate recall. You acquire information or training to respond not at random but to the right stimulus and on the right occasion. Total reproduction may sometimes be what is wanted (though actually this is hardly ever a practical need; learning a part in a play or a speech for formal delivery are almost the only kind of example) but even so it will not be reproduction just anywhere or at any time! It will be in response to a cue. One reason why old-fashioned book-learning has fallen into disfavour lately is that it often appeared to ignore this important condition of effective learning. Information is acquired only because some time it will be wanted and if no such occasion is ever likely, then it is better not to take the trouble. Thus you will want to recall the Latin word *manus* when you are to translate the English word *hand*; and it is much better to practise this particular cue-response connection than to memorize *manus* in a list of fourth-declension nouns.

By the same token the words you want to spell correctly will occur in the context of writing. Visualizing them is a better form of recall than spelling them aloud (which is really only a useful quick check for the teacher's information) and practising them in a written sentence is best of all. You are responding with appropriate writing movements to the imagined cue of the word as you say it to yourself—just as you will when making up a sentence in a letter or an essay.

There is no need to multiply examples. For a helpful account of the appropriateness factor in recall, in both the recognition and reproduction form of response to a cue-stimulus, readers should turn to the chapter entitled 'Teaching for Recall' in Thyne's book on applying learning theories to classroom procedures (2). To sum up we may say that a good deal of 'forgetting' is not failure to retain (since so often the wretched item is recollected afterwards!) but is due to absence of an effective reminder in the context because the response has never been practised in it.

However, some forgetting is the simple loss of learned material— a function of the passing of time and quantitatively measurable by Ebbinghaus's methods. One of the best known findings was the *immediacy* of loss. This happens in ordinary activity. The sensory input begins to decay at once unless noted and used. It is, you remember, the device which prevents overloading of our functioning mechanisms. In the same way as soon as we have memorized something we begin to forget it. The biggest loss is at the start (when obviously there is more to *be* forgotten) and anything that survives it has a chance of lingering on. The only practicable antidote is *overlearning*, revision that is literally immediate, followed by frequent repetitions. This accounts for the apparent indestructibleness of an old skill, not something special in the nature of sensori-motor connections themselves. As soon as we have practised a sensori-motor skill we overlearn it by using it, so reinforcing the responses. We seldom re-activate memorized material so regularly.

Ebbinghaus also showed that learning a large amount at once was uneconomical. Doubling a list of nonsense syllables more than doubled the time it took to memorize. This partly results from the well-known phenomenon called *retroactive inhibition*, now known as the chief culprit in the forgetting process.

We have seen that to function effectively we must jettison much of our sensory intake and use only what fits our present purpose. This is a self-motivating device and largely unconscious. Unfortunately we transfer this natural tendency or habit (it is probably a bit of both) from our spontaneous learning to our formal learning. Thus when we have just learned something and go on immediately to another activity, the first learning is driven out, or blurred, and it appears impossible to prevent it.

There is plenty of experimental evidence of the control- or matched-group type. A group who go on from learning one task to a second task remember it worse than another group who rest in the interval. But we all know how in ordinary study by the end of the third paragraph we have forgotten what the first was about. Again, a crowded school timetable impairs the effectiveness of the individual lessons. Forgetting of this kind seems an essential condition of continuous activity. What can be done?

Luckily it is known that the worst effects of retroactive inhibition come about when the two successive activities are similar but not similar enough to reinforce each other. So they can be avoided. For example a French lesson could be followed by biology or music rather than German or Latin. Alternatively, you could shift your context. If you associate your Latin responses with room 14 and your French responses with room 33 in the new wing, you may start either where you left off even though other new learning has intervened. This is why people whose foreign languages have grown rusty find themselves quite fluent again when they go abroad. Similarly it is better to have a fixed place for working where you can pick up the threads again quite promptly. It is because our various performances are insulated from each other in time and location that we can progress in several over the same period.

Sometimes, of course, new learning reinforces older, and there is positive instead of negative transfer (see page 216 above). Interference occurs when the same stimulus or situation requires a different response; but there is facilitation when a new performance has many stimulus-response units in common with an older one, or even when many of the motor responses have been practised to other stimuli.

A neat way of measuring positive transfer or facilitation is by the difference between the time it takes to re-learn something and the time the original learning took. The interesting thing is that we find this even when the material originally learnt seems to have been completely forgotten. Ebbinghaus demonstrated that there is still a considerable saving at the second learning. There must have been latent retention. We have no way of telling how often this benefits us in ordinary life. But one of the causes of difference in the learning speeds of individuals must be due to transfer effects through latent remembering.

We have seen that the causes of remembering and forgetting which affect our spontaneous learning apply also to our formal learning, and that our techniques for learning and memorizing should make the most economical use of these natural tendencies. Some remembering is selective (substance learning) and sometimes word for word retention is required. Individual differences in learning facility must be partly due to previous learning experience. Economical methods of instruction and allowance for individual learning speeds are the two main objectives in *programming*.

2 *Programmed instruction*

Programming is a word often used nowadays. Applied to a machine it means that it is pre-set to deal with whatever is fed into it—the weekly wash or a string of numbers. In education it means something quite different—a way of arranging and presenting information. A teaching programme may seem, by traditional standards, a little unusual, but it contains much that teachers have always accepted as good procedure and the novelties are extensions of this. The actual showing of the material to the pupil may or may not be done with the help of a gadget or machine. But it will not (except in a very special case to be mentioned later) be a machine programmed in the first sense mentioned. The programming refers to the sequence of items which is aimed at making the intake just as complete and just as quick as the learner's ability allows. Its success depends on the programme writer: his beliefs about the difficulties in the material and how they should be clarified as well as his skill in inventing an order of presentation and words that do this. Naturally the programme must be adjusted to the medium, which can be a printed textbook, or a flat box with a small exposure aperture beneath which is a strip that unrolls as the pupil turns a handle. There are more complicated arrangements, with the programme divided among alternative item sequences which are released by the different answer buttons pushed by the learner. They are often presented in a television-type screen.

In theory a teacher could even present a programme by scribbling each step on the blackboard and having the class either write the answers or chant them in chorus in the old-fashioned way. This would not destroy the teaching effectiveness of the programme's plan and word-ing—the statements, the questions, the examples and the practising of the responses. But it would throw away its two advantages over class presentation—the saving of effort by neater methods of showing the information and the different speeds of working that it allows.

No doubt the best education for any child would be to have a gifted teacher all to himself so that his own questions and his own responses to tasks could control the timing of lessons and the form of presenta-tion. But since this is impossible ways ought to be found of giving mass education more individuality by devices like personal work assignments. Programming is such a device. The pupil literally gets the source of information into his own hands, works through the sequence at his own rate and is more at his ease because if he answers wrong nobody knows but the patient machine, which either lets him go back again through the sequence or directs him on to a special loop sequence by way of his own mistake so as to clear it up.

Programming has been found particularly successful with slow learners. It also seems to ensure longer lasting mastery and may even modify the old educational axiom that the quick memorizers remember best and the slow learners forget quickly. It may well be that if slow learners are allowed to reach full mastery they will retain just as well. In other words, all learners will get there in the end; some will take longer, that is all, and it will be because of differently developed learning competencies for which environment has been partly respon-sible.

This brings us to Skinner's beliefs on the subject. He shares with Norman A. Crowder the credit of founding the programmed instruc-tion movement although their views and techniques are different. Skinner thinks that learning need not seem difficult, or at least difficult for some pupils. Learning, or the adoption of a complete sequence of new responses, should come about by steps so small that each one is managed with no sense of effort. Only at the end in looking back can the extent of difference be seen between the starting behaviour and the final behaviour. Programming for Skinner is the kind of competent,

complete teaching which he does not believe possible by class instruction, since what it implies is mastery by every pupil, slow as well as
quick, and class teaching does not even aim at this, let alone achieve it.

Edging a pupil by a sequence of sub-responses towards the complete
total response is a human adaptation of the shaping process in animal
experiments. But the shaping expedient is different. Animal behaviour
is induced gradually to the final form by an adjusted series of *reinforcers*
which follow the crucial moves. But the human learner can be got at
by verbal instruction *before* the response and in fact the question is
worded in such a way that the learner cannot help getting the next
answer right—unless he is positively not attending.

Each step in a programme (called a *frame* because it is usually enclosed
in an aperture) contains by convention a statement and a question or
request asking the learner to *do* something even if it is only to copy a
word. Skinner believes very strongly in the teaching effectiveness of
doing something, making an *overt* response. He is probably justified,
insofar as practising doing the right thing is always useful, and worth
inducing by almost any device, especially at the start of the learning.
Secondly, he believes that to find oneself right (as the next frame shows
before going on further) is the human substitute for the animal's
reinforcer, the material reward of a food pellet, and equally essential
to learning.

Always to be right can be boring if one can take no credit for it,
especially to bright learners for whom being right is no novelty. This
is another reason why learning by programmes of the Skinner type
makes a more marked difference to the performance of duller children.
As time goes on overt responses may be replaced by *covert* ones and
the very strong hints or prompts may be modified, at least for the
bright learners who can get there without so many safeguards against
mistakes or reassurances that they are successful.

A thoroughgoing Skinner-type programme has its first draft tried
out on a sample of children and is then re-worded according to their
answers, so as to get, in its final form, almost 100 per cent correctness
of response. This is very different from the aim of (say) a standardized
test which is to maximize not minimize the spread of individual
differences in performance. Now it is true that there are routine drills
and skills which not only demand perfect accuracy of reproduction if
they are to be workable (spelling and the arithmetic tables are the
obvious cases) but which are well within the compass of *most* pupils.
Turning all this over to programming could lift a burden off the class
teacher, who cannot possibly have all the time and patience the slow

ones need without penalizing the able. Factual knowledge which does
not allow much variety of interpretation, like the purely chronological
aspect of history, might well be done in this way, and if the pupils can
get it letter perfect, all the better for their sense of competence. Furthermore, Skinner's practical insistence on deciding beforehand exactly
what the final achievement is to be, and then planning the requisite
sub-steps, is useful when applied to a class lesson taught in the ordinary
way. Exercise in programming is good teacher training.

Naturally this kind of instruction does not apply to all learning,
especially not to learning of the exploratory or creative kind. It is a
supplement to, not a substitute for, the communal activity of a classroom. As has been suggested above, many of the features of the rather
rigid Skinnerian model may be modified or dropped to allow for
individual learning patterns. The other programming technique, which
was developed by Crowder, does this by incorporating alternative
frame-sequences in the one programme. Thus one frame contains a
fair amount of information (not a tiny fraction as with Skinner's
method) asks a question about it and offers a choice of three or four
responses (like a multiple-choice test). Having chosen the one he thinks
correct, the learner pushes the corresponding button. This releases
the next frame in the logical sequence, if he is right, and an alternative
corrective sequence if he has judged wrong. These corrective sequences
eventually loop him back on to the main line and are called branches.
Conversely a student who has been consistently right may be jumped
a frame or two.

The wrong responses offered have not just been invented at random
by the programme writer but carefully designed to cover the sort of
misunderstanding learners have been found to need help with—and
can actually learn from. Crowder thinks of this as the sort of inter-
change that actually goes on between student and tutor, the tutor using
the responses, including the mistakes, to frame his next explanation.

One disadvantage, at present unavoidable, is that the learner cannot
be allowed actually to invent his own responses constructively, only
to select from three or four ready-made ones. Even so, the 'works' in
a teaching machine that carries a branching programme must be
intricate, and making up all the permutations of different frame-
sequences is hard work for the programme writer. (*Scrambled* books,
which refer the learners to different pages for their answers, do the
same thing but in a more limited way.) Work is going on just now on
machines of the computer type, capable of far more variations of
sequences. When a learner plugs in and pushes the response buttons

(he may even be allowed to write his own response) the machine collects all the responses like data; and, being programmed in the other sense mentioned on page 244 to handle this information, can switch the student on to a special one of many circuits that exactly suits his ability as it has added up so far.

It is tempting to think of the teaching computer as 'judging' the learner and providing information to suit him out of its own resources, just like any intelligent teacher. But of course the material stored in its network is like the material carried by any other teaching machine. It is collected by human instructors and arranged so as to anticipate as many as possible of the individual learning patterns. Records of learning are accumulating from the automated instruction which is already in progress and who knows but a complete theory of learning may emerge from it in the future. But it will not be a simple one and the tendency will be towards techniques with greater variability of application, not greater rigidity.

BIBLIOGRAPHICAL NOTE ON PROGRAMMING

This is a brief account of the psychological origins of programming. For descriptive details readers should consult such textbooks as W. K. Richmond's *Teachers and Machines* (Wm. Collins Sons & Co. Ltd., 1965) which gives a historical survey of the movement, some explanatory samples and some account of research into the comparative effectiveness of teaching by programmes. The terminology of programming (often rather technical and stereotyped) is well assessed by John Leedham and Deric Unwin in their *Programmed Learning in the Schools* (Longmans, 1965). The appropriate chapter in J. M. Thyne's book, mentioned in the reference list, relates the techniques to practical learning requirements.

REFERENCES

(1) Hunter, I. M. L., *Memory*, Penguin Books, 1964.
(2) Thyne, James M., *The Psychology of Learning and Techniques of Teaching*, University of London Press Ltd., 1966.

6

Language

1 The nature of language learning

Language is characteristically human behaviour and plays a leading part in most human activities. It is of special importance in education and behavioural development and could have been dealt with as part of almost any of the topics in this book; its significance can be conveniently introduced by a review of certain points made in connection with some of them.

You will remember from the chapter on intelligence that verbal performances (for example, making an absurdity explicit as well as being able to laugh at it) showed the highest correlations with the overall intelligence score. This could mean only that most mental tasks are verbal, but then such tests show a high correlation with later ability in education, and there is plenty of evidence that an enriched language environment stimulates intellectual development.

Middle childhood may be regarded developmentally as the season of accelerated cognitive growth. The systematization of concrete experience into concepts, as Piaget describes it, must be partly due to the extended use of language in formal education and reading in particular. Reference was also made in the chapter on mental development to the motivation of language learning by the worthwhileness of communication, and while any satisfactory family setting will provide this motive, it will be remembered that Bernstein believes that children from more articulate homes develop more sensitive speaking and thinking mechanisms. Conversely, it may make matters worse to assign a linguistically deprived child to a lower stream in school. In this connection should be mentioned Luria's study of twins who had a restricted language code but became more active and purposeful with better language experience.

The belief of the Russian psychologists in the importance of words for crystallizing concepts was noted in the section on thinking. By language, action becomes internalized as thought and need not be carried on overtly. Words become a system of signals (in the Pavlovian sense) for responses. Vygotsky has been chiefly associated with this idea.

We saw, too, that children's concepts are less often worked out by independent experience than attained by social transmission through the language of a human culture. Not all psycholinguists would accept Whorf's suggestion that our language *decides* our picture of reality, but it must have considerable influence upon the availability of ideas (page 218) and our ability to recall them (page 241). This is not to recommend a return to the old verbal methods of imparting information which Pestalozzi objected to, but to say that just as words alone are not enough, neither is activity without language enough for human learning. Children accompany their pre-school exploration of the world with a running commentary; we ought to continue this in formal education and help them to make their discoveries explicit.

Concepts in human societies have emotional as well as cognitive meanings which Osgood tried to measure. They are important for imaginative thinking and for our choice of action in real life, especially when it concerns other people. This brings us to the other psychologically important aspect of language. It is central to personal-social development. Through verbal exchange a child gets the idea of himself as a person, and later on the special language of the juvenile sub-culture mediates group-membership and strengthens personality. On the other hand a child deprived of close communion often gets his own back at society by refusing to talk and by being linguistically retarded in other ways, as Spitz and Goldfarb showed. Problem and delinquent children and adolescents often have poor speech habits.

Language has been defined as characteristically human, a kind of behaviour for which we find no parallel in animal behaviour and which must be learned, at least in part, in ways that animal learning does not help to explain. How far is this true?

In the first place language is not tied to an overt physical action. It need not be *vocal*. Lenneberg noted that deaf children in a certain school, where they were being specifically taught to adjust to *speech* signs through lip reading and also to vocalize themselves, had nevertheless invented an elaborate code of *gesture* signs which they used behind the teacher's back; a newcomer to the group picked it up effortlessly. Language in fact is a mental not a physical pre-disposition (1). Lenneberg and other psycholinguists call it a species-specific ability which cannot be understood by the abilities of other organisms. You will remember that Harlow accepts this much although he is trying to demonstrate that intelligent insight may be learned in a simple version by animals.

After all, many primates have a similar vocal equipment to ours and most vertebrates make some sounds—squeals, grunts, and hisses. When excited, human children make the same kind of noises! But animal vocalizations do not function as symbols of things that are not there (as a child's do when he demands a toy from a closed cupboard) let alone of abstract properties which can be shifted about from one thing to another. This is, in effect, what a child does when he calls a rose 'pretty' and mother's dress 'pretty' although as visual stimuli patterns the two are quite different and (most important of all) the 'pretty' response to his mother's dress is not imitative. Not only has he never seen the dress before, but no one has ever made the vocal response of 'pretty' to it in his hearing. The uniqueness of our language behaviour is one of its most important properties, and very hard indeed to explain as the product of conditioning as it has experimentally demonstrated so far.

Certainly the learning factors are important: the speech environment itself and the strong reinforcements which children get from adults when they do make speech responses. Ability to speak a given language is not an instinct! The mechanisms of any language, its particular code or system of defining its referents have to be perceived by children and gradually assembled into rules that they can use.[1] The point is that although the 3,000-odd languages in the world use all sorts of different systems for distinguishing between referents, native speakers become competent in them all without ever thinking of them as 'difficult'—or easy for that matter. Language competence is universal. All children without an abnormality learn to speak.

Furthermore, the learning is apparently of the spontaneous type and certainly very rapid—the usual indexes of an innate tendency. It follows that language development will show a characteristic maturational pattern. Surveys of the Gesell type—the old *normative* studies, as they are now called—charted normal speech performance at successive ages. There is considerable agreement among the tables of results. The first word: towards the end of the second six months;

[1] A referent is the object event or idea to which a word refers, or the inflection of a word. In English and in several other languages the letter s at the end of a noun is one way of distinguishing the presence of more than one of the thing in question. Children learn this rule and apply it spontaneously to make plural forms they have not heard—like *foots* and *sheeps*—another indication that language acquisition is not simply imitative.

two- to three-word sentences or sentence-phrases: at age two. And so on. A standard textbook of this period was A. F. Watts's *Language and Mental Development of Children* (2). The second and third chapters give the age-achievements for the two main aspects covered by the normative surveys, vocabulary and sentence formation.

Vocabulary counts in the case of young children could be done directly, but for older children estimates must be made by sampling. Needless to say, they varied. Apart altogether from the variation caused by environmental factors, investigators did not follow the same policy about adding in parts of the verb, plurals of nouns and other grammatical forms as separate words. Not to do so was to omit an important aspect of language competence, yet morphology (the inflection of nouns and verbs) and vocabulary are two separate things. To give readers some notion of the actual figures: while new words were found to accumulate only slowly for a month or two after the first word, when the child appears to be preoccupied with his developing motor skills, there is a great surge when the naming age is reached, about the end of Piaget's sensori-motor period of mental growth, and a two-year-old might have 500 words and a three-year-old almost 1,000. Watts himself estimated that the school entrant would have between 2,000 and 3,000 with an increase of about 700 a year in the primary school period.

Vocabulary competence was sometimes assessed by the occurrence of the different parts of speech. But this was a measure of syntactical rather than lexical competence,[1] and modern linguistic techniques tackle it better upon the whole. Similarly, sentence length, a great favourite of the normative studies, was really less significant than grammatical structure which was harder to assess quantitatively. But the *control* of sentences, with proper observation of the function of subject and predicate and few omissions or wrong inflections, was recognized as the typical achievement of the five-year-old as Gesell describes him. His language is in fact complete in the sense that anything he wants to say, or can think of, he *can* say. Teachers have noticed that a child is seldom stuck by 'not knowing the word'. He will invent one, or a circumlocution. His thoughts, within the limitations of his age, are fully explicit.

The different language skills measured by the normative surveys correlated highly with each other and, needless to say, with mental age. It was assumed that the advancement of girls over boys in most

[1] Terms in use in present-day linguistics and roughly synonymous with grammar learning and vocabulary learning respectively.

of the assessments was due to an actual difference in maturation rate, a typical conclusion of the period. You may remember, however, that Mildred Templin in her later survey (3) found evidence of a diminishing sex difference, suggesting that it might be more environmental than genetic. She also found a smaller socio-economic factor (that is, as between children from different home and educational backgrounds) and this also could be environmentally explained. It seems that there is now a more widespread habit of talking to children conversationally, once commoner in middle-class families, and that outside media like television are creating a more uniform speech environment.

Her conclusions are typical of the general trend towards environmental explanations of ability which came after the normative emphasis of the earlier studies. This was discussed fairly fully in the chapter on intelligence. There should now be mentioned one or two of the attempts to explain language acquisition in terms of the scientific learning theories. They have been mostly directed at the problem of explaining how primitive vocalization (babbling) becomes shaped into true speech behaviour by the selection of certain phonemes from the baby's extensive repertoire of noises. Later language, with all its complexities, is presumed to follow the same learning patterns.

A phoneme is a sound which is actually used in a language to mean something. We can all make clicking and smacking sounds with tongues and lips but they are not so used; likewise the Welsh breathed l and French rolled r are not English phonemes. How does a baby pitch upon the useful ones? Some psychologists like M. M. Lewis explain the first pseudo-speech sounds as organic reactions to comfort-discomfort, since the physical apparatus that we use for language is not primarily designed for it but for biological functions like breathing and chewing. The glottis itself is meant to exclude foreign bodies from the windpipe as we find out soon enough if we try to talk and swallow at the same time! (4)

A typical reinforcement explanation of the vocal responses of a baby would be that an accidentally emitted phoneme elicits his mother's approval, which has become a secondary reinforcer to him because of its association with primitive satisfiers like being fed and cuddled. Therefore this particular vocal response is repeated and non-rewarded items discarded. In the same way imitation is a generalized habit because imitative noise-making is always reinforced. This simple formula is taken as the basis of all language acquisition, including the later stages. Skinner, for example, classifies all language acts according to the nature of the reinforcement that clinches them. Echoic responses have already been described from this point of view. What Skinner calls *mands*, things directed at people like questions and threats, are reinforced by their social effectiveness; *tacts*, labels for objects and events, function in the same way as the presence of the things themselves.

We have already come across the Pavlovian explanation of words as conditional stimuli, responded to like the concrete stimuli themselves, of which words are signals. This is the very difficult sign-theory of language which has been developed by Osgood (5).

The learning theories are all very speculative and, as we saw in reference to education in general, do not give much practical help about how to promote really complex language competence after the stage of very early childhood. There is sound psychological guidance for the pre-school years, for example about the intimate connection between the child's cognitive and emotional development and his early experience of communication. But there is not much knowledge about the specific language needs of middle childhood and nothing at all that correponds to Piaget's experimental demonstrations of how the *closed* (scientific and logical) concepts develop. Piaget, you will remember, has given curiously little attention to language's share in structuring those schemas and operations which form his model of organized thought. Children's talk, the titular subject of his first well-known book, interested him chiefly as a way of access to their thinking; and his view of egocentric talk as a primitive stage has been replaced by Vygotsky's, that it is the medium by which experience is internalized.

From a review of the points made about language in preceding chapters, we went on to consider its claim to be a special form of human behaviour, not to be explained in terms of imitative learning alone. If, as Lenneberg and others believe, there is an innate predisposition to acquire language, then there should be a genetic maturational sequence by which this happens. The normative surveys laid down the general lines of this sequence, although the age-norms do not adequately represent the wide range of individual differences in performance which are probably more the result of environmental factors than the earlier surveys suggested.

A particular language must of course be learned, and this must come about in part through the operation of the conditions common to all learning, such as reinforcement and association. But we have no comprehensive account of how the more complex forms of language competence are achieved.

Changes in language teaching have been due to experiments with new classroom methods and to changes in the views of language scholars about the nature of language itself. The present mode is for productivity, not formal correctness, and for using language for all sorts of human purposes, buying a loaf as well as writing an exercise. This is typical of the socio-scientific study of language called linguistics, and particularly of its psychological implications.

2 Linguistics and the psychology of language

There are many investigations going on just now in the field of linguistics and like the learning theorists, linguists insist that there is nothing like a complete theory. But they take the view that since language is human behaviour of the most characteristic sort, analysing it will give a clue to the very nature of behaviour itself. If this ever happened school language teaching could be effectively programmed.

There is a plastic period in the pre-school years during which spoken language is spontaneously acquired. It is not a very long one, beginning in earnest about the middle of the second year and laying all the necessary foundations in about twenty-four months. Provided the environmental opportunity is there, that is. Now there must be a succeeding plastic period for acquiring the later forms of competence. Traditionally, little attention has been given in formal schooling to extending the two auditory skills of speaking and listening; the school's job has been to add the two *visual* language skills of reading and writing. This is what M. A. K. Halliday and his collaborators have called productive instruction in their book *The Linguistic Sciences and Language Teaching* (6).

There has usually been agreement that this is now the time for children to learn *about* language as well as use it spontaneously without thinking as they have done in the pre-school learning stage. The children are to be asked to think about how language functions and what it does, for example, by a change in word order. Both the productive instruction and this descriptive instruction are harder to motivate than the pre-school learning of the spoken language, and the children's present language activities outside the school. What suggestions are offered by linguistics?

The first is on the nature of language itself. It is behaviour; not something inside a dictionary or a book of poetry but something that people *do*. Language happens when somebody speaks or writes, just as running happens as a means of escaping danger or pushing a needle in and out occurs in making a row of cross-stitch. Like the running or the needle-thrusts language is manipulating responses for a calculated effect. They might be obvious (like the object of yelling 'Look out!') or more subtle like the exchanges of lovers—or professional rivals politely doing each other down.

This view, that the meaning of language is how language operates in a social and physical context, has the advantage of recognizing various kinds of meaning—personal and emotional as well as literal. It was put forward by an anthropologist, Malinowski, and developed by J. R. Firth, who has greatly influenced linguistics in Britain and the kind of language teaching which corresponds. That is why a language lesson in school nowadays is just as likely to take the form of play-acting a visit to the grocer's as of writing down the answers in an English exercise, since its object is to show that language is effective behaviour which alters situations. (*No, give it to me. It's too heavy for you. Or, Do you have a shorter one please? This doesn't fit.*)

There are different fashions of being effective. Certainly a line of poetry can be effective for its rather special purpose, but so can a newspaper headline or the instructions which a qualified journeyman gives to the apprentice on a job. Only, the vocabulary and phrasing would be different and we might say that they are drawn from different *registers*. There are restricted registers, that is limited systems of language-signs with fixed uses, some with international currency, like the terms used in air-transport and certain verbal traffic signals. A school activity could be to list a group of terms from (say) a weather forecast or a sports commentary and have the pupils identify the context, as they readily will.

Most of us can draw on one or two special language registers that have to do with a profession or a craft and which convey meaning much quicker than ordinary circumlocutions in that particular context. But some registers are social, not technical. A young woman teacher does not select her words, or even her syntax, from the same register during a lesson as in the staffroom among her equals. Her pupils, and particularly the boys, will have their playground talk and their classroom talk—more extensive, thanks to books and the teacher, but certainly not more effective as behaviour. The language registers used in a school neighbourhood may enrich the school language activities, for example in a country district with a sturdy dialect, or they may be a problem like the restricted codes, as Bernstein describes the communication in under-privileged homes.

The difficulty, as Randolph Quirk points out in his discussion of the uses of English (7), is to persuade a pupil of the need for widening his range of communication when he has been completely comprehensible in his own community all his life. Quirk points to another psychological problem when he distinguishes the linguistically 'assured' from the linguistically 'anxious' who have been made to feel inadequate by the educational stress upon the need for correctness. It is the same thing as makes the natural left-hander feel anxious and disturbed. (See above, page 236.)

Received pronunciation and standard grammar are important parts of language teaching not because they are socially acceptable but because they constitute the most widely comprehensible *code* that makes language behaviour more effective in more contexts. The linguistic concept of *code* is quite difficult but it is the basis of the new psychological approach to sentence structure and a short explanation is necessary. Readers may remember that the way the nervous system discriminates between one pattern of sensory stimulation and another was described as a kind of coding. Language patterns work in the same way by gradually narrowing down the message contained by speech sounds to the one meaning out of a great many possible things they might say. For example if a sentence starts with *The* it narrows down the choice of the kind of words that can fill the second position. Or in a three-word group like *he has gone*, there are only one or two words that can fill the middle space but each would say a different thing from any of the other ones that are possible. A five-year-old has learned an important part of English coding, the word order; because while he might be heard to say 'Johnny and me has buyed lots of fings' he will not say 'buyed has' nor else 'Lots of fings has buyed Johnny'. (He has learned at least one other important code-convention as well, the form of the verb that normally tells an action belongs to the past. He has not got it right, but his intention is quite unambiguous.)

The grammatical choices are usually limited. If you want to 'encode' the idea of *continuous* action you must use -ing. Vocabulary choices are more open; nevertheless there is an important coding device by which certain terms belong in a word group or context. Linguists call it their *collocation*. Thus if someone says 'May I have a slice of—?' we expect to be asked to pass bread or cake but hardly the sugar. The collocation rules are more flexible but they have to be learnt and are an important way of conveying intentions.

These very sketchy illustrations show how coding can be done through sentence-structure and what is called the morphology, the shaping of the words by prefixes and endings like -ful, which signifies an adjective usually. We could easily fit real words into the appropriate slots in a nonsense sentence like *The fripious clones tondled insifflably*.

Finally, the smallest units that distinguish one intention of the speaker's from another are the single sounds called phonemes, which we have come across already in connection with infant vocalization. Curiously enough children may be later in establishing some of their phonemic distinctions than quite complex grammatical ones. We heard our five-year-old get his word order faultless but he cannot encode the contrast between *fin* and *thin*. His range of discriminations is not fully operative. At the start of speech, indeed, one phoneme has to serve several of his intentions to communicate. In time, this one sound will have expanded into several, all properly allocated.

We find exactly the same process of expansion in the development of his sentence-forms. At first the same primitive two-word sentence serves all functions. Thus 'Mummy shoe' may mean either discovering mummy's shoe or a request to have one's own shoe put on by mummy; and later separates into 'That mummy shoe' and 'Mummy put shoe' respectively.

Through linguistics there has been a new approach to the psychology of language development, as the above examples indicate. Its first and most important feature is the fresh emphasis upon the genetic factor as opposed to imitation and learning. But unlike the old normative surveys with large samples, the observations are made as longitudinal studies of individual children. Their utterances are shown gradually evolving from primitive to fully expanded forms that operate differentially as in the example just given. Most of the investigations have been carried on at various American universities, for example by Roger Brown and others at Harvard and by Miller and Ervin at the University of California. Some of their theories are difficult but readers will find a useful general account of procedures and findings by David McNeill entitled 'Developmental Psycholinguistics' in a symposium on the origins of language (8).

The starting point for most psycholinguists is that imitative learning and Pavlovian conditioning may explain how single words are acquired, for instance, but fail to explain the two most striking things about language growth. First, its speed. As McNeill observes, grammatical speech (that is, with a sentence-structure of some kind) does not begin till about eighteen months but the basic structural rules are meaningfully applied at three and a half. Secondly, every utterance is a unique response. Even when it is a repetition of a former utterance, it can be made in situations where it was never made before. But in any case, we all turn out, adults and children alike, dozens of new utterances in a day, with arrangements of words that never occurred before nor in reference to the same things. Listening to a young child one finds that he does not echo parrot fashion nearly so often as he initiates.

The ability to spin out endless new variations on the basic structures (which it should be noted again is acquired by all children, unlike many other skills) has been called a child's linguistic *competence*. On the evidence of the expanding sentence structure Brown argues that young children have a grammar of their own that is not imitated from adults (adults do not say things like *fall the ladder* even as baby talk) and which is not a cut-down version of what they do hear. When an adult tries to get the child to repeat the expanded form, the child obediently modifies his speech but to his own grammar pattern! In his own good time he will get it right—again provided the models are there to help him expand and differentiate. However ready he is maturationally, he obviously cannot acquire the syntactical rules if he does not hear them functioning in his speech environment.

We have seen that children learn by rule rather than imitatively by their well-known habit of regularizing irregular parts of speech. They will say *buyed* and *mouses*. Russian psychologists quote many examples of this in their more highly inflected language. Jean Berko has very ingeniously demonstrated this learning of the morphological rules. She would ask a child to fill in the missing word in 'This man is spowing and yesterday he—.' The children had no trouble in supplying the code-sign for the past tense of an action they had obviously never heard of in their lives. She goes on to point out, however, in a survey of investigations into language learning (9) that this rule-learning, like the effective phonemes, is spontaneous and unconscious. We have to accept it that most of the children's language competence even after they come to school continues to be self-taught and beyond the teacher's direct control.

What we can do is make the speech models they are going to choose from effective and distinct in their functions, and motivate them to use language themselves—in dramatic play, for example, where different situations call for different kinds of linguistic handling. It has been said that productivity is at the moment regarded as more important than correctness; and educators in the past have relied too much upon children's ability to listen, useful though it is.

Speech is not the only form of language behaviour, though it is the most effective. There are other communication signs to help it besides the words and word-groupings, such as intonation (think of all the things you can say with the one word *Well!*). Besides, speech happens in a living situation. That is why ordinary talk is not always fully expanded grammatically and would sound odd if it were. But written language has none of these helps and must be fully expanded. It has no other way of defining what it is referring to and fulfil its intention. There is no listener there to be smiled at or asked to supply a comment or question. Secondly, written language must be fully expanded phonemically; a word may be spoken as a vague, general whole but it must be written letter by letter. And the intonations and pauses must be represented by a new code system altogether, the punctuation.

These are some of the difficulties of teaching the second extension of language behaviour. Another is how to motivate it. Writing is not learnt spontaneously, even with the help of 'live' activities that can be written up like classroom news items. As Vygotsky points out, in what must be one of the most brilliant passages known to developmental psychology (10) written expression does not come by nature. A new, difficult, and entirely conscious skill is involved. Because we learn to talk unconsciously we need not *think out* or think *about* the grammatical rules for saying what we mean; but writing is not learnt this way and some kind of grammar teaching is now necessary. There are, of course, misleading ways of thinking about English grammar and children are often asked to 're-write correctly' usages which are perfectly sound. The passage from Vygotsky should be read along with Randolph Quirk's chapter headed 'Problems of Usage' (7). Between them they give a well-balanced statement of the function of conscious learning in language production.

We have been considering in the last few pages some of the concepts of psycholinguistics. Language is behaviour designed to have some effect upon a situation, usually a social situation. Meaning, or intention, is conveyed by the particular code that a language uses. Speakers draw upon a *register* of terms and forms of speech. Some registers are limited in application. The most widely communicative register is standard usage, and it is an educational problem to motivate the learning of these more effective forms of language in children from a restricted speech environment. We considered next the psycholinguistic view of language acquisition, as spontaneous learning. The extension of speech activity in school can be similarly motivated; but writing involves learning of an entirely different kind. Although the ancillary skills of spelling and punctuation may become automatic, it is probably fair to say that the act of composition never does.

3 Reading

Unlike writing, reading becomes spontaneous very readily. You can no more stop yourself from reading a printed word you are looking at than from hearing a spoken word you are listening to, and nine times out of ten the sense is taken in as fast as the visual sign. Writing is an uncommon skill; reading is not. It comes perhaps not exactly naturally to human beings (but then, strictly speaking, neither would speech without speech models) but rapidly enough for most people to forget how they learned it. A teacher can rely, in fact, upon a fair proportion of latent or spontaneous learning in reading as in speaking. In a minority of cases this is not so and the total reading response has to be broken down to diagnose some individual language disability. But most children acquire reading *competence* in about the same number of years as speech competence. This does not mean that they can read anything and everything; but it does mean that they are ready to go on to self-teaching by reading for pleasure. A number learn it in a month or two and can read silently as a matter of course before they leave the infant school. All children within the very wide range of normality, are *able* to read sooner or later.

There are two points which are complementary to each other in F. J. Schonell's preface to his *Psychology and Teaching of Reading* (11). First, that only a small minority of children positively cannot be taught to read, the severely subnormal and the rare cases of cerebral damage; second, that there is a very wide age-range over which individual children will learn to read. Between them, these two statements should help educators to keep a sense of proportion about the problems of teaching reading, which come under two headings, the nature of the learning process itself and the individual readiness of the learner.

Reading is perceptual learning. The pattern of it, in its simplest form, is Pavlovian conditioning—recognizing a neutral or meaning-less stimulus (little black marks on paper) as signalizing the meaningful stimulus with which it has become firmly associated. As in Pavlovian conditioning, the *overt* response is only important as an indicator that the learning has taken place and the association has been formed. The handiest check for the teacher that in looking at the print-sign the pupil has at least 'heard' the spoken word is to have him say it aloud.

But saying it aloud is a *test* that a part at least of the teaching has been effective; it is not the *object* of the teaching. Reading is visual *listening*, not visual speaking (writing is that). All the essential responses in reading are covert ones and have to do with the activation of the cortical association networks. They are not directly measurable and if a teacher wants to assure herself that they are happening, as she usually does, then it must be some other way, such as asking the child to turn his eyes away from the book and tell her what he has just understood from it.

Reading is Pavlovian learning in another respect. The pupil is being trained to perceive finer and finer distinctions in the signs, just as Pavlov's dogs learned to discriminate between the circle (worth salivating for) and the ellipse. Thus when he sees a strip-shaped pattern he knows it is the label for *gramophone* and a short one with two little eyes in the middle is to be pasted below the face of the man in the *moon*. Readers will recognize the familiar *look-and-say* technique which proceeds on the assumption that print signs should be 'meaningful' and that word shapes are easier to distinguish from each other than the minute markers that distinguish the letters. A typical look-and-say primer has a light vocabulary of words contrasted for length and format. They may also be aware that doubt has been cast on the usefulness of the theory, particularly by advocates of the neo-phonic methods like J. C. Daniels and Hunter Diack. They believe that the concept of word-patterns or *gestalts* is a fallacy; that fine discriminations between letters can be learned as readily by young children as between printed word-signs, since *all* print is an unfamiliar medium; and that the whole object of reading is the *phonemic* analysis by which a child can break down words for himself which he has not happened to come across.

Of course this raises the characteristic problem of English reading—the lack of consistent correpondence between the phonemes and the graphic symbols, which does away with some of the advantage of alphabetic writing. Not so much, though, as the older *sentence-method* and *look-and-say* theories would have us believe. There have been recent experiments in augmented alphabets (one letter to each sound) and in colour-printing (like-*sounding* syllables as in *ray*, *weight*, and *make* are coloured alike but conventionally spelt) to help children to step out confidently. Readers will find a useful survey of the pros and cons of the various methods and the psychological thinking behind them, in a volume published by an international reading symposium in 1964 (12).

Reading uses visual cues but it is also language behaviour in all its complexity. It carries possibly a rather heavier load of memorizing than speech, though not necessarily of concepts and active thinking. These are the *covert* reading performances which tend to mature concurrently with thinking ability in Piaget's sense. The two kinds of performance undoubtedly reinforce each other and a good reader is usually the pupil who can solve mathematical and other logical problems especially when they are put verbally. But occasionally a pupil can be quite far advanced in conceptual maturation (by the Piaget problems) and a poor reader for one or another of the reasons we shall be considering in a moment.

Turning now to the old-established question of reading readiness. In the period when intelligence was thought of as a central power with effects that could be measured on the separate performances of an individual, it used to be said that before a child could read he must have reached a mental age of six and a half. Nowadays we are just as likely to think of the mental age rating as a *consequence* of reading experience—or at least of stimulating language experience. Reading will come earlier to children who are linguistically fortunate and will in its turn stimulate other abilities. As John Downing points out in the first chapter of the reading symposium just mentioned, the readiness depends on what kind of task you are confronting the children with. It is a matter of methods and presentation as much as of maturation. On the other hand, he goes on to say, the readiness concept has a value on humane grounds by reminding teachers, as Schonell repeatedly did, of the harm that can be done to the confidence of the slow and poor-average learners.

Most teachers are alert nowadays for signs of sensory and motor immaturity. Although the physical function in reading is not the main one it requires considerable steadiness to move the eyes along a line of print without many regressive movements. If the print is big enough, a young child of normal maturity should be able to hold the book at a comfortable distance so that he can develop a rhythm in his eye-movements, which, as most people know, are a series of jumps. It is in the pauses or fixations in between them that the actual print-signs are taken in. It takes time for the saccadic jumps (as they are called) to settle down, but gradually they become longer and fewer, with bigger eyefuls of print taken in at each pause. This all happens much faster than speech and is another reason why oral reading should be dropped for comprehension purposes just as soon as it has served its turn of linking the print signs with their spoken referents. Naturally, teachers must continue to use it as a check that pupils have in fact been able to read words, and secondly for elocution purposes.

Small inaccuracies of articulation are not necessarily a sign that the child is still too immature to read. Often the reading itself helps him to establish phonemic distinctions and to realize that strings of speech can be broken up into words and, conversely, synthesized from them —which pre-reading children do not fully perceive. Mispronunciations and visual difficulties with the mirror letters (like b and d) wear away together as phonic analysis replaces the pseudo-reading of the preparatory lessons.

Nowadays a new kind of stress is laid upon what is sometimes called, for want of a better term, emotional readiness. This is the curiosity about the act of reading itself and the wish to try it which normally comes about in a child who has been encouraged to be communicative, and has been used from babyhood onwards to having the pages of books turned for him and talked over by interested adults. Conversely, a child from a poor linguistic background is likely to be retarded in his idea of communication in general and to understand very little of the use of printed words, let alone how to enjoy them. It is not surprising that such children are unresponsive to the first reading lessons, and unfortunately linguistic deprivation is apt to be a cumulative handicap.

We have been considering reading as a part of general language ability. We have seen that if the apparent predisposition to acquire spoken language is to be fulfilled then certain learning conditions must be present in the environment, particularly speech models and social reinforcements of speech behaviour on the child's part. In reading the learning requirements are more obvious but we are entitled to assume that almost all human children will develop the capacity to acquire visual language sooner or later. It is, then, important to understand the nature of the reading task and the meaning of readiness for it.

Learning to read is learning to make conceptual responses to the print-signals, which of course is *covert* behaviour. The *overt* response of saying the words aloud is an index that the pupil has probably made the right connections but this must be confirmed by tests of comprehension. To make the right responses the learner must discriminate exactly between the print signs, and some educators believe that word-wholes are *gestalts* or patterns more 'natural' for a beginner to distinguish.

Designed material that reduces the task difficulty will naturally lower the readiness requirements. In any case we do not now think of reading readiness as being an entirely maturational stage that must be waited for. Mental growth is affected by environmental, and above all linguistic stimulation. In regard to the physical pre-requisites of reading we may reasonably argue that being able to discriminate small auditory and visual differences is as much the result of training as of maturation while motor control of the eye-movements needs practice and the articulation of phonemic distinctions often improves along with the phonic analysis of printed words.

We have also seen, however, that there is a wide range of individual differences in the maturation of the ability to read and therefore that with any instructional method there is going to be an irreducible percentage of pupils who have not learned to read by the time they leave the infant school. Again, according to the spread of measured intelligence in the school population (still a useful independent estimate against which the spread of other mental performance can be tried for fit) there will be among the pupils retained in ordinary schools a percentage of each year of age who have not reached the mental level for insight into reading. It will of course be a diminishing percentage and should in theory be worked out completely by the end of primary school (a child only just ready to read at age eleven must be reckoned to have an I.Q. as low as 60).

In *practice*, of course, this is not so and there are pupils in secondary schools who have a reading age of seven or less, which really means that they cannot read at all. It is obviously important to try to find out what other factors are at work, and whether they are largely environmental or even educational in origin.

4 *The nature of linguistic backwardness*

We have seen that individual variation in the growth of language ability is to be expected and that the observed percentage of children who cannot read when they leave the infant school is perhaps not disturbingly high (it is about 15 in some surveys). Provided junior school teachers are prepared to teach reading from its beginnings by a continuation of the infant school methods, as M. F. Cleugh recommends in her book on the education of slow learners (13) these slower developing children will most of them be reading by eight and a half or by nine and a half. But conversely without the special teaching needed at this critical maturation period, the handicap becomes cumulative. The greatest sufferers on the whole are not those who are more obviously sub-normal in natural ability (with I.Q.'s below 70) since there is often provision for them in special schools where they are encouraged to reach their fullest potential (see Appendix III) but the much larger group, about 10 per cent of all children, who by I.Q. standards are classified as dull. A few may be sent to the special schools, since educational subnormality can be interpreted fairly widely at the discretion of the local education authority. But the great majority must remain in the ordinary classrooms where it is unlikely that their special developmental needs can be fully met.

The linguistic attainments of dull children tend to become progressively less in comparison with the rest of their year-group. They often come from homes where the talk is poor and books, or almost any kind of reading material, practically non-existent. It would be strange if they did not build up an attitude of anxiety or resentment. Reading failure causes more heart-burning than failure in, say, arithmetic. Arithmetic is expected to be 'difficult' for many, whereas reading is, as we have seen, a skill that is ordinarily acquired and one that is essential to the business of living.

In *Half our Future*, a report of the Central Advisory Council on Education (14) it appeared from the survey sample of the then secondary modern school population that roughly a quarter of fifteen-year-old pupils had a reading age of thirteen or less.[1] Now this is not a desperate situation. It is characteristic of slower learners that they have difficulty with the kind of conceptual responses that are mediated by language and our educational expectations should be correspondingly realistic. The Ministry of Education pamphlet, 'Slow Learners at School', indicates that simply being able to read what is necessary for functional purposes is probably as much as can be attained by many slow learners (15).

On the other hand to do this is within the *mental* scope of the great majority. The problem is a personality one. With the non-reading secondary school pupils it is to overcome the resistence which cumulative failure has built up. Readers will find it more fully described in the introductory chapter of the book on the secondary education of dull children published by Cheshire Education Committee (16). Altogether it appears a fair summary that the percentage of backward

[1] It should be noted, however, that the reading test used was the same as in the Ministry of Education reading surveys of 1949 and 1956 and showed a significant advance in reading-age scores in the survey carried out for the 1963 Report. This could tentatively at least be attributed to improved conditions and methods of teaching.

readers is higher than the percentage of innately 'dull' children, and that complete reading failure happens oftener than it should on the basis of ability expectation. This is partly due to inadequate educational provision for differences in developmental rate and partly to environmental causes which are beyond the jurisdiction of the school.

Such ideas, of course, are not new. Thirty years ago Sir Cyril Burt, while stipulating that inherent lack of ability was the characteristic condition found along with school backwardness (17) also listed peripheral ones like illness or physical handicaps, and environmental ones like poor home backgrounds and frequent absences from school. There is probably very much less nowadays of the gross cultural deprivation that some children suffered from thirty years ago. Nevertheless, psychologists take environmental factors more seriously than ever since the idea of a fixed innate intelligence has been modified.

It would be nonsense to deny that there must be great differences in intellectual endowment. Putting it very simply some children will have a bigger number of cerebral neurons, or perhaps a better physiological arrangement of them through family inheritance! So we may expect a spread of performances—like school attainments—to match the spread of ability. But ability can be boosted and we are never able to say that its upper limit has finally been reached.

Educators in the past have worried about the 'gap' between natural ability and performance. Even the backward ought to be living up to their potential and not doing worse than they can. Some writers have wanted to confine the term backwardness to these under-achievers, as they are sometimes called. (Note that by this argument a child of *any* level of natural ability could be backward, and this is, upon the whole, the attitude taken by the Cheshire committee in the study just mentioned). At one time Schonell wished to see the term retardation adopted to indicate a gap between measured ability and measured achievement. But we do not now think of measured ability (on an intelligence test) as a separate independent thing which causes other performance to be good or bad. As we have repeatedly seen, intelligence tests have a large overlap with English attainments in school—hence the name verbal reasoning tests is often preferred. Any environmental experience which boosts one will boost the other.[1]

A hint of this was given in connection with the mathematical type of concept and backwardness in arithmetic or other school activities of a mathematical nature (see above, page 222), but it is upon

[1] Readers are reminded of what was said about the significance of educational quotients in Part II, Chapter 2, page 52.

linguistic development that the boosting or depressing effect of the culture is clearest. A child has a natural predisposition to progress in language and this includes learning to read. Therefore failure rightly makes educators uneasy, though not exactly by reason of the under-achievement theory.

Of course, school is only a part of the speech environment. But when home language models are poor, the school has a responsibility to compensate, if possible. The Cheshire committee urge that in the case of the poor readers at the secondary stage, effort should be made to bring their performance up to a *reading age* of about eleven. It appears from surveys that pupils of this level of attainment will go on improving their language and reading habits after school, whereas those who leave with a reading attainment age of nine and a half, do not. Some surveys, notably one carried out in Kent by Joyce Morris, do not hesitate to identifiy teaching conditions and procedures as a main factor in reading backwardness (18).

There is a complex relationship between the spread of general ability and the incidence of reading backwardness. Obviously we cannot put the blame fair and square upon a pupil's dullness or write him off permanently as belonging to the educationally subnormal category. There remains, however, another possibility to consider. Is there such a thing as an innate, specific, *language* disability?

First of all we must remember that slowness of language development is not in itself a defect. Every child goes through the sequence at his own characteristic pace. Mildred Templin found, for instance, that on an average the three-year-olds in her sample showed 50 per cent correctness of articulation, while 100 per cent accuracy was the rule by age eight (3). Phonemic errors are to be expected in some children in the early years of school and it is also to be expected that they will correct themselves. Stephen Jackson in his little account of special education in the country (19) suggests that up to 5 per cent of infant school children will need some help with speech in the normal run of things. It is only when serious irregularities persist beyond six and a half that specialist diagnosis and corrective therapy should be sought. It is important to find out if the child is only copying poor models, or if there is some organic disability. Only in some very rare cases are there deeper-seated conditions like brain damage or emotional disturbance.

Stammering and stuttering occurs in about 3 per cent of children (more boys than girls). It should again be noted that it is quite a common occurrence for a two-year-old to stutter and the habit can be carried over, especially if parents make a fuss about it. Some stammerers (stammering is sometimes distinguished from stuttering as inability to get the words out) are suffering from anxieties which 'throttle' speech. Some, not so many as was once believed, are victims of a forced changeover from left to right hand. The point is, there is no one explanation of articulation difficulties; some are to be expected in a proportion of children and will be outgrown; some are environmentally reinforced and need remedial methods; a very few are symptoms of deep-seated personality disorder or of cerebral damage. Both conditions are rare.

Withdrawal into silence is the refuge of a badly disturbed child, and a truly autistic child, who appears unaware of the existence of others, is a medical case requiring psychiatric treatment. *Aphasia* likewise is a medical term and ought to be restricted to instances of physiological brain lesions, which create inability to use or understand word symbols—not used, as it sometimes is, to account for subnormality in the maturation of language functions and even at times for specific reading disability. This brings us to the present use of the term *dyslexia*.

Although there is some confusion of reference, *dyslexia* is a psychological and developmental term and does not in itself mean a physiological condition or explain anything. Its meaning is malfunctioning of language behaviour, but it is restricted in practice to the effects of this supposed malfunctioning upon reading. The idea of a mental abnormality so specialized that it affects only a specific skill like reading is at first sight rather strange. There is, however, a tiny but distinguishable percentage of children who have not learned to read, although they have normal vision, hearing, and articulation; show normal competence in ability tests not involving reading performance; and are not linguistically or educationally deprived. The typical 'dyslexic' failure appears to be in associating the graphic symbols with spoken language and its meanings, which is a cerebral function.

About thirty years ago there was an attempt to identify specific reading disability as 'word-blindness' and tests were invented for diagnosing the child's power of distinguishing between tiny visual patterns other than print. But the failure, whatever it is, is not in simple perceptual discrimination. There are three characteristic language zones in the dominant cerebral hemisphere and countless neural pathways for assembling the verbal input; at any junction there could be a break in communication which would be impossible to locate because of the inter-relationships. Some of the many possibilities are mentioned by K. Lovell in his historical survey of research into the question in the symposium on reading mentioned on page 262 (12).

Not all investigators accept dyslexia as a direct cause of failure. In her book on reading backwardness M. D. Vernon avoids the term advisedly (20), although latterly she came round to a cautious belief in a particular type of reading failure found in an otherwise non-handicapped child. On the other hand Joyce Morris did not identify an instance in the Kent survey.

Dyslexia is believed to be like aphasia but caused developmentally, not by damage. Normally, as you will remember, correlations between the various mental functions tend to be high, as mental development advances at about the same rate on all its fronts simultaneously. Thus children bright in other ways have usually begun to speak early, score higher on assessments of language acquisition like vocabulary counts and sentence length and will have reading ages well in advance of their birthday ages. Conversely, at the lowest extreme, children with intelligence of the imbecile grade (below 55 I.Q.) may never develop speech. Low-grade feeble-minded children, including typical mongols, go through the same sequence of language acquisition as normal children but more slowly, and at the end of the plastic period, which Lenneberg and others believe to be in the early teens, the ceiling they have reached will be lower, according to the individual degree of retardation. Now, supposing there is marked developmental retardation in one mental function, or even one part of a function, and this should have to do with speech, then you may well get such a case as the dyslexic child even when there is no environmental aggravation.

Children who are late in reading may be in fact fulfilling their own maturational pattern and the percentage of non-readers within an age-group in the ordinary schools should diminish steadily with each year. Unfortunately they may not get the necessary help as they reach the critical point of readiness, so that a handicap which began in part from pre-school cultural deprivation will be cumulative. Consequently at any age-level there will be a higher percentage of backward readers than would be predicted theoretically from the I.Q. range.

Some children, of course, have congenital handicaps of vision, hearing, and articulation, which unless corrected by aids and special educational methods will certainly retard their language abilities and their conceptional development. But it seems possible that there is such a thing as a rare condition of specific abnormality in the development of the mental functions of language, and this would be different in nature from the retarding effects of cultural or educational deprivation.

Only brief reference has been made in this chapter to the relationship between language difficulties and emotional disturbance. Severe impairment through personality disorder is rare. But it has been repeatedly emphasized throughout the present book how important effective human communication is for the development of a personality that is both individual and functionally sound.

REFERENCES

(1) Lenneberg, Eric H., 'The Capacity for Language Acquisition' in *The Structure of Language* (ed. Fodor and Katz), Prentice-Hall, New Jersey, 1964.

(2) Watts, A. F., *The Language and Mental Development of Childen*, Harrap, 1950.

(3) Templin, Mildred, *Certain Language Skills in Children*, Oxford University Press, 1957.

(4) Lewis, M. M., *How Children Learn to Speak*, Harrap, 1957.

(5) Osgood, Charles E., *Method and Theory in Experimental Psychology*, Oxford University Press, New York, 1953.

(6) Halliday, M. A. K. *et al.*, *The Linguistic Sciences and Language Teaching*, Longmans, 1964.

(7) Quirk, Randolph, *The Use of English*, Longmans, 1962.

(8) McNeill, David, 'Developmental Psycholinguistics' in *The Genesis of Language* (ed. Smith and Miller), Massachusetts Inst. of Technology Press, 1966.

(9) Berko, Jean, Chapter 13 in *Handbook of Research Methods in Child Development* (ed. Mussen), Wiley, New York and London, 1960.

(10) Vygotsky, L. S., *Thought and Language*, M.I.T. Press and Wiley, New York, 1962.

(11) Schonell, F. J., *The Psychology and Teaching of Reading*, 1951. (Third edition.)

(12) Downing, J. (ed.), *The First International Reading Symposium*, Cassell, 1964.

(13) Cleugh, M. F., *The Slow Learner*, Methuen, 1957.

(14) Report of the Central Advisory Council for Education, *Half our Future*, H.M.S.O., 1963.

(15) Department of Education and Science, pamphlet No. 46, 'Slow Learners at School', H.M.S.O., 1964.

(16) Cheshire Education Committee, *The Education of Dull Children at the secondary stage*, U.L.P., 1963.

(17) Burt, C., *The Backward Child*, U.L.P., 1937.

(18) Morris, Joyce, *Standards and Progress in Reading*, National Foundation for Educational Research, 1966.

(19) Jackson, Stephen, *Special Education in England and Wales*, Oxford University Press, 1964.

(20) Vernon, M. D., *Backwardness in Reading*, Cambridge University Press, 1957.

Appendices

Appendices

Appendix I

A note on educational and vocational guidance

An important aim in assessing pupils' abilities and attainments is vocational guidance. In most schools this is closely bound up with educational guidance since at various points in his scholastic career a pupil is required to make choices between subjects and between courses, which has the effect of restricting the range of available choices in further education or in job selection. More occupations are requiring special preparation or special qualifications as our technology becomes more complex. The Report of the Central Advisory Council for Education published in 1959 by H.M.S.O. under the heading 15–18 (the well-known Crowther report) recommends careful guidance of pupil's choices since this must be done as early as 13 for some subjects and the vocational decision may be made unintentionally in this way.

The trend in the present educational policy is away from early selection and specialization. Vocational guidance aims accordingly at widening the range of choices rather than narrowing them down. The part played in it by special aptitude testing is therefore not so crucial as, theoretically, it might appear. We do not, in this country, practise a regular programme of ability diagnosis matched with a corresponding analysis of the various occupations into their specific performances. Thus even the twenty-one separate aptitudes once listed by Oakley and Macrae in their classical volume *A Handbook of Vocational Guidance* (U.L.P., 1937) would nowadays be regarded as too cumbrous and too precise in its objectives; and the idea of a one ideal type of occupation is not practically useful.

When the Youth Employment Officer interviews a school leaver he usually does so on the broader 'seven-point plan' described in Paper One of the National Institute of Industrial Psychology after an article by A. Rodgers in the periodical *Occupational Psychology* (Volume 13). These seven points are: (1) physical make-up, (2) school attainments, (3) general intelligence, (4) special aptitudes, (5) interests, (6) disposition, and (7) circumstances. A few Y.E.O.'s issue questionnaires and give aptitude tests but most depend upon the teachers for detailed information about individual pupils. For each of the seven points (except the first and last which are usually discussed informally and confidentially) the careers specialist on a school staff would be responsible for collecting reliable assessments and keeping systematic records.

275

Thus, for attainments, in addition to school reports of actual marks and grades, some plan must be followed for evaluating comparative standards of different courses, and for equating teacher's estimates and impressions.

A measurement of general intelligence would not add much significant information in the case of the highly selected group who go on to the upper levels of fifth- and sixth-form work. But it does differentiate more practically among pupils of the middle and lower ranges of ability, who form the bulk of school leavers, since every occupation can be taken as having first a *minimal* I.Q. requirement and secondly a 'ceiling' beyond which individual ability would not be made use of. This would give a realistic start to a guidance programme, since young people are prone both to under- and over-estimate their own capabilities.

The school records will often be the best index of any special aptitudes. But some of these are well-established as being independent of each other in testing and one or two are correlated very slightly with general intelligence: this does not apply to traditional verbal ability, but it does to manual dexterity, artistic and musical ability, and even to certain types of facility with spatial and numerical calculations. The National Institute of Industrial Psychology publish occupational-aptitude tests related to some of these factors.

The large and exhaustive interest 'inventories' which are widely used in the U.S.A. (one of them can be scored by machine in forty-seven different ways to suit different occupations) may be adapted for classifying interests broadly into: intellectual, practical-constructional, physical, social, and so on. Some schools ask pupils to write essays about the careers they would choose, and some of these are informative and realistic.

Some form of fixed rating scale might be used for assessing disposition. The seven-point plan stresses as 'key' characteristics: acceptability to others, dependability, and self-reliance. Scientific personality measurement is a skilled psychological function (see Chapter 5) and informal methods are more practical with large numbers, provided they are used with reservations.

Assessment and educational guidance is the psychological aspect of the career teacher's function. The other is informative and a question of curriculum and administration. Instruction about industry and commerce should be part of a course in all secondary schools, except perhaps for the small minority of academic sixth formers. A handy survey of the topic of vocational education is to be found in the pamphlet of the Department of Education and Science (H.M.S.O., 1965) called 'Careers Guidance in Schools'.

Appendix II

Developmental disorders. Maladjustment and delinquency

The behavioural problems which come under these two headings are nowadays regarded as developmental in nature with emphasis upon the interaction between the growing personality and past and present environment, rather than on the possibility of a genetic or constitutional predisposition to maladjusted or delinquent responses. Difficult children are not a type apart. Normal children show abnormalities from time to time in reaction to stresses in their adjustment tasks; ordinary childish tiresomeness or adolescent defiance shades into the outright anti-social acts which are usually called delinquent. We must remember that the term has legal rather than psychological significance. Many apparently law-abiding young people are capable of dishonesty and aggressions. One case of pilfering, for example, may be quietly dealt with by the school authorities. Another happens to be brought to the notice of the law.

What is regarded as normal or acceptable will obviously vary with the culture and above all with the expectations of the adults. This makes the *ascertainment* of maladjustment quite complex and estimates of its actual incidence vary quite considerably. Fuller discussion of these points are to be found in the then Ministry of Education's *Report of the Committee on Maladjusted Children* (H.M.S.O., 1955) particularly Chapters Three and Four which discuss the nature of maladjustment in relation to normal development; secondly in the report of the working party appointed by the Secretary of State for Scotland, published by H.M.S.O. (Edinburgh) in 1964 under the title of *Ascertainment of Maladjusted Children*.

There is, of course, a group of children with organic disorders or constitutional handicaps whose behaviour cannot be expected to be quite normal in any ordinary sense. Those include (besides those with gross mental subnormalities like the mongols and cretins) some children who have suffered from such neurological conditions as epilepsy or meningitis, as well as the small percentage of extreme cases classified as psychotic, like the autistic children mentioned elsewhere. Psychotic children are not always readily identifiable. Defectives have a characteristic 'look' but a psychotic child remains attractive in appearance and may give no clue but a curious detachment from people and events. Prompt diagnosis of psychiatric and neurological disorders is obviously desirable so that provision can be made for the severely disturbed outside the regular educational system. In other cases when the true nature of a handicap is recognized, sympathetic treatment in the ordinary classroom may be enough and may prevent the development of secondary maladaptive behaviour.

Turning now to the regulations for various categories of handicapped pupils we find the *maladjusted* described as those who 'show evidence of emotional instability or psychological disturbance and *require special educational treatment in order to effect their personal, social or educational readjustment*'.[1] To this the 1955 report added that a child may be 'regarded as maladjusted who is developing in ways that have a bad effect on himself or his fellows *and cannot without help be remedied by his parents, teachers and the other adults in ordinary contact with him*'[1]. In other words referral for specialist guidance and therapy is recommended when the child's handicap, whether environmental or temperamental, is such that he cannot get through his present developmental difficulty by himself or with the help of ordinary control.

There is something to be said for roughly classifying maladjustment symptoms as a guide to teachers who may be in doubt whether or not to refer a particular child to the appropriate service[2] although this can be misleading on other grounds. The same apparent symptom (e.g. bed-wetting or excessive tempers) can be part of many different behavioural patterns and call for different kinds of treatment.

The most significant general sign is a lack of *expected* developmental progress —an unaccountable standing-still, or deviation, or regression to earlier habits. Within his individual capabilities a child should be solving his two main developmental tasks of happy adjustment and of living up to realistic social requirements. A maladjusted child is *primarily* unsuccessful and unhappy. He may, or may not, show clear failures in learning, or the kind of 'bad' behaviour which attracts a teacher's notice. All writers on the subject of child guidance warn teachers to be on the look-out for 'withdrawal' symptoms (e.g. day-dreaming, solitariness) as well as the more irritating ones like exhibitionism or abnormal fidgetiness.

Some disorders are typically *nervous* or emotional. Such children react with excessive anxiety to simple setbacks, and develop (for instance) school phobia, with real illness manifestations like active vomiting which make attendance effectively impossible. Some acquire obsessive habit rituals like counting every

---

[1] My italics.

[2] In England and Wales the school psychological service is particularly concerned with educational problems while emotional and psychological difficulties would tend to be referred to the child guidance clinic which is normally under psychiatric or medical direction. However, there will be in the employ of the clinic at least one educational psychologist who is also in the school psychological service. In Scotland child guidance is entirely an educational service and staffed by educational psychologists. Medical or psychiatric specialists may be called in for consultation. Other child guidance specialists include speech therapists and social caseworkers.

second stair, and get out of bed to perform them if they have forgotten. These are often children of parents who are insecure themselves, with rigid standards; or else who are unpredictable from the child's point of view, veering from fussy over-protection to sudden capricious rages.

There are typically nervous *habit* disorders. These may range from 'allergic' reactions like asthma to the persistence of a childish self-comfort like thumb-sucking. Often the root anxiety is made worse by the parents' anxiety and clinical psychologists find these among their most stubborn problems. There is no single cure. Bed-wetting may yield to a straightforward de-conditioning therapy (a systematic technique of habit-breaking) or it may not. There may be deeper-seated conflicts originating in the former antagonisms between mother and child over toilet-training—often the first occasion for him to discover his own inadequacies in her sight. Or, of course, his power of dis-pleasing her!

The *behaviour* problems likely to come to the school's notice during child-hood, apart from defiance and unruliness in class, are truancy, pilfering, and excessive aggression or cruelty in the playground. These unacceptable attempts at self-assertion can be regarded as abnormal in the sense that a child developing satisfactorily in his personal-social relationships, and mastering his learning requirements, should not need to fall back on taking things or bullying for reassurance—or at least not often and not for long. Teachers frequently report a history of this sort of behaviour in a child who becomes a delinquent in the teen years. Terms like *rebellious* and *sullen*, or *querulous* and *unsatisfied*, or *sly* and *evasive*, are typically applied to the child whose sense of personal worth is shaky. Persistent delinquents, the stubborn cases, often have unstable excitable temperaments and are prone to boasting, quick temper and jealousy.

Very often the school, and afterwards the child guidance counsellor or the probation officer, are having to cope with the results of bad psychological conditions in a home (which need not always be the poor or low-grade home). Parents who are unstable, self-obsessed and immature in their personal contacts can make their children feel rejected or inadequate, since there is no steady reassurance of affection, and such parents do not build in them the necessary sense of responsibility for one's own actions, since they understand it very little themselves.

Family relationships form an enormous developmental topic and readers will find many accounts of it in textbooks both British and American. One which covers many essential points in a short space and relates the organizational aspects of child guidance usefully to real life behaviour is Isabella Clark Maclean's *Child Guidance and the School* (Methuen, 1966). In reference to school situations the author makes comments on what has become a subject of much psychological study—the group and inter-personal relationships inside the four walls of the classroom. A teacher's own personality, including her insecurities as well as her assets, will be reflected in the quality of her leadership and the children will be correspondingly relaxed or uneasy. Again, in a big group a personality problem in one child is likely to be frustrating to a teacher's plans and the pupil who is difficult is likely to be confirmed in his antagonism. Readers will find various topics of this kind discussed in the symposium edited by O. A. Oeser, *Teacher, Pupil and Task* (Tavistock Publications, 1955). Elizabeth Richardson's *Environment of Learning* (Nelson, 1967) is a study, according to its sub-title, of conflict and understanding that results from different kinds of group organization in secondary school forms.

Although there is an overlap between maladjustment and anti-social behaviour not all maladjusted children become delinquents. And not all delinquents are maladjusted. Many bold young culprits show few or no neurotic symptoms. There is no one delinquent type. Many surveys have been carried out in an attempt to establish common factors in delinquency—either in the social context or in the form of personality traits. There is a higher incidence for juvenile offenders of all the familiar social conditions listed long ago in Burt's London survey (*The Young Delinquent*, U.L.P., 1925) such as relative poverty, 'black spot' neighbourhoods, broken or irregular parental ties, poor family standards. Yet only a percentage of children so handicapped become juvenile offenders.

Age surveys show a peak age for trouble round about 14 with strong evidence that the majority of these adolescents do in fact cease to commit offences as they mature. This suggests, as Burt himself believed, that delinquency in most cases is only an extreme version of ordinary youthful bad behaviour and revolt. There is a sex factor. Far fewer girls than boys are delinquent in the sense of being convicted for offences against property and persons, and this too may be considered as socially normal.

There has, however, appeared at least one new social theory in recent years, linked with the teenage explosion. This is the view that the gang member is completely socialized within his own sub-culture and therefore not a deviant in the eyes of his chosen society.

There are some psychological theories about the non-development of any recognizable conscience which characterizes certain individuals. H. J. Eysenck suggests that they do not *condition* readily—that is, do not acquire guilt or avoidance reactions to wrong acts. Psychologists in the Freudian tradition (e.g. Bowlby, Goldfarb, and Winnicott) believe that children who have no close relationship with parents in the early years, cannot develop a sense of identity with them and their moral restraints, and secondly do not learn how to postpone immediate gratification for other advantages (Freud, you remember, calls this the *reality principle*). Moral or social indifference of this kind is actually far harder to deal with than the boldness of the gang, or the hostility which is so often a defence against feelings of failure or rejection. A teacher with the courage and perseverance to carry it through, can often make something like a co-operative group out of silly, uninterested girls or jeering louts. But those other effects of a disastrous early upbringing appear to be indelible.

The literature of delinquency is extensive. D. J. West gives a very fully documented account of it in the first half of his book *The Young Offender*

(Pelican Books, 1967) with a summing up of the usefulness of the findings, both sociological and psychological. In addition the 'feel' of modern approaches to the problem might be got by reading one of the individual investigations, such as T. R. Fyvel's *The Insecure Offenders* (Chatto and Windus, 1961) which considers in particular its educational significance.

Appendix III

A historical note on the definition and treatment of backwardness

Of the ten categories of handicapped children for whom the Education Act of 1944 (and subsequent regulations) recommended special educational provision, there was one defined as *educationally subnormal*. It was to include all children who by reason of innate mental disability or *for any other cause* were failing to progress by ordinary educational methods. This implied that educationally subnormal was not identical with mentally handicapped. A child backward in school attainments because of a behavioural problem might be recommended for the special school in certain educational areas. Thus school performance alone was to be the criterion and this meant that a large percentage of children could theoretically qualify for special education.

The percentage of children in any 'backward' category will vary according to the definition of backwardness used. It is different with the categories of measured intelligence which give a fairly steady 2 to 3 per cent of children with I.Q.'s below 70 and approximately 10 per cent in the range between 70 and 80. The Ministry of Education Pamphlet No. 5 suggested that a pupil should be regarded as backward whose attainments are 80 per cent, or less, of what is normal school performance for his age-group. But this would give a high percentage of children (about 15).

We find, therefore, since it was clearly impractical to provide special education for all this number and probably highly undesirable to remove most backward pupils from the ordinary schools, pamphlet No. 30 of the Ministry of Education (1956) describing the e.s.n. children as 'about 5 to 10 per cent of the school population who need special help' but going on to add that most of them should be taught in the ordinary schools.

The position has been confusing but lately has clarified to some extent. In 'Slow Learners at School', the title of pamphlet No. 46 as published in 1964 by the new Department of Education and Science, the term *slow-learning* is recommended for children who are failing to some degree in school work, with *educationally subnormal* restricted to the much smaller percentage within this group who need special education.

The provision for these children, methods of ascertainment, and the organization of special schools and special classes, is gone into thoroughly by M. F. Cleugh in *The Slow Learner* (Methuen, 1956). Stephen Jackson's

Special Education in England and Wales (Oxford University Press, 1966) contains handy information of the official and administration sort, with list of suggested readings.

There is, of course, a specialist qualification for teachers of the handicapped. But teaching slow-learning children is one of the responsibilities of the teacher in the ordinary classroom. M. F. Cleugh's book has a chapter on this difficult job. Readers may also care to consult *The Education of Slow Learning Children* by A. E. Tansley and R. Gulliford (Routledge and Kegan Paul, 1960) and the recommendations about the curriculum in *Slow Learners at School.* Tansley's *Reading and Remedial Reading* (R.K.P., 1967) brings the instruction methods down to practical details and analyses the diagnosis of particular learning deficiencies. The two publications by Cheshire Education Committee, *The Education of Dull Children at the Primary Stage* and *The Education of Dull Children at the Secondary Stage* (U.L.P., 1956 and 1963) contains many samples of appropriate work in main subjects and hints on the aims and techniques of instruction.

Appendix IV

Further reading on current personality theories

There have been several attempts at a comprehensive theory of personality and its development. Educators may be guided by them in understanding young people and in forming their own attitudes. Systematic application is another matter, and in the best-known example, Freudian psychoanalysis, the doctrines are highly technical and can be properly used only by trained practitioners. However, in his own *Outline of Psychoanalysis* (Hogarth Press, 1963) Freud gives a readily understandable account of how the ruthless animal lusts of infancy are supposed to come under the control of the child's increasing awareness of the real world which gradually forms the conscious self, or ego. Among the most important realities are restraints imposed by parents which are ultimately accepted and identified with as the so-called superego. The main personality structure is essentially complete by five years of age and throughout life the driving force of action is the primitive sensuality in socially acceptable guises. Some followers of Freud confirm this; others depart from strict orthodoxy by stressing not bodily but social-personal needs. Parents loving and reliable, though not necessarily permissive, give the impression of a stable world in which a child can assert himself without anxiety. Conversely if the world seems hostile and unpredictable neurotic symptoms develop as a form of self-defence. Typical *neo-Freudian* views like Karen Horney's in American social psychology are described by J. A. C. Brown in *Freud and the Post-Freudians* (Penguin Books, 1961). Bowlby, Goldfarb, Winnicott, and Erikson, as we saw, are 'Freudian' to a greater or less degree in their developmental views.

Many personality psychologists think that it is unsatisfactory and forced to explain later activity as extensions of primitive bodily wants. According to A. H. Maslow, as we saw, a need is only active when unsatisfied and there is a developmental drive towards the freedom of self-actualization once the specific wishes for affection, esteem and so on are securely taken care of (see the fifth chapter of his *Motivation and Personality*, Harper and Row, 1954). An important group of the so-called 'self' theorists (notably Carl Rogers in his *On Becoming a Person*, Constable and Co., 1961) explain individuality through the growth of the *self-concept*. This is an old psychological idea going back to William James in the last century and to William Macdougall's classic *Introduction to Social Psychology* (Methuen, 1908). It assigns less motive force to the so-called unconscious appetite and far more to the conscious idea of oneself as a person, which, as we saw in the text, grows out of experience and out of the attitudes to oneself of other people.

Thus an individual sees in his present environment what he needs for his own purposes. It is his *personal construct* or *perceptual field*; it is different from someone else's, and he acts accordingly. Readers may care to link this with the chapter section headed 'The Problem of Individuality' in Part III of this book. *Individual Behaviour* by Arthur Combs and Donald Snygg (Harper and Row, 1959) is a useful text on this perceptual view of personality.

Index

(Psychologists and titles of books substantially mentioned in the text are included in the index or appended index of names. All page numbers refer to the text and not to the formal reference lists at ends of chapters.)

habits, 227, 234
  attention habit, 202–3
  nervous, 278–9
  skills and, 234–7
habit-breaking, 230, 236
  in therapy, 279
habit-learning, 230, 232, 234 ff
Hadow Report, 117
Half our Future (Newsom Report), 266
handedness, left-, 107, 112, 119, 236–7
handwriting, 235
Harvard growth studies, 116
hemisphere, dominant, *also* cerebral dominance,
  and hand preference, 237
  and speech areas, 191
heredity and environment,
  in twins, 108–9
  in brain maturation, 157–61
heredity and family intelligence, 157
histogram, 31
Home and the School, The, 114, 116, 140, 154
homes, studies of, 96
How we Think, 212

identical twins, *see* monozygotic
identification,
  with authority figures, 13, 146, 280, 284
  in sex-typing, 140
illusions, 198, 203
images, memory, 240
imitation, 89
  as habit, 235
  in language learning, 251, 258
impression scoring, 44 ff
individuality of environment, 183–5
  of heredity, 103–5
insight, 217
intelligence, 65–6, 72–3, 77–8, 81 ff
  and (school) backwardness, 266, 267–8
  and creativity, 66, 82, 86, 224 ff
  composition of, *see* composition *and* factors
  cultural content, 77, 97, 100, 183
  decline of, 153
  defined by Binet, Burt, Spearman, 82
  defined by Hebb, 81
  developmental changes in, 75, 79–80
  distribution of, 74–5
  environment and, 79–80, 153 ff
  heredity in, 157
intelligence quotient, 24, 40, 63, 65 ff
  and school backwardness, 206, 267–8
  and creativity scores, 87, 226
  and reading ability, 265, 270
  by age ratio method, 73, 87, by deviation method, 74–6
  coaching effects on, 79
  constancy of, 69, 75, 79 ff
intelligence tests, 66–80
  and information, 68, 77–8
  and language, 72, 153, 267

Binet type, 66 ff, 82, 87, 201
creativity type 226, group type 78 ff, performance type 71, 76, 127, 153, single ability type 85–6, 226, verbal type 71–2

language, 17, 25, 72, 101–2, 125, 134–5, 138–9, 152–3, 155–6, 168, 175, 177, 191, 207–8, 210, 212, 215, 218, 237, 241, 249–71
  and concepts, 207–8, 218–20, 249
  and intelligence, 72, 267, 270
  and remembering, 241, 250
  and thinking, 155–6, 249
  as behaviour, 210, 250 ff, 255 ff
  codes, 155, 250, 257, 260
  registers, 256
  written, 260
Language and Mental Development of Children, The, 252
Language and Thought of the Child, The, 168
language development: (1) linguistic account of, 257–9; (2) normative studies and norms of, 101–2, 125, 251–3
  and backwardness general, 265 ff, specific, 268–9
  deprivation factor, 134, 135, 155–6, 249
  environmental factor, 152 ff, 251, 253, 256
  personal-social factor, 132 ff, 138–9, 250
  neural and physical factor, 191–3, 237, 258, 269
  sex difference factor, 101, 252
language-learning, 251 ff
  and teaching, 256 ff
  conditioning (sign), theory of, 208, 249
  reinforcement theory, 253–4
  theories of Lewis 253, Luria 156, Piaget 168, 254, Vygotsky 156, 168, 249
Language, Thought and Personality, 139
latency period (development), 137
law of effect (learning), 231
learning, and attention, 202, 204
  and brain maturation, 159–60
  and development, 113
  and habits, 234 ff
  and practice, 241
  and psychology, 161, 178
  and thinking skills, 212, 215
earning, formal (*see* memorizing), 239 ff
  overlearning in, 242
  whole and part learning, 241
learning, forms of,
  avoidance, 231
  concept-attainment, 217–24
  perceptual, 193, 196–7, 204
  programmed, 49, 239, 244 ff
  skill, 234 ff
  spontaneous, 239, 243, 244
  trial and error, 214, 235

Index of Names

Bartlett, F. C., 215, 216, 225, 240
Berko, J., 259
Bernstein, B., 155, 249, 256
Bowlby, J., 17, 91, 134, 280
Brown, R., 258
Bruner, J. S., 215, 220, 224
Burt, C., 39, 41, 49, 82, 168, 267, 280
Cleugh, M. F., 265, 282
Combs, A. and Snygg, D., 285
Crowder, N. A., 245, 247
Daniels, J. C. and Diack, H., 262
Dewey, J., 213
Douglas, J. W. B., 114, 116, 140, 154
Ebbinghaus, H., 38, 39, 239, 243
Erikson, E., 130
Firth, J. R., 256
Freud, A., 135
Freud, S., 12, 129 135, 137, 147, 280, 284
Fyvel, T. R., 281
Gabriel, J., 126, 132, 148
Galton, F., 55, 56, 201
Gesell, A., 39, 94, 95, 98, 99, 101, 115, 135, 251
Goldfarb, W., 17, 91, 134, 147, 250, 280
Guilford, J. P., 86, 87, 156, 225–6
Harlow, H., 139, 215–6–7
Hall, S., 117
Halliday, M. A. K., et al., 255
Havighurst, R., 129, 142, 215
Hebb, D. O., 81, 97, 157, 176
Hilgard, E. R., 97, 214, 232 footnote, 238
Horney, K., 284
Humphrey, G., 213
Hudson, L., 156, 224, 226
Hull, C. L., 163, 229, 232
Hunter, I. M., 239, 240
Isaacs, S., 13, 95, 168
Jackson, S., 268, 282
Jersild, A., 96, 132
Koffka, K., 199
Kohler, W., 199, 213, 217
Lashley, K., 191
Lenneberg, E., 191, 250, 254, 270
Lewin, K., 163, 183, 199
Lovell, K., 174, 222
Lunzer, E. A., 149
Luria, A. R., 156, 177, 207–8, 249
McClelland, W., 42, 45
Macdougall, W., 130, 284
McKellar, P., 224
McNeill, D., 258

Maier, N., 214
Maslow, A. H., 130, 284
Mays, J. B., 142
Mead, M., 142
Miller, Neal and Dollard, J. C., 232, 235, 237
Miller, W. and Ervin, S., 258
Morris, J., 268, 270
Morse, M., 146
Mowrer, O. H., 232
Opie, I. and P., 138
Osgood, C., 208, 220, 254
Oeser, O. A., 280
Pavlov, I., 9, 38, 156, 191, 199, 205, 231–2
Piaget, J., 6, 12, 17, 95, 99, 124, 125, 127, 139, 156, 161–76, 177, 184, 215, 218, 221, 223, 254; see also main index
Peel, E. A., 167
Peck, R., 129
Pidgeon, D. and Yates, A., 42, 45, 72
Quirk, R., 257, 260
Richmond, W. K., 248
Rogers, C., 284
Schofield, M., 145, 146
Schonell, F. J., 46, 49, 261, 263, 267
Sheldon, R., 109, 111, 114
Shields, J., 121
Skinner, B. F., 39, 230, 232–3, 237, 245–7, 253
Spearman, C., 38, 82, 83 ff
Spence, K. W., 229, 230
Spinley, B. M., 130
Spitz, R., 134, 250
Stephenson, G., 146
Tanner, J. M., 97, 102, 111, 119
Tansley, A. E. and Gulliford, R., 283
Templin, M. C., 253, 268
Terman, L. M., 40, 71
Thomson, R., 167, 214
Thorndike, E. L., 9, 38, 199, 230–1, 237
Thurstone, L. L., 85, 86, 87, 156, 226
Thyne, J. M., 201, 242
Vernon, M. D., 270
Vernon, P. E., 49, 86, 153
Veness, T., 144
Watts, A. F., 252
Wechsler, D., 86
Wertheimer, M., 199, 214
West, D. J., 280
Whorf, B. L., 217, 218, 241
Winnicott, D. W., 147, 148, 280